ASTRONOMY MADE SIMPLE

by

Kevin B. Marvel, Ph.D.
Deputy Executive Officer
American Astronomical Society

BOOKS

A Made Simple Book
Broadway Books
New York

Produced by The Philip Lief Group, In

ASTRONOMY MADE SIMPLE

For information, address: Broadway Books, a division of
Random House, Inc., 1745 Broadway, New York, NY 10019.

Printed in the United States of America

Produced by The Philip Lief Group, Inc.
Managing Editors: Judy Linden, Jill Korot.
Design: Annie Jeon.

Broadway Books titles may be purchased for business or promotional use or for special sales.
For information, please write to: Special Markets Department, Random House, Inc.
1745 Broadway, New York, NY 10019.

MADE SIMPLE BOOKS and BROADWAY BOOKS are
trademarks of Broadway Books, a division of Random House, Inc.

Visit our website at www.broadwaybooks.com.
First Broadway Books trade paperback edition published 2004.

Library of Congress Cataloging-in-Publication Data

Marvel, Kevin
    Astronomy Made Simple: a clear guide to the workings of the universe / by Kevin B.
    Marvel; produced by the Philip Lief Group, Inc.
        p. cm. — (Made simple)
    Includes bibliographical references and index.
        ISBN 0-7679-1704-9 (alk paper)
        1. Astronomy. I. Philip Lief Group. II. Title. III. Made simple (Broadway Books)

QB45.2.M.37 2004
520—dc22

2004054437

10 9 8 7 6 5 4 3 2 1

DEDICATION

As this book was nearing completion, a close and personal friend passed away after a brave fight against a rare form of cancer. Dr. Janet Akyüz Mattei, the longtime director of the American Association of Variable Star Observers, died on March 22, 2004. She represented the best in astronomy and the best of humanity. A tireless advocate for variable star observing, she managed to connect professional astronomers with eager and talented amateur astronomers to build something larger than both groups. She was a longtime friend and colleague, and I dedicate this book to her because she always tried to make astronomy simple.

ACKNOWLEDGMENTS

Writing a book of this type in the Internet era means that I owe much to many. I would like to thank the innumerable instructors and educators who posted to the Internet their versions of explanations of physical phenomena and astronomical facts. You have no idea how useful your alternative explanations were. Different points of view are tremendously valuable.

I would like to thank the National Observatories and NASA missions, which have placed a fantastic amount of current and past astronomical knowledge in the hands of all with access to the Internet, as well as the international organizations that have done the same.

I would like to thank my editors, Jill Korot and Jeffrey Golick, who both tweaked my writing so that it was better. I want to also thank my pal and confidant, Chris De Pree, the author of *Physics Made Simple*. We both enjoyed working on these books and worked hard to connect them in some subtle ways.

Most of all I want to thank my wife Tamara, who gave me the time at home to work on the book and made sure I had plenty of sustenance during the process.

Finally, I would like to thank my employer, the American Astronomical Society, and—most especially—my boss, Dr. Robert Milkey. He gave me the flexibility I needed to complete this project and has always been a champion for me when I want to work on projects outside my current realm of endeavor, lobbying for science and astronomy in particular.

In conclusion, I was privileged enough in my graduate school days to have known Dr. Clyde Tombaugh, the last living discoverer of a planet within our solar system. And his inspirational discussions about the long nights at the telescope that finally paid off in discovery are one of the main reasons I sweated through my own Ph.D. research project.

After a long and productive career at the White Sands missile range in New Mexico, Clyde took up a teaching position at the New Mexico State University in Las Cruces. He began working at White Sands in 1946 after getting his master's degree from the University of Kansas in 1939 and subsequently teaching at Arizona State College (now Northern Arizona University in Flagstaff). He started teaching at NMSU in 1955 and ultimately helped make an independent astronomy department at the university in 1970. He was an emeritus faculty member by the time I arrived at NMSU in 1990, but he still regularly attended department colloquia. The graduate students and even the faculty would occasionally fall asleep in colloquia and Clyde was no exception. He was better than the graduate students though. Somehow, despite dozing off during parts of some lecture or the other, he always snapped awake during question time, always managing to ask a real zinger that would go straight to the heart of the speaker's presentation. Sometimes he would question material presented while he (and often I) was snoozing. I don't know how he did it, but his questions were always very insightful and caught many speakers off guard.

He came in nearly every day of the week to work in his office, which was filled with interesting memorabilia of his days at White Sands and even from Lowell. The astronomy department also benefited from his telescope-making skills. One of the best examples is a (still-used) solar telescope, with about a 5-inch unsilvered mirror. The mount was made of plumbing pipe and the telescope itself was made out of scrap wood painted a light blue. I can still remember using the telescope for the first time to show my laboratory students the Sun. I noticed some writing on the telescope structure: "Image of Sun dimmed by 700,000 times. Telescope made by Clyde Tombaugh." I was flabbergasted. Here was a telescope made by a living legend and I was using it to show a bunch of undergraduate students sunspots. But, his skill in making telescopes wasn't the only thing great about Clyde. He had a true love of astronomy and a wonderful way of always smiling at everyone.

He did have one nasty—but endearing—habit: he enjoyed making puns. I remember one day in particular when I was happily arranging for a weekend boating trip on Elephant Butte Lake about 2 hours away from the university. Clyde listened in while the photocopier was running. He was making some copies of something he was sending to a reporter interested in the discovery of Pluto. When his copies were done, he walked into the Department office where I was standing and speaking with some fellow students.

Clyde said, "So you have a boat, huh?"

"Yes," I said, "twenty-two feet long."

"Is she for sail?" Clyde asked and then broke into a huge grin at how funny his pun was. All we could do was groan.

What I liked about Clyde was that he was approachable and humble. Despite his fame and worldwide acclaim, he remained a normal person with a sense of humor and a delightful view of the world. I imagine that other famous people of science, Galileo, Newton, Faraday, and Michelson, were equally approachable. Some probably were, most probably were not. Clyde was a great man, not only for his discovery of Pluto but also for his great personality, warm heart, and constant patience. It was an honor to know him.

CONTENTS

INTRODUCTION

Astronomy is arguably the oldest science. Since ancient times, people have looked up and wondered about the stars, planets, and other celestial phenomena. Although the true scientific study of the heavens has been with us only a few hundred years, in that time we have learned much about the objects in the sky and even learned the origin and ultimate fate of our universe.

Astronomy is fundamentally the study of everything we see in space: the Sun, the Moon, other planets in our solar system, stars, planets around those stars, our Milky Way Galaxy, other galaxies, and even the whole universe itself. For most of these objects, the only way we can learn about them is from the light they give off or reflect. Luckily for astronomers, light carries much information about the object and about the space between the object and us here on Earth.

Astronomers have two basic activities. They seek to map the heavens, to produce a complete inventory of our Universe, and they seek to understand how objects in the universe, and even the whole universe itself, change over time. Astronomers refer to this as the study of the evolution of objects (though they are not referring to the theory of evolution developed by English naturalist Charles Darwin). Evolution in an astronomical context simply means how something changes over time.

The Sky Above

Nothing in human culture is shared and appreciated by as many people as the night sky and the objects it contains. Whether you are in the United States (even in our largest cities), the Serengeti Plains of Africa, the Gobi Desert of central Asia, or on a boat in the middle of the Pacific Ocean, the night sky can be seen, studied, and enjoyed.

Before electricity, early peoples used the night sky as inspiration for their stories and passed those stories along to their children. The night sky is at the heart of the legends and myths of many cultures. What draws civilizations to the sky is no doubt its majesty. When you go to a dark location, away from the glare of city lights, and look up at the sky, you can lose yourself in its beauty. A myriad of stars twinkle above you. A few bright planets are perhaps visible, along with their distinctive colors_red for Mars, yellow for Jupiter. You may see a meteor leave a bright trail as it blazes into our atmosphere. Even manufactured objects such as the *International Space Station*, Space Shuttle, or low-orbit satellites can add to the nightly performance.

In our entertainment age, fewer and fewer people go outside simply to enjoy the night sky. This is a tragic loss. The heavens above are the one universal art. We should all make time to understand and enjoy this dramatic canvas. It is hoped this book will help you gain a deeper appreciation of those twinkling lights overhead.

The Basics

Astronomers are still working hard to understand the details of our universe, but they already have a good understanding of many things.

We know that Earth is a sphere that spins on an axis and orbits the Sun. Earth is a member of a solar system of nine planets and the Sun. The planets are also spherical bodies_some made of rock, some of gasses_that also spin on their axes and are in orbit around the Sun. Some planets have moons like our Moon, but smaller. Lots of smaller objects, such as comets, asteroids, small rocks and even sand-like dust grains, also orbit the sun.

Our solar system is a small part of a very much larger system of stars, gas, and dust called the Milky Way, or sometimes simply the Galaxy. Billions of galaxies (systems of stars like our Galaxy) exist in the universe, the Milky Way being just one, and kind of an average one at that.

Astronomers know that distant matter is the same as matter here on Earth, and chemical elements such as hydrogen, oxygen, and iron appear to be the basic building blocks of the whole universe. Surprisingly, the rules, or physical laws, that govern how matter interacts work the same everywhere in the universe. Gravity works on the same principle on Earth as it does on the Moon or at any other spot in the universe. This is fortunate for all of us that wish to study the stars, because it simplifies things considerably.

Those tiny, bright points of light we see in the sky_the stars_are really extremely large and hot balls of hydrogen and helium gas. They give off light because nuclear reactions take place deep in their interiors, giving off energy that makes its way to the surface in the form of light. They exist for finite lengths of time, slowly changing as they age. They initially form out of dust and gas, usually in clusters or groups known as stellar nurseries. Also, we now know that planets exist around other stars, although we have no direct image of them yet.

Understanding the Sky

So why should anyone bother trying to understand astronomy? Just looking up at the sky is interesting enough, right?

Long ago, people enjoyed finding patterns, such as lions, bears, and hunters, in the alignments of the stars. They then made up stories about these constellations, or patterns of stars in the sky. As different constellations became visible during the year, different stories could be told. This is perhaps the simplest way to enjoy and understand the sky.

But this book will try to teach you a bit more about what you might see in the sky. Seeing Mars as a bright red dot in the sky might brighten your night, but knowing that this red dot is a whole planet like Earth with its own ice caps, dust storms, sand dunes, and the largest volcano *and* the largest canyon system in the whole solar system would probably enhance the experience. Knowing that Mars has a thin atmosphere composed almost entirely of carbon dioxide and that there is likely water just below the surface in the form of ice could make Mars seem a bit more interesting and exotic than a simple red spot in the sky.

If you are curious about astronomy and want to understand more or if you are taking an astronomy class in school and hope to understand things more completely, this book will clearly explain the fundamentals of astronomy and enhance your enjoyment of the night sky.

About This Book

This book begins by exploring some of the basic facts concerning how the universe works before moving on to the specific contents of the universe and their interactions.

Chapter 1 talks about the origins of astronomy, and Chapter 2 presents some historical ideas about the universe. Chapters 3, 4, and 5, review some of the basic physical laws that govern the universe and how astronomers use these laws to learn about the universe. Chapter 6 discusses the tools of astronomy, whereas Chapters 7, 8, 9, and 10 provide an inventory of our solar system, with detailed information about the planets, Sun, and other objects such as comets and asteroids. Chapters 11, 12, and 13 discuss stars and their life cycles, and chapter 14 moves us outward to other galaxies. Chapter 15 discusses exciting recent developments in cosmology and theories about the whole universe.

The last chapter talks about life in the universe and the possibility of detecting life elsewhere. Because we know that we are composed of the same basic stuff we see everywhere in the universe and because we don't think we live in a particularly special place, we suspect life must exist elsewhere. But right now we don't know for sure. Astronomers will make great efforts in the coming decades to answer this question. Whoever first confirms the existence of life elsewhere will be recorded in history books forever. It could be the last truly significant discovery in the field of astronomy.

Finally, two appendices provide information about using a telescope and doing further work in astronomy. I hope that this book helps you understand astronomy; but more importantly, I hope it allows you a greater satisfaction when you look up at the night sky. Enjoy!

THE BIRTH OF ASTRONOMY

KEY TERMS

equinox, transit, eclipse, occultation, magnitude, parsec, light year

THE MYSTERY OF THE LIGHTS ABOVE

It is difficult to imagine what ancient humans thought about the sky. Ancient hunter-gatherer cultures had little reason to use the sky as a calendar; the animals they hunted and the wild plants they harvested served as much more relevant indicators of when the time had arrived to move on to the next hunting ground. But as agricultural civilizations spring up around 5000 B.C.E., we begin to find early traces of astronomy.

Imagine being an ancient farmer in 5000 B.C.E. Winter is ending and you want to plant your crops as early as you can to maximize the growing season, but not so early that your seedlings are damaged by frost, heavy rain, or wind. Without a calendar (let alone a *Farmer's Almanac*, Internet connection, or GPS device), how would you know when to plant?

Early peoples found that the sky and its motions could be used to tell them with some accuracy when to plant their crops or move their herds to other pastures. So, broadly speaking, the first astronomical measurements led to calendars, calendars based on the motions of the objects in the night sky.

THE SKY AND ITS MOTIONS

When we watch the sky, we see a whole range of motions. The Sun appears each morning, moves across the sky, and ultimately sets. Most stars copy this motion at night, but some never rise or set and are always visible. Our nightly star show slowly changes during the year. The Moon moves in a similar way, but it appears in a slightly different place in relation to the stars each day. The planets, too, follow this general trend but have their own special motions as well. In this section, we explore all these motions and what causes them.

The Origins of Timekeeping

Before clocks, ancient people used the sky to tell them what time and date it was. Our clocks and calendars today are based on this practice. The year, month, day, and hour are all intimately tied to the motion of the Sun, the Moon, and the stars.

The Day

The most basic motion we see is the regular rise of objects in the east, their movement across the sky, and then their setting in the west. All celestial objects we see in the sky share this basic motion, most visibly the Sun. Although early peoples thought that this motion represented the heavens whirling about Earth, we know now that this motion is caused by the rotation of Earth on its axis. An axis is a line about which an object rotates and can be thought of as an imaginary rod stuck through the object, like a chopstick through a peach. The peach is like Earth and the chopstick is its axis; the planet turns on this rod. Earth's axis is defined by the two poles, North and South; these are the points where the chopstick enters and exits the peach. The definition of a day is based on this fundamental rotation of Earth about this axis. One full rotation of a planet on its axis is one day.

The ancients used the Sun's location in the sky as a measure of the time of day. Life was simpler then, so if you were told to arrive at a field just after sunrise, you knew more or less when to show up, although not everyone would get there at exactly the same time. Today we use mechanical or digital clocks to mark time and people still show up late. Our technology may change, but people seem to stay the same.

CIRCUMPOLAR MOTIONS

From some points on Earth, some stars appear never to set. Imagine standing at the North Pole, the exact point where Earth's axis resides, the spot directly under the Pole Star. From this special location on Earth, every star we see is circumpolar. Being at the North Pole is like standing on a merry-go-round and looking straight up. Everything you see is rotating around you: Nothing enters or leaves your vision; everything just whirls around in a circular motion. Back at the North Pole, this is circumpolar motion. Conversely, if we stand on the equator, every star we can see rises and sets. This is just like being on a merry-go-round and looking directly away from it; everything we see enters and then leaves our vision as it rotates around, similar to the rise and fall of the stars. Figure 1.1 shows that this is caused simply by your location on Earth, and is not a fundamental property of the stars themselves. Going back to the merry-go-round, if we looked up at a 45° angle, some things would never leave our vision, whereas others would enter and leave, just like the stars if we are at a latitude between the North Pole and the Equator. The closer we are to the pole, the more stars appear to be circumpolar.

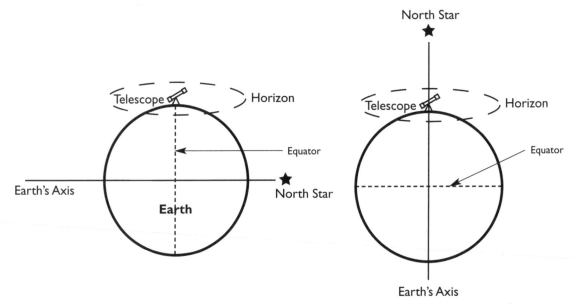

Figure 1.1—Observing the Celestial Sphere at the Equator and at the North Pole

The Month and the Moon

The Moon, of course, changes its appearance from day to day. The moon has phases, which are apparent changes in illumination of a celestial object over time. Some days the Moon appears completely illuminated, and on other days it is only partially lit. Some days it is not visible at all or is visible only as a very slim crescent. It takes about 29 days for the moon to cycle through its full set of phases. This steady and repetitive cycle became the basis for our *month*, which is a period of time originally derived from the amount of time it takes for the Moon to cycle through its full set of phases, caused by its orbit around Earth. Our modern months do not match this cycle exactly. Venus, Mercury, and the Moon all exhibit phases as seen from Earth.

The Moon's phases are due to two basic facts: the Moon is a sphere, and it orbits Earth. Because Earth and the Moon are fairly far away from the Sun (about 93 million miles away), the light from the Sun hits them as parallel beams of light. When parallel beams of light hit a sphere, they can illuminate only one side of the sphere. Because we are on Earth and it spins once each day, we move into and out of the Sun's light, which is illuminating only half of Earth at any one time. As we look at the Moon, we see only one side, the side facing Earth, but the light from the Sun is fully illuminating one whole side. When the Moon is full, the side facing Earth is fully illuminated by the Sun. When it appears only half-illuminated (called a quarter phase), half of the side facing is illuminated and half is left in the dark. As the Moon orbits Earth, we see the fraction of the Moon's side that is illuminated change over time, from full (completely illuminated) to new (completely dark) and back again through the crescent (partially illuminated), quarter (half-illuminated), and gibbous (mostly illuminated) phases. See Figure 1.2.

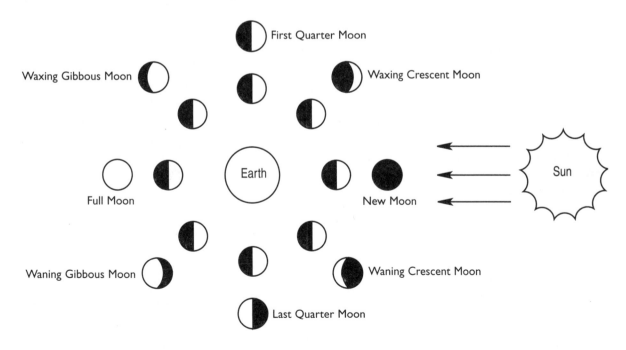

Figure 1.2—The Origin of Lunar Phases
Inner circle represents how it is; outer circle represents how it looks from Earth

Interestingly, we always see the same side of the Moon. Although slight wobbles allow us to see slightly more than half of the face, substantially we see only the same side. Until the Soviet Union sent a lunar probe to orbit the Moon and return pictures of its surface to us here on Earth, we had no idea what the far side might look like. Not too surprisingly, it is only slightly different than the face we know. The reason for this odd situation is that as the Moon moves in its orbit around Earth, it rotates on its axis at exactly the speed needed to keep the same side facing Earth.

THE DARK SIDE OF THE MOON

The side of the Moon we can't see, the so-called dark side, has spawned debate, discussion, and contemplation, not to mention art and poetry. Because we can see only one side of the Moon, it was assumed by the ancients that the far side, the side we could not see, was in perpetual darkness. Some thought that odd creatures lived there, building elaborate temples and civilizations. Others thought it would be covered in ice and snow, because the light of the Sun never reached its surface. The common misconception that if one cannot see the far side, it must be dark could not be further from the truth. As the Moon orbits Earth, we see different fractions illuminated. But, the Moon, a spherical body illuminated by the distant Sun, is always half lit. We see only the portion of the Moon that is facing Earth, and the illumination of that half changes based on where the Moon is in its orbit. The side of the Moon facing away from Earth is like a negative image of the side facing us. The fraction of its surface that is illuminated is the same fraction that is not illuminated on the side facing us. The fraction of its surface that is dark is the same fraction that is illuminated on our side of the Moon. Song lyric aside, the far side of the Moon is not "dark"; we just can't see it.

The Year

The other fundamental motion observed by ancient astronomers was the change in position of the rising and setting Sun. We can measure this motion by observing the Sun as it rises and sets and recording where along the horizon it appears to rise. Over time we see that the position changes each day. In winter in the Northern Hemisphere, the Sun rises at a point south of straight east and sets at a point south of straight west (the opposite is true in the Southern Hemisphere). In the Northern Hemisphere summer, the Sun rises north of east and sets north of west. The day when the Sun rises directly east and sets directly west is called an *equinox*. On this day, there is an equal amount of daylight and nighttime. See Figure 1.3. An equinox occurs once in the spring (*vernal equinox*) and once in the fall (*autumnal equinox*). These special days typically fall on March 21 and September 23 each year, although the exact date can vary slightly due to leap years and a slow but steady wobble of Earth on its axis.

There are two other notable days, called *solstices*. A solstice is a special day when the Sun rises or sets the furthest north or south during the year. On the *winter solstice* (December 21), we have the least amount of daylight in the Northern Hemisphere and greatest amount of daylight in the Southern Hemisphere. On the *summer solstice* (June 21), we have the greatest amount of daylight in the Northern Hemisphere and the least amount of daylight in the Southern Hemisphere.

This daily motion of the Sun along the horizon, steadily moving north in summer (in the Northern Hemisphere) and south as winter approaches, is exactly the motion used by ancient peoples to plan their farming activities. They could, for example, use natural

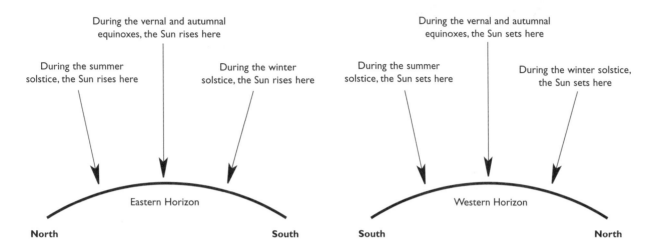

During the vernal and autumnal equinoxes, the Sun rises here

During the summer solstice, the Sun rises here

During the winter solstice, the Sun rises here

Eastern Horizon

North

South

During the vernal and autumnal equinoxes, the Sun sets here

During the summer solstice, the Sun sets here

During the winter solstice, the Sun sets here

Western Horizon

South

North

Figure 1.3—The Rising and Setting Points of the Sun at Solstices and Equinoxes

markings along the horizon to serve as indicators. When the Sun rose near an oddly shaped mountain or hill, it would indicate the planting time. In places without significant natural markers on the horizon, people set up their own markers. Stonehenge, a circle of large stones of uncertain origin in southern England (Fig. 1.4), was used to mark the special rising and setting locations of the Sun and also the Moon. We know this because the alignments can still be seen today; we didn't find a user's manual buried near the stones. Because the rising and setting positions repeated regularly about every 365 days, they could be used to mark the seasons over and over again. This motion is the foundation of our calendar year.

Photo courtesy of Tamara Koch

Figure 1.4—Stonehenge

THE SEASONS

Each year we experience changes in the typical daily temperatures, the weather, and the length of the day. We call the cold times winter and the warm times summer; the time between winter and summer is called spring, and the time between summer and winter is called fall. What is the origin of these changes? Because Earth is warmed by the light of the Sun, changes in the length of the day (and, subsequently, in the temperature and weather) must cause the seasons. Earth's axis is not perfectly perpendicular to the plane of Earth's orbit, its motion around the Sun. The axis is slightly tilted. This tilt causes the length of day to vary. In winter we have short days and in summer, long days. The tilt also spreads the Sun's light over more of Earth's surface, decreasing the amount of heat we receive. Imagine shining a flashlight straight down onto a sheet of paper and drawing a circle around the brightest region of the light. Now tilt the flashlight away from perpendicular. You will find that the brightest portion of the light is now elliptical, not circular, and that it would cover more area, its intensity significantly decreased. The tilt of Earth's axis is about 22.5° and is enough to cause our seasons. This also explains why it is summer in the northern hemisphere while it is winter in the southern hemisphere and vice versa. When the Northern hemisphere is tilted away from the Sun (decreasing sunlight intensity), the southern is tilted toward the Sun (increasing sunlight intensity). Near the equator, the impact of Earth's tilt is not as significant, because the Sun stays more or less straight overhead and the length of day stays more or less the same. The tilt of Earth is best seen from one of Earth's poles. During summer at the North Pole, the Sun stays above the horizon all the time; and during the summer solstice, it is 22.5° above the horizon. Some people have the mistaken idea that the seasons are caused by how close Earth is to the Sun. Although the distance between Earth and Sun does change slightly during the year, it is not great enough to cause the seasons and also doesn't explain why the seasons are reversed in the two hemispheres.

The Planets

With the Sun at its center, the solar system has nine planets, of which Earth is the third. Just like Earth, the others revolve about the Sun at certain rates. Planets closer to the Sun move more quickly than Earth, whereas planets further out revolve more slowly. Many of the planets are especially bright in Earth's night sky and move differently than the rest of the stars due to their orbital motion around the Sun. The word planet derives from an ancient Latin word meaning "to wander," a reference to the special motions of the planets. The planets move around in the sky over time in dramatic but smooth sweeping motions that are easy to follow even without telescopes or careful measuring.

The planets Mercury, Venus, Mars, Jupiter, and Saturn are visible with just the naked eye and can be tracked by comparing their positions each evening with the positions of nearby bright stars. Perhaps because of this nighttime prominence, they have often played important roles in the stories of ancient cultures. Today, most people don't even know which planets are visible on any given day. (The resources in the appendix will help you make sure you aren't one of these folks!)

Although the planets follow paths in the sky that are similar to the Sun (east to west during the day and slowly moving eastward relative to the background stars during the year), they have some special quirks in their motion, since they, too, are orbiting the Sun like Earth. We know now that the reason the planets follow paths similar to the path of the Sun is that all the planets orbit more or less in a plane around the Sun, similar to the flat surface of a compact disk, with the Sun at the location of the hole in the disk. A *plane* is an imaginary geometric construct that is perfectly flat, like a sheet of paper. The odd motions we see are caused when Earth catches up to and passes one of the planets, which travel at different speeds (see Fig. 1.5).

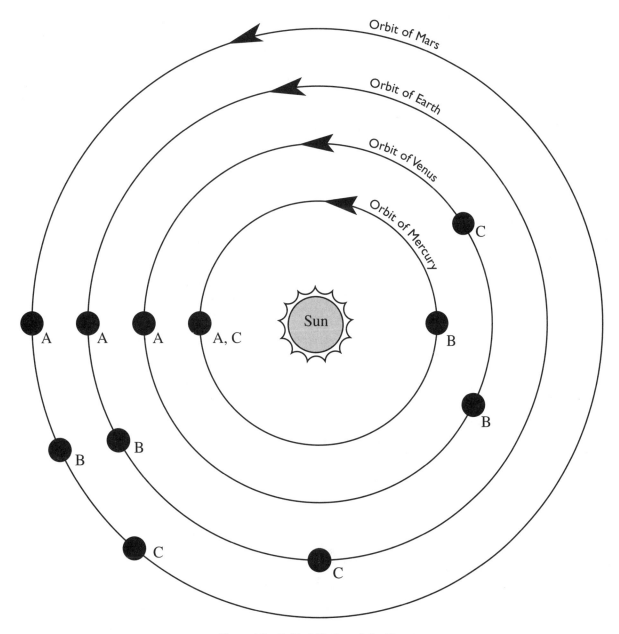

Figure 1.5—Orbital Motion of the Planets
The planets are aligned at A. After three months, the planets are at location B. Three months later,
they are at location C. Differing orbital speeds cause our view to change dramatically.
(Please note, these positions are illustrative, not accurate.)

SPECIAL EVENTS

In addition to the regular motions of objects in the sky, many special events take place that are either hard to predict (such as the appearance of some comets) or that happen very infrequently (such as two planets being covered up by the Moon at the same time). An exciting example of a special event is the transit of Venus. A *transit* is simply an event seen from Earth when an object passes across the face of the Sun. The best-known transits are those of Venus. In this case, Venus, as seen from Earth, appears to move across the face of the Sun. Because Venus is so much smaller than the Sun, it doesn't cast a perceptible shadow here on Earth, but during the transit a small black circle can be seen moving across the face of the Sun. Venus transits occur in pairs separated by 8 years and happen about every 105 years.

After the first transit of Venus was observed in 1639 (the one in 1631 was not seen in Europe due to bad weather), astronomers discovered that such a transit could be used to determine the actual distance between Earth and Venus using geometry. Therefore, they could establish a scale for the solar system. Although expeditions were sent all over the globe to observe the transits of 1761 and 1769, the results were not so great. The next set of transits, which took place in 1874 and 1882, turned out better and the overall scale of the solar system was established. It was later refined in the twentieth century by radar measurements of the Earth-Venus distance.

The next set of transits will occur in 2004 and 2012. Because the next transits after these won't happen until 2117 and 2125, you should make every effort to see one of these. The 2012 transit will be easily visible from Europe and the United States, although not in its entirety. The reason transits are visible from some locations and not from others is the same reason that we have night and day. The Sun is visible from Jakarta, Indonesia, at the same time that it is night and the Sun is not visible from New York. We live on a spherical Earth, and from

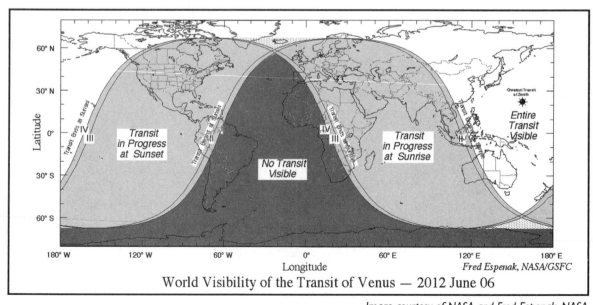

Image courtesy of NASA and Fred Espenak, NASA

Figure 1.6—Geographic Visibility of Venus Transits

any given location you can only see half the sky at a time. If a transit is taking place, it will not be visible from some fraction of Earth if it takes less than 24 hours (h) to occur. Venus transits usually last only a handful of hours.

Mercury also transits the Sun and, because it orbits the Sun more quickly than Venus, its transits are more frequent, with one taking place thirteen or fourteen times per century. The magazines listed in Appendix 1 provide up-to-date information about special events such as transits and eclipses that are visible from inhabited portions of Earth (i.e., places with hotels for eclipse viewers, unlike the open ocean or the Antarctic, where some eclipses are visible but are hardly convenient to view).

Eclipses

An *eclipse* is the blocking of one celestial object by another. *Solar eclipses* are events that take place when the Moon blocks the light of the Sun, casting a shadow onto Earth. There are partial, total, and annular solar eclipses. *Lunar eclipses* are events that take place when Earth passes between the Sun and the Moon, casting a shadow across the surface of the Moon. Because of Earth's atmosphere,

the shadow is often reddish in color. Eclipses don't just happen here on Earth; we see shadows move across the face of Jupiter cast by its moons, Io, Ganymede, Callisto, or Europa. Eclipses can happen for any planet and moon combination. However, except for one moon of Uranus, no other moon-planet combination makes such perfect eclipses as we have here on Earth. This is because the angular size of the Moon as seen from Earth is nearly exactly the same as the angular size of the Sun as seen from Earth. Despite the vast difference in the actual sizes of the Moon and the Sun, they both appear to be the same size because of their distances from Earth. The Moon is much, much closer to Earth than is the Sun. There is no physical explanation as to why the two angular sizes are similar. We just got lucky. See Figure 1.7.

This similarity in size leads to two kinds of eclipses, total eclipses and annular eclipses (Fig. 1.8). *Total eclipses* occur when the face of the Sun is completely blocked by the Moon as seen from Earth, and *annular eclipses* occur when the Moon is closer to Earth in its orbit, appearing slightly smaller and leaving an annulus, or ring, of the Sun still visible. When the surface of the Sun is only partially obscured by the Moon, it is called a partial

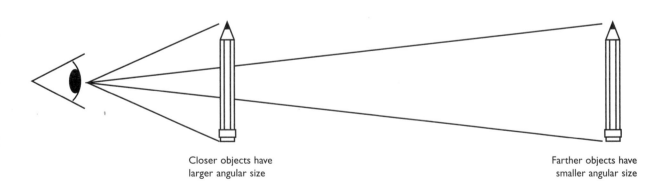

Closer objects have
larger angular size

Farther objects have
smaller angular size

Figure 1.7—Illustration of Angular Size

Figure 1.8—Explanatory Picture of Eclipses
Eclipse as seen from above (Note: not drawn to scale)

eclipse. These are fairly common. Be sure to properly protect your eyes before you look directly at the Sun at any time, not just during an eclipse.

Lunar eclipses, which occur when Earth passes between the Moon and the Sun, are visible from slightly more than half of Earth, because Earth rotates a bit while the eclipse takes place.

Occultation

An occultation is the observable passage of one object in front of another. Technically, eclipses are occultations, but because eclipses involve the Sun they get a special name. Occultations occur anytime one celestial object passes in front of another. The most interesting and dramatic occultations for amateur astronomers are when planets are covered up by the Moon. Nothing makes the solar system appear so fully three-dimensional as the image of a distant Saturn being covered up by the closer—and, therefore, apparently larger—Moon. However, another occultation is of great interest scientifically: the occultation of a distant star by an asteroid in our solar system. An *asteroid* is a large chunk of rock, not large enough to be a planet but still large enough to block the light of a distant

star. Most asteroids are located between the orbits of Mars and Jupiter. By carefully watching these occultations, scientists can measure the size and shape of asteroids, something not usually possible.

When these occultations take place, astronomers carefully measure the light from the distant star as it is covered by the asteroid and then quickly uncovered (asteroids are small, typically no more than 50 miles (mi) across, so they don't block the star for long). By observing from multiple locations on Earth and keeping careful records, some concept of the shape of the asteroid can be determined. Most are very rough in shape, usually potato- or peanut-shaped.

Alignments

A few years ago you probably heard of the so-called great alignment of the planets. Occasionally, when viewed from Earth, the planets appear in the same general location in the sky. Some people predicted the end of the world or at least worldwide calamities. Such alignments can be interesting, but they rarely have any astronomical significance. They are important to know about because they often make the front page of newspapers or the evening news. The most famous one took place in the 1980s, when all the planets visible with the naked eye were close together in the sky, an event dubbed by the media "the grand conjunction."

Objects in the solar system orbit the Sun and moons orbit their planets. Comets whiz around, and miscellaneous asteroids and other debris are zinging around us every day. If some of the objects appear close together sometimes, it is just a happy accident. No major disasters will ensue and the end of the world will not come. Such alignments are merely a good opportunity to get out and enjoy the wonder of the night sky, not fear it.

MAPPING THE SKY

Although the sky seems to always be changing, much of the sky stays fixed. Most of the stars we see remain fixed relative to each other over human lifetimes. But certain things do change. Given the sky's importance to them, many early peoples worked hard to map the sky, enabling them to track the items and objects that actually change. The earliest maps of the sky were associated with stories. They were passed down through generations and starred heroes and mythological creatures. The subjects of the various stories and myths took physical form as patterns of stars in the sky,

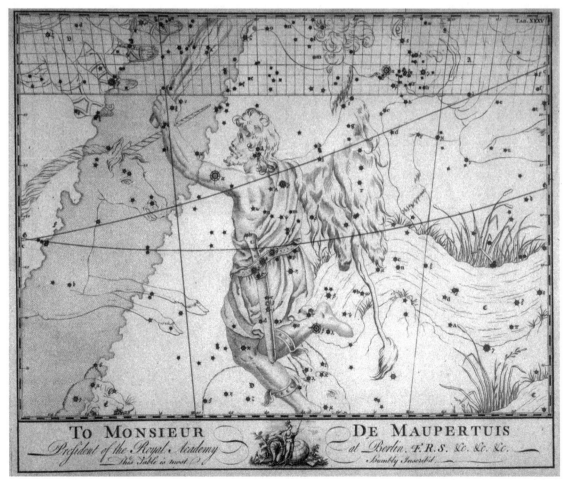

Image courtesy of Michael Oates

Figure 1.9—An Image from an Early Star Atlas

the constellations mentioned in the introduction. Over there in the fall rises Orion the Hunter, the son of the Queen of the Amazons and Poseidon, the God of the Sea. Circling the pole star with her head always tipped down is the vain queen Cassiopeia, who ended up in the sky by inciting the wrath of Aphrodite, the most beautiful of the gods. The small group of stars called the Pleiades were known as the seven sisters, who were placed in the sky by the king of the gods, Zeus, to protect them

from an over attentive Orion. Each group of stars had a story (or stories), and each grouping was remembered by their name, story, and time they were visible in the sky.

Modern times call for modern maps, and as geographers have done for the Earth, astronomers have made maps of the heavens. By recording the locations of bright stars and their relative brightness, astronomers can discern the approximate layout of the

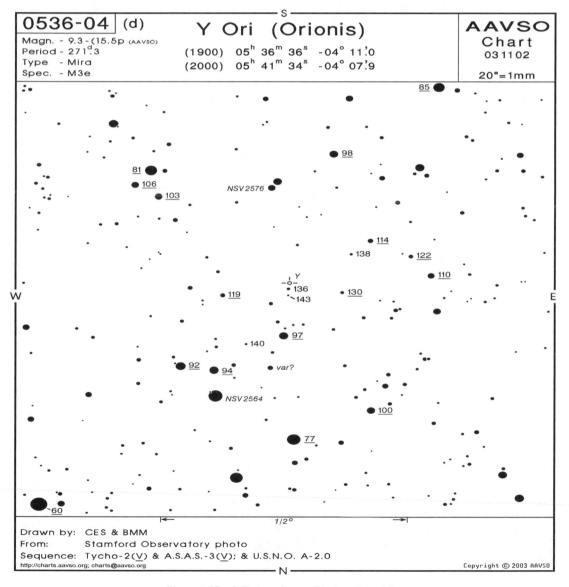

Figure 1.10—A Picture from a Modern Star Atlas

observable universe. Begun by the ancient Babylonians (in the area that is now modern Iraq) in 3000 B.C.E. or earlier and brought to a fine art by the Chinese and Greeks, such maps can also be useful for navigation. Because the stars remain fixed in the sky and fixed relative to each other (at least over human lifetimes), we can predict where the stars should be in the sky.

Early star atlases often had fanciful drawings of the creatures and people associated with the constellations (Fig. 1.9). Modern star charts are somewhat boring in comparison but are more accurate and informative. They include not only the position of the star, but also its brightness, whether it is a double or multiple star, and other information about other kinds of objects (Fig. 1.10).

Coordinate Systems

Just as we have latitude and longitude on Earth, so we have declination and right ascension in the sky. *Latitude* and *longitude* are coordinates laid down in a grid on the spherical Earth that measure north-south positions. Latitude measures how far north or south you are from the equator and is measured in degrees, with the poles being 90° away from the equator, which has a latitude of 0°. Longitude measures east-west positions in degrees eastward or westward from a point directly south of Greenwich, England, which has a longitude of 0°. Declination and right ascension are coordinates projected outward onto the sky, as if it were the inside of a giant *celestial sphere*, which is an imaginary sphere above Earth that appears to hold all the planets (Fig. 1.11).

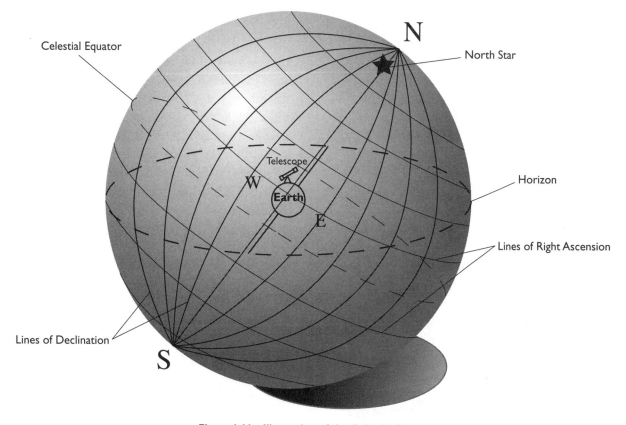

Figure 1.11—Illustration of the Celestial Sphere

Right ascension is similar to longitude in that it measures positions east or west of the point on the celestial equator where the Sun appears to be on the vernal equinox. *Declination* measures positions north or south of the *celestial equator*, which is the projection of Earth's equator outward onto the celestial sphere, just as latitude measures positions north or south of the equator on Earth. Like latitude and longitude, the sky coordinates of right ascension and declination have angular units. Right ascension is measured in hours, minutes, and seconds instead of longitude's degrees, minutes, and seconds. The motion of the sky is the root of our units of time, so 360° is equivalent to 24 h, and both systems are used to measure angles. Astronomers use these coordinates to pinpoint the locations of stars, galaxies, and other objects.

Sky Catalogs

Catalogs of the sky are not modern inventions but have been made throughout history. The first significant star catalog was compiled by a Greek astronomer known as Hipparchus of Rhodes (ca. 160–127 B.C.E.). He observed the bright stars in the sky and recorded their locations. He also assigned categories of brightness for the stars, known as *magnitude*, which is a unit for measuring the brightness of stars. The brightest stars were of the first magnitude and fainter stars were of the second, third, or fourth magnitude, and so on. Hipparchus' original system had six classifications, such that stars of the first magnitude appeared about 100 times brighter than stars of sixth magnitude. Each change in magnitude represents a ratio in brightness of about 2.5.

This ratio system is still in use today, but it has problems. Faint objects have large magnitudes, the reverse of how we normally think about

numeric quantities. The very brightest objects (like the planets or the Sun) have negative magnitudes.

The magnitude of an object in the sky as we see it is known as the *apparent magnitude*, which is how bright a star appears from Earth, a combination of the Star's inherent brightness and its distance from us. But sometimes we are interested in the true brightness of an object in the sky. This true brightness is known as the *absolute magnitude*, which is the actual brightness of an object when seen from exactly 10 parsecs away from Earth. A star 1 parsec away displays a parallax effect of 1 arcsecond (arcsec). One parsec is a unit of measure that is 3.26 light years. A *light-year* is equal to the distance light travels in 1 year, about 9,500,000,000,000 kilometers (km). To calculate absolute magnitude, we must know either the distance to the star or its inherent brightness or luminosity.

A truly monumental catalog of stars, the *Bonner Durchmusterung*, was created by Friedrich Wilhelm August Argelander (1799–1875) using a newly constructed telescope in Bonn, Germany, to make observations of more than 500,000 stars. He hired a sculptor to etch the stars and the coordinate grid into granite blocks and used the blocks to make printed star maps. This catalog, also called the *Bonn Sky Catalog*, is still in use today. Stars are noted by their BD number, such as BD 40362.

This catalog was the backbone of most astronomy work until the publication of the Palomar Sky Survey, undertaken by the National Geographic Society and the Palomar observatory from 1950 to 1957. Using large photographic plates and a special telescope, the program took pictures of the sky over a period of a few years. The plates weigh about a pound each

NATIONAL VIRTUAL OBSERVATORY

A new system called the National Virtual Observatory will connect all existing and future sky catalogs and observations. The idea is to use computers and the Internet to allow astronomers and the public access to stored astronomical data without having to use a telescope. Because there is no "real" observatory, only astronomical data, it is called a virtual observatory. This U.S. observatory will ultimately include the resources and data of astronomers worldwide, when it may have to be renamed the International Virtual Observatory.

This virtual observatory will make it far easier to compare objects in different catalogs, which can lead to new scientific knowledge. There will even be a user interface to allow amateurs or the just curious to access the data, look at images taken with different telescopes, or learn about some particular object. This is a developing resource that will be fully enabled only in the future, but the carefully archived sky catalogs will always be available, whether online or in the library. Web addresses for some of these resources are provided in Appendix 2.

and are delicate, but they give great views of large portions of the sky. Printed versions of the survey also exist, but the most compact form is a set of about 20 CD-ROMs that contain digitally sampled images of all the plates.

These days, astronomers produce catalogs all the time on a wider and wider range of objects. Because computers make storing data so easy, most catalogs are now digital, and books listing all the objects are not published very often. An interesting galaxy survey, the Sloan Digital Sky Survey project (http://www.sdss.org), will soon publish a final catalog, listing millions of objects, their magnitudes, and spectral characteristics, as well as the distance to the nearest million or so galaxies. This unprecedented catalog will give us our first comprehensive picture of a large portion of the universe.

SUMMARY

The sky has played an important role throughout history. The objects in the sky change position hour by hour, day by day and month to month. Objects rise and set each day. The Sun, Moon, and planets change position against the background stars throughout the year. The motions of the objects in the sky have, therefore, been used for timekeeping. The day is defined by the rotation of Earth. The month is tied to the motion of the Moon around Earth. The year is defined by the Sun's apparent motion through the sky, which is caused by Earth's year-long orbit around the Sun. The planets, because they orbit the Sun independent of the Earth, move at different rates and are in different positions in the sky over time.

Some special events take place due to alignments of the various solar system objects. These include transits, when a planet passes between us and the Sun, eclipses (either lunar or solar), when the Sun, Earth, and Moon are aligned, and occultations, when the Moon or a planet blocks the light of a distant star.

Just as on Earth, coordinate systems are used to locate the objects in the sky and map their locations over time. On Earth we use longitude and latitude. For celestial objects, we use right ascension and declination. Astronomers use sky atlases or catalogs to record where objects are in the sky.

UNDERSTANDING THE UNIVERSE

KEY TERMS

constellation, cosmology, heliocentric, supernova, geocentric, retrograde motion, astronomical unit, inertia

EARLY IDEAS

Soon after humans established the first farms in 5000 B.C.E., they settled in towns, took up trades (not everyone had to gather food all the time anymore), and even began to study the sky. Let's look at the contributions to astronomy of five ancient cultures and summarize what they thought or knew about the heavens. Understanding the origins of our knowledge of the sky will allow us to appreciate our current knowledge even more and will, we hope, show how science progresses—in fits and starts.

Mesopotamia

Ancient Mesopotamia was a broad region of the Middle East that is now the territory of several countries, including most of modern-day Iraq. The earliest records of organized civilization come from this area. Some of the earliest recorded towns are found here, established as far back as 7000 B.C.E. The region boasted two substantial rivers that provided a regular water supply. They also flooded occasionally, bringing fresh nutrients to the soils in the floodplain. Farming developed in this lush zone, which became known as the *fertile crescent*. Many different distinct cultures flourished in

particular towns or regions. These cultures included the Babylonian, Assyrian, and Sumerian civilizations, which each flourished at different times. By 3000 B.C.E., clay tablets were being used to record information using *cuneiform*, an early form of writing developed by Mesopotamian cultures. Some deciphered tablets include records of the motion of planets or the occurrence of eclipses, the earliest records of humans viewing the universe. Some were just calendars. Most were business transactions, just like our paper records today.

These early tablets indicate that the Babylonians and Sumerians had begun to name some groups of stars, or constellations. A *constellation* is a group of stars in the sky, usually identified by a mythological creature or character. Some of the ancient Mesopotamian definitions are still in use today, such as Leo, Taurus, Scorpio, Ursa Major, Gemini, Capricorn, and Sagittarius. They also had begun to track the motions of objects in the sky, eventually developing a calendar based on these motions. They even formed a basic star catalog known as the zodiac, which they could use to record the general location of any astronomical phenomenon. The *zodiac* is an ancient star catalog from the Babylonian culture composed of 12 roughly equal constellations through which the Sun and planets were observed to move along the *ecliptic* (the plane of the Earth's orbit around the Sun). The Babylonians also attempted to predict eclipses, and many tablets from about 1000 B.C.E. forward contain eclipse references.

Modern constellations are marked by boundaries in the sky and not by the lines connecting the brightest stars, as in the constellations defined by ancient civilizations.

Although ancient Mesopotamians appear to have actively studied the motions in the sky, they used this information for astrological purposes—to predict when events would happen on Earth or to see if undertaking a particular activity would result in a positive outcome. No distinction was made between religion/astrology and early astronomy. They were essentially indistinguishable. However, the priest-astronomers performed many functions that modern astronomers carry out: tracking the planets, recording star positions, and following the lunar phases. And Mesopotamian culture did give us some fundamental units still in use today. These people broke a circle into 360 slivers of equal size. This unit of angular measure, the *degree*, is defined as 1/360 of a circle. They also broke the day up into 12 equal portions of time of two hours each. Our modern reckoning of time is derived from this system.

India

Just a few thousand miles away and a few thousand years later, the civilization that took root on the banks of the Indus river developed another view of the universe. The first reference to astronomical topics in ancient Indian culture appears in about 2000 B.C.E. in the *Rig Veda*, a religious text. The positions of the planets and stars were used to cast horoscopes. Ancient Indian astronomers believed (correctly) that the Sun must be the same as the stars but that the stars were more distant or, perhaps, less important. They also believed (incorrectly) that the Sun was at the center of the universe and that Earth and other planets

moved around the Sun. There is no recorded evidence supporting these facts in ancient Indian texts, however. They simply accepted these ideas on faith as the foundation of their understanding of the universe. The formulation of theories about the origin and change over time of the entire universe is known as *cosmology*. Indian cosmology was revolutionary in that it tried to connect the movements of the planets and stars with a working model of the universe.

Aryabhatta (476–520 C.E.), an Indian astronomer well ahead of his time, developed a cosmology that was fundamentally *heliocentric*, or sun-centered (usually used in reference to a model of the solar system or cosmology), which explained (correctly) that moonlight was reflected light from the Sun and guessed (correctly) that Earth was a sphere that rotated on an axis. Because his work was not translated into Latin, the primary language of early science, until the thirteenth century—after these facts had been explained and accepted by European astronomers—he did not have a significant impact on western astronomy (although some of his mathematical methods were eagerly adopted). Brahmagupta (ca. 598–ca. 668 C.E.), another Indian astronomer, estimated the circumference of Earth. Using his own approximation for the value of pi (the square root of 10; pi is usually represented as π), he determined that the Earth was about 36,000 km in circumference—not too far off the modern value of 40,075 km.

Other than these two astronomers, much of ancient India's contribution to early astronomy was mathematical, such as the development of the decimal system, including the use of zero and negative numbers, and contributions to algebra.

China

For millennia, Chinese culture was cut off from the rest of the world by the large central deserts of Asia, the cold northern plains of Siberia, and an immense ocean to the east. Developing in isolation, China had a well-advanced culture by about 2000 B.C.E.

As in Mesopotamia, much of Chinese astronomy was centered on creating horoscopes or predictions, and little work was carried out trying to understand what the stars and planets were. Even so, the Chinese kept careful records of the sky, such as the first recorded eclipse of the Sun, recorded in 2136 B.C.E. The earliest written record of a *supernova*, a true stellar explosion that destroys a star, was made by Chinese astronomers in 1054 B.C.E. Although they called it a "guest star," because it stayed visible only a short period of time, their accurate record of its location has allowed modern astronomers to identify the remains of the star in the sky today, now called the Crab Nebula. A *nebula* is a cloud of gas and dust that appears cloudlike in space.

The Chinese are also responsible for the oldest known printed star chart. This chart shows the positions of stars as recorded by Chinese astronomers in about 350 B.C.E.; the chart was subsequently etched onto bronze and then copied onto paper in about 940 C.E. Today you can see this manuscript in the British museum in London.

The Chinese were also the first to record *sunspots*. Sunspots are darker regions on the surface of the Sun that appears as dark blotches (we talk in detail about them in Chapter 10), and records of the number of sunspots covering nearly 2000 years exist in documents from ancient China and Korea. Although the first Western detection of sunspots was made

THE ORIGINAL TEXT RECORDING THE DISCOVERY OF A GUEST STAR

Here is the text from the manuscript that recorded the guest star:

In the second year of the reign of the Zhongping Emperor, 10th month, day kuei hai, a guest star appeared within the Southern Gate [a constellation]. It was as large as half a mat. It showed the five colors and it was happy-angry [it twinkled]. It gradually became smaller and disappeared in the 6th month of the second year after. According to the standard prognostication this means insurrection. When we come to the 6th year, the governor of the Yuan-shou region punished and eliminated the middle officials. WuGuang attacked and killed HeMiao, the general of chariots and cavalry, and several thousand people were killed.

Luckily today, no rulers use the appearance of supernovae to guide their decisions (let's hope so anyway).

by Italian astronomer Galileo Galilei (1564–1642) in 1610 using his self-made telescope, ancient Chinese astronomers were recording the existence of sunspots as long ago as 800 B.C.E. Sunspots were key in determining that the Sun rotates. These spots exist on the surface for quite a while, and astronomers can track their motion by observing the Sun with properly filtered telescopes.

Greece

It is not until the ancient Greeks that astronomers actually thought about ways to explain what they saw in the sky as opposed to using heavenly motions to predict Earth-bound events. From about 600 B.C.E. to about 200 C.E., Greek philosophers attempted to understand the world around them—and the universe—in a physical way. Some of their ideas included the concept that Earth was a large sphere and that the Sun and the stars were burning much as fire burns on Earth.

Aristarchus of Samos (ca. 310–ca. 230 B.C.E.) was the first to propose that the universe was heliocentric, or sun-centered, although his idea did not catch on. Indian astronomer Aryabhatta came up with the same idea independently some 700 years later. Even though his original book on the heliocentric theory did not survive to the modern era, his ideas had currency at the time. The Greek scientist Archimedes (ca. 287–212 B.C.E.), whose father was an astronomer, quoted Aristarchus in one of his books, *The Sand-Reckoner*:

> His hypotheses are that the fixed stars and the sun remain unmoved, that the earth revolves about the sun on the circumference of a circle, the sun lying in the middle of the orbit, and that the sphere of fixed stars, situated about the same center as the sun, is so great that the circle in which he supposes the earth to revolve bears such a proportion to the distance of the fixed stars as the center of the sphere bears to its surface.

This ancient quote shows that the ideas of this one lone thinker more than 2000 years ago were shockingly accurate.

Aristarchus also tried to measure the distance between Earth and Sun by measuring the angle between the Moon and Sun at exactly the moment when the Moon is half-illuminated. This is a challenging observation, and the calculation itself, once the measurement was obtained, would have been hard at the time (before trigonometry was invented) too. Needless to say, he got the wrong answer, but the method could have worked, had he had better tools and calculation methods.

The Greeks also began to develop ways of measuring the size of Earth. Greek astronomers believed Earth was round because Earth's shadow appeared round on the face of the Moon during lunar eclipses. Eratosthenes (ca. 276–194 B.C.E.), who lived in Egypt, designed an experiment using two sticks and the shadows they cast at noon to measure the circumference of Earth. Although his calculation ended up being wrong (probably due to the uncertain distance between the two sticks), the idea that the world was round and measurable was truly revolutionary. To be fair, he wasn't too far off. His calculated size of Earth was correct to within 4% of the true value (Fig. 2.1).

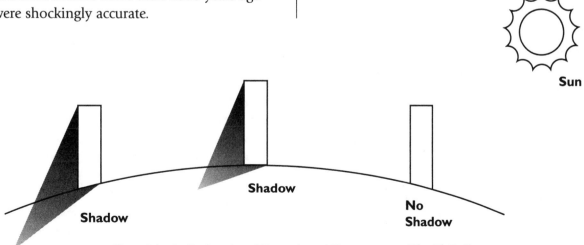

Figure 2.1—An Explanation of Eratosthenes' Measurement of Earth's Radius
Shadow length and direction at some times on Earth depend on location and size of Earth itself.

The true giant of Greek astronomy was Ptolemy (ca. 85–165 C.E.). He wrote many books on a wide variety of topics, many of which established fields of study and summarized the then current understanding of geography, mathematics, and optics. Many of his works have survived into the modern era. Ptolemy's major astronomical work was *The Almagest* (the title is a corruption of an Arabic title for the work, *Al Majisti*, but Ptolemy originally called the book *The Mathematical Companion*). In *The Almagest*, Ptolemy laid out mathematical theories for predicting the positions of the Sun and Moon based on observations and a model for the solar system in which Earth is at the center and all solar system bodies orbit the Earth. This idea of a geocentric solar system was to last nearly 1600 years. A *geocentric* system is earth-centered; the term is usually used in reference to a model of the solar system or cosmology. He also developed a theory for eclipses and produced tables that could be used to make predictions of eclipses and the positions of the planets. Some of the models and methods he published derived from the work of Aristotle, and Aristotle's giant reputation helped convince Ptolemy's readers of their validity.

How would human history have unfolded had the Greek civilization not fallen apart? The Romans, inheritors of Greece's legacy and knowledge, were good at building empires, vast aqueducts, and tremendous buildings, but they were not as good at astronomy as the Greeks. Further developments in astronomical knowledge had to wait until after the so-called dark ages, when new ideas about the world began to be shared through the medium of printed books.

Arabia

The dark ages did have their bright spots. As Greek civilization faded, Arabic civilization began to emerge as dominant in the Middle East and North Africa. After a brief period of war and unrest, which finished about 750 C.E., Baghdad became a center of culture and learning with the caliph, or king of the time, establishing what was essentially a university. Many of the Greek texts that survived the period of instability were translated into Arabic. Refinements to the calculations and tables in the books were made, and new results and studies began to be published by Arabic scientists.

Abu Ali al-Hasan ibn al-Haytham (965–1040 C.E.), later known to Europeans as Alhazen, produced a seven-volume work on optics, *Kitab al-Manazir*, which was translated into Latin in 1270 as *Opticae Thesaurus Alhazeni*. It is considered the next major contribution to the field of optics after Ptolemy's *Almagest*.

One of Alhazen's most important contributions to astronomy and to science in general was the formulation of the scientific method. He stated that experiments should be systematic and repeatable. Also, they should produce quantitative measurements that could lead to the formation of hypotheses that could then also be tested by experiment. Alhazen also theorized (correctly) that vision was made possible by rays of light falling on the eye. This disagreed with Ptolemy's theory that the eyes themselves emit light rays that bounce off of objects and return to the eye.

Another Arabic astronomer, Abu Rayhan Al-Biruni (973–1048 C.E.), measured the size of Earth very accurately using triangulation techniques; his value was not improved upon in the West until the sixteenth century. Al-Biruni made qualitative observations of the velocity of light and correctly surmised it was immense compared to that of sound.

Arabic astronomers also made extensive catalogs of the stars, naming the brightest ones. Their catalogs were ultimately reintroduced to Europe through Spain, where Arabic culture held sway from about 712 to about 1450 C.E. Many modern star names, including such stars as Betelgeuse, Algol, Fomalhaut, and Deneb, are Arabic in origin.

THE RENAISSANCE

Copernicus

Nicolaus Copernicus (1473–1543) is credited with the modern introduction of a heliocentric theory for the solar system. Copernicus was born in Torun, Poland, where his father had moved to establish a copper business. His father died when Nicolaus was 10 years old, and young Nicolaus remained in Torun until he entered the University of Krakow. He later went on to the University of Bologna in Italy, where he studied astronomy and mathematics extensively.

In 1514, after returning to Poland, he shared a small hand-written book with his circle of friends, outlining his theory of the solar system and establishing the seven basic facts at the heart of his theory. Among these were the following notions:

- Earth was not at the center of the solar system
- The center of the solar system is, in fact, near the Sun

- The stars are tremendously far away from Earth compared to the Sun
- The rotation of Earth about its axis accounts for the daily motion of the stars and Sun across the sky.

The most important aspect of his theory, detailed in the book *De Revolutionibus*, was the explanation of a quirky motion of the planets that had long been observed but never adequately accounted for. Known as retrograde motion, it was easily observed by tracking the daily position of the planets in the sky. Planets usually move smoothly across the sky in a more or less straight line. With *retrograde motion*, a given planet appears to make a slow reversal in its motion, completes a small loop in the sky, and then continues on in its original path. Since the motion could be easily observed, it had to be explained in any successful theory of solar system motions.

Retrograde motion had always been a problem for Ptolemy's model of the solar system. To account for it, Ptolemy put Earth at the center with the other planets orbiting in circular paths about Earth. The other planets also moved in much smaller circular paths of their own as they went about Earth. These little curlicues, called epicycles, took place every so often and, when viewed from Earth, could more or less explain the retrograde motion. Almost. To fully explain the motion, Ptolemy further had to have the planet move at a non-uniform speed as it went around the epicycle, staying almost completely still at some times while moving quite quickly at others. This was a rather complicated and ungainly model, but since Ptolemy, the great Greek scientist, couldn't be wrong, the complexity was tolerated. *Epicycles*, observed reversals of a planet's motion in the sky, were ultimately explained by Copernicus' heliocentric model of the solar system.

After Copernicus' death, his work became known by European astronomers and his model was quickly accepted, because it was simpler than Ptolemy's model and yet explained all the observed phenomena. This is the hallmark of good science: abandoning complex models for simpler ones that still explain what we see.

In Copernicus' model, the Sun resides near the center of the solar system, with the other planets orbiting about it on circular paths. The order of the planets given by Copernicus was Mercury, Venus, Earth, Mars, Jupiter, and Saturn, which we know today is the right order. The outermost planets had yet to be discovered.

The beauty of this model was that retrograde motion was explained simply as a geometric effect caused by the motion of Earth and by the fact that we, the observers, are watching the other planets from a moving platform. In this model, the Sun sits at the center, with Earth and Mars orbiting it. Mercury and Venus have been left off for clarity. Because Mars orbits more slowly than Earth, Earth catches up and passes Mars as Earth moves about the Sun. As it does so, Mars appears to slow down, reverse direction, and then start forward again. You may have experienced retrograde motion yourself if you have ever been in a car with a manual transmission. Such cars can drift backward slightly when driving uphill from a stoplight. As the driver engages the transmission, the car drifts backward (because the driver took his or her foot off of the brake); nearby objects appear to drift forward slightly, then stop, and finally appear to drift backward again once the car is accelerating.

Tycho and Kepler

The next breakthrough in our understanding of our solar system came from northern Europeans. Danish Astronomer Tycho Brahe (1546–1601) began his career by studying law, but he was so impressed by the ability of some astronomers to predict a total solar eclipse that he changed career paths and moved to astronomy. Designing his own instruments, he was able to improve the accuracy of contemporary astronomical measurements. Brahe carefully observed the positions of the stars and planets in the sky over time, keeping careful records of all of his observations. He published his observations of a so-called new star, or nova, in 1573. The publication got the attention of King Frederick II of Denmark, who awarded him his own island and substantial funding to continue his observations. On his island, Hven, he built an observatory/castle that he called Uraniborg. At one point, nearly 1% of the Danish budget went toward the construction of Uraniborg. For perspective, the entire NASA budget (about $15 billion in 2003) is only about 0.7 % of the U.S. budget (about $2140 trillion).

After the death of King Frederick II, Tycho's funding dried up and he had to move elsewhere. The king's son was not willing to continue supporting Tycho's observations. Settling in Prague, Tycho partnered with a young, energetic astronomer named Johannes Kepler (1571–1630). Kepler was an avid student and would eventually use Tycho's observational records to improve Copernicus' model of the solar system. He knew from Tycho's careful and copious observations that Copernicus' model did not perfectly predict the locations of the planets and that it was slightly wrong most of the time. After years of work, he had a stroke of genius. Instead of the circular orbits introduced by Copernicus, Kepler hypothe-sized that the planets traced ellipses in space. This small change, when worked through mathematically, greatly improved the predic-tive capability of Copernicus' model and led Kepler to develop three fundamental laws of planetary motion.

Kepler's Laws

The amazing thing about Kepler's work was that three simple rules seemed to be all one needed to predict the motion of the planets. Let's look in detail at these laws to appreciate Kepler's triumph. Kepler's first law states that the paths of motion of the planets are ellipses,

THE ELLIPSE

The ellipse resembles a squashed circle. More formally, an ellipse is a special mathematical curve known as a conical section. As its name implies, it can be thought of as the intersection of a flat sheet of paper with a cone (Fig. 2.2). If this paper intersects a cone parallel to the cone's base, the intersection is a perfect circle. At any other angle, the intersection is an ellipse. An *ellipse* can be defined mathematically as the set of points whose combined distance from two selected points is a constant. This definition is most easily understood by looking at the way an ellipse can be drawn using a long piece of string, two thumbtacks, and a pencil. By tacking the two ends of the string to a piece of paper and then using the string as a

sort of holder for the pencil, you can easily draw an ellipse (Fig. 2.3). Each thumbtack is a focus. As they get further apart, the ellipse gets more elongated. When they move together, the ellipse looks more circular. The planetary orbits are so close to being circles (with the exception of Pluto) that the two foci are near-ly on top of each other. (When they are on top of each other, you get a circle.) A line extended through the two foci that intersects with the ellipse itself is known as the major axis, whereas the line perpendicular to the *major axis* that goes through the center of the ellipse is known as the *minor axis*. The length of these two axes can be used to help charac-terize the ellipse.

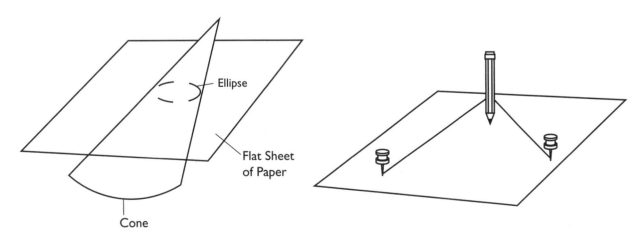

Figure 2.2—A Plane Slicing through a Cone   Figure 2.3—Drawing an Ellipse

with the Sun at one focus. The second law states that, as a planet moves around the ellipse, the line connecting the planet and the Sun sweeps out equal areas in equal amounts of time. Although this idea is a bit hard to visualize, it simply means that as the planet moves along the ellipse, its speed changes. When it is furthest from the Sun, it moves the slowest; when it is closest to the Sun, it moves the fastest. The third law, which appeared later than the other two, states that the length of time it takes a planet to move around its orbit is related to the size of the ellipse.

THE NITTY-GRITTY OF KEPLER'S LAWS

Kepler's laws are fundamentally mathematical in nature. Although we can appreciate them qualitatively, to actually work with them, we have to use formulas. The nice thing is that the formulas are pretty simple. If the letter P stands for the period of the planetary orbit and the letter a stands for the semimajor axis of the ellipse, then Kepler's third law states that the two quantities are related by the equation $P^2 = C \times a^3$, where C is a constant value. If the units of the period are in years and the semimajor axis is in *astronomical units* (a unit of distance equal to the average distance between the Earth and Sun, about 93 million miles), then the constant C is just 1.

Kepler's laws were amazing predictive tools. By knowing (in some sense) the distance of a planet from the Sun, you could predict how fast it moved. This statement, when you think about it, means that the Sun must have some kind of influence on the planet. It took a while before anyone seriously confronted why the planets moved in this way, aided in part by a new invention from an experimenter in Italy.

Galileo and the Birth of Physics

Galileo Galilei is easily one of the most fascinating Renaissance scientists. Born in Pisa, Italy, he attended the university there in 1581. His father hoped he would study medicine, but Galileo had other ideas. He became fascinated with trying to explain the world around him. His first efforts, studying the motion of a pendulum, a weight swinging at the end of a string from a fixed point, were successful, and he was able to find that the amount of time it took a pendulum to swing back and forth (its period) was not related to the arc of the motion. He is also famous for disproving one of the key ideas of Ptolemy—that heavier objects fell faster—supposedly by simultaneously dropping a heavy object and a light object off of the Leaning Tower of Pisa and noting that they hit the ground at the same time. In fact, Galileo used small balls rolling down ramps to disprove Ptolemy's idea. A modern version of the legendary Pisa experiment was carried out using a rock hammer and a feather by astronauts on the Moon during one of the Apollo moon landings. Both the feather and the hammer hit the lunar surface at the same time.

The underlying theme of all of Galileo's work was experimentation and a questioning of any assumed truth. If something was true, he reasoned, it should stand up to rigorous testing and experimentation. His studies of motion laid the foundations for the science of physics.

In astronomy, he is most famous for pointing a telescope at the objects in the heavens and publishing his results. He built his first telescope in 1609 (polishing the glass lenses by hand, a very tedious job) and quickly made three very important discoveries. These discoveries were so important that some people claim that no greater discoveries have followed so quickly after the construction of a new telescope. The first discovery was that Jupiter had moons that orbited it in a regular way, just as the Moon orbited Earth. This was the final death knell for the geocentric model of the solar system, for how could moons be orbiting another planet if all objects had to orbit Earth?

He also found that our Moon had mountains and craters and must be a body similar to Earth, only smaller in size. And he found that the fuzzy light of the Milky Way was really the combined light of many faint stars that the eye could not distinguish without the aid of a telescope. These three discoveries rocked the world of science and set off a flurry of telescopic investigations, resulting in the discovery of sunspots, the phases of Venus, and many other ideas.

Galileo, after publishing his first observations, immediately built a larger telescope and attempted to convince supporters of the geocentric model that they were wrong. Unfortunately, many of these individuals were either members or friends of a conservative movement within the Catholic Church. Beset by the inquisitors of the church and threatened with excommunication and, potentially, death, he recanted his position supporting the heliocentric model of Copernicus and Kepler.

However, the sun-centered cat was out of the bag, and observations by others with increasingly larger telescopes led to the acceptance of Kepler's heliocentric model. This period of discovery in all areas of human endeavor—not just science—is called the Renaissance. In the closing years of the Renaissance, a young scientist in England of unprecedented genius explained why Kepler's laws worked and opened the door to a new understanding of our universe.

Newton and His Laws

Isaac Newton (1642–1727) trained as a mathematician at Cambridge and, during the plague years of 1665 and 1666, returned to the countryside, where he continued his work on a number of physical phenomena.

In one of the most important books of all time, *The Principia*, Newton finally explained why Kepler's laws worked. He had succeeded by finding that three simple assumptions and some complicated mathematics not only predicted Kepler's laws but answered many other questions as well, such as how far a cannonball could be fired. Newton's first law states that all objects at rest will stay at rest and all objects moving will continue moving in a straight line unless acted upon by an outside force. This property is known as *inertia*. The measure of an object's inertia is its mass. The more mass an object has, the greater is its inertia.

Newton's second law relates *acceleration*, or the rate of change of velocity (usually given in meters per second per second, or m/s^2) of an object to the object's mass and the force acting on the object. Written symbolically as $F = m \times a$, where a is acceleration, m is mass, and F is force, this law is one of the fundamental cornerstones of basic physics. If an object has a large mass, more force will be required to change its motion. We all know this intuitively. Imagine trying to push a Volkswagen Beetle that is sitting at rest and compare it with trying to push a cement truck at rest. Which is harder to push? The cement truck, of course: it is bigger and made of more matter and, therefore, has a larger mass.

Newton's third law describes how forces interact: for each action, there is an equal and opposite reaction. Forces act in opposition. Earth may tug on the Moon, keeping it in orbit, but the Moon also exerts a tug on Earth and they both rotate about a center of mass, a kind of balancing point located somewhere between the two objects. A cement block sitting on a table doesn't move, even though the force of gravity is pulling on the cement block. This is because the table, made of wood or metal, holds the cement block up against gravity by exerting an opposite force on the block.

From these three laws, Newton derived some interesting properties about gravity, although he was unable to explain why gravity existed. Scientists are still working on this problem today. One interesting property of gravity is that the force between two objects decreases as they get further apart. Also, the force of gravity appears to be universal. It seems to work for objects here on Earth, the Moon in orbit around Earth, Earth and the other planets in orbit around the Sun and, as we know now, for our Sun in orbit around the center of the Milky Way, and even for galaxies moving in orbit around the center of great clusters of galaxies. One simple rule applies to objects of almost every imaginable size and across immense distances.

Newton's ideas have lasting value because they can accurately predict a wide range of phenomena. People found that Newton's laws correctly predicted the motions of the moons of Jupiter, the flight of cannonballs (or feathers) through the air (or the near-vacuum of the Moon), as well as the orbits of the planets about the Sun and even the Sun about the center of our galaxy. Newton's *Principia* allowed scientists finally to see the true power of a complete scientific theory, and

NEWTON'S LETTERS

Communication between scientists is very important today as it was in the past. Today, emails zip back and forth between collaborating scientists on an almost minute-to-minute basis. Before the Internet or phones, the written letter was how communication took place. Scientists would often begin their workday with the arrival of the post. Reading letters from their colleagues describing current work could lead to new ideas. News of new observations and theories quickly spread through the network of scientists. Much of the knowledge we take for granted today is owed to the reliable postal system of the late 1600s and 1700s. Isaac Newton was no exception to this letter-writing habit. In a letter to a French scholar and colleague later in his life, he described the nature of the astronomical work he performed during the productive period he spent away from Cambridge during the plague years of 1665 and 1666:

I began to think of gravity extending to the orb of the Moon & (having found out how to estimate the force with which a globe revolving within a sphere presses the surface of the sphere) from Kepler's rule of the periodical times of the Planets being in sesquialterate proportion [$P^2 = C \times a^3$] of their distances from the centers of their Orbs, I deduced that the forces which keep the Planets in their Orbs must be reciprocally as the squares of their distances from the centers about which they revolve: and thereby compared the force requisite to keep the Moon in her Orb with the force of gravity at the surface of Earth, and found them to answer pretty nearly.

What a profound letter to receive in the morning post. Imagine being the first reader of this remarkable missive. Somehow emailed discoveries just don't seem to pack quite the same punch as this carefully worded, handwritten letter.

its publication in 1687 stands as the gateway to modern scientific understanding of the universe and signaled the death of all early ideas about the universe, from the Mesopotamians to the Indians, through the Chinese, to the Greeks and the Arabic peoples. Experiment and observation, theory formulation, and testing were to be the new basis for our understanding.

SUMMARY

Cultures throughout history have added to our knowledge of astronomy. Constellations were identified and named, and stories were told about the characters these sky drawings represented. Mesopotamian culture gave us our unit of angular measure, the degree. Indian mathematicians developed the concept of zero as well as making early cosmological models of our universe. The Chinese actively observed the sky, recording celestial events in written documents and creating star charts. The ancient Greeks established the roots of science by attempting to understand the world around them in a physical way and even attempted to measure the size of Earth and make accurate catalogs of star brightnesses. The Arabic cultures gave us many of the names of the stars we use today and tried to understand how we see. The Renaissance opened up our astronomical understanding, as well as our growing knowledge of all the sciences. Copernicus was the first western scientist to develop a workable sun-centered model for the solar system. Tycho and Kepler paired their respective skills as observer and mathematician to determine some predictive laws (Kepler's laws) governing the motion of the objects in the solar system. Kepler determined that the planets moved in elliptical orbits around the Sun and that their rate of motion was related to the size of their orbit. Galileo used simple experiments to try and understand the physical laws and also published the first observations of celestial objects made with a telescope. Isaac Newton built upon the scientific knowledge developed during the early Renaissance to develop and publish comprehensive books detailing how the physical laws worked. He used calculus, a newly developed mathematical tool, to predict the motion of objects and made the intuitive connection between motion of objects here on Earth and in space.

LIGHT

ELECTROMAGNETIC RADIATION (A.K.A. LIGHT)

All kinds of objects emit light. Some things in the universe absorb light and some reflect light. By studying the light that ultimately arrives here on Earth, we can learn not only about the distant objects that originally emitted the light, but also about the material or objects that the light encountered on its way here. Light is the fundamental carrier of information in the universe and an astronomer's most fundamental tool.

Technically speaking, light is electromagnetic radiation, which combines some of the properties of electricity and magnetism, as the name implies. *Electromagnetic radiation*, or light, is the fundamental carrier of information in the universe. It has a constant speed—the speed of light—and is characterized by its wavelength. Light is a traveling wave of electromagnetic energy usually formed by the repetitive motion of a charged particle.

When electricity was first being investigated in the mid-1700s, it was found that certain things could be made to have an electric charge, whereas others could not. If a piece of amber were rubbed with silk, an electric charge would build up on the amber that could be used to attract small bits of dust or paper. These charges could also be manipulated: for example, stored for future use or transferred from one item to another.

As scientists learned more about electricity, they found that simply the presence of electric charge could influence material nearby. Scientists developed the concept of an *electromagnetic field*, or the area surrounding an electrically charged particle, to explain how one object might influence another without actually touching it. A field is just a mathematical way of describing the fact that objects can exert forces on one another at a distance. It was found that electric charges had an electric field and that these charges felt a force when other charged particles were brought near them. Charged particles created an electric field. Magnets could also be explained in this way. Magnets had a magnetic field, and when certain kinds of objects—magnetized objects—were brought close to them, they felt a force.

The study of charges ultimately gave way to the study of moving charges, or electricity. Electricity generated great excitement in the scientific world of the late eighteenth and early nineteenth centuries. Here was a way to send energy along a wire that could do work, carry messages, and light our homes. Much of our modern civilization is based on a basic knowledge of electricity and how to manipulate it. In the early days of electricity, scientists spent a lot of time studying how flows of electricity, or currents, moved along wires. English scientist Michael Faraday (1791–1867) discovered in 1831 that a current moving in a wire could deflect a compass needle and that a changing magnetic field could induce an electric current. This discovery of *electromagnetic induction* showed that a moving electric field causes a magnetic field and that a moving magnetic field can induce electricity. These results led to the development of the electric motor and, ultimately, the electric generators that power our world.

Scottish scientist James Clerk Maxwell (1831–1879), born the same year that Faraday discovered electromagnetic induction, derived a set of equations, later simplified to just four, that completely described electric and magnetic phenomena and also predicted the existence of traveling waves of electromagnetic radiation. Using the equations, Maxwell was able to show that the speed at which these waves moved was close to the measured speed of light, and in a brilliant bit of deduction, he guessed that they were one and the same phenomenon. He was right. We know today that electromagnetic radiation, traveling pairs of electric and magnetic fields, is light.

BASIC PROPERTIES OF LIGHT

Electromagnetic radiation is so fundamental to astronomy that it is worthwhile to understand a few of its most basic properties. Although scientists can now easily summarize the properties of light and how it is formed and interacts with matter, this is hard-won knowledge; it took hundreds of years for investigators to figure this out. As Albert Einstein said, "The most incomprehensible thing about the world is that it is comprehensible."

Wavelength

One significant property of light is that it travels as a wave. Waves are energy in motion. They occur in water, air, and even in solid objects, such as earth's crust during an earthquake. Waves are characterized by their wavelength. The *wavelength* is the distance between successive peaks or troughs of a wave. In the case of water waves, we simply find the highest part of the wave and then wait until the next high part comes by. This

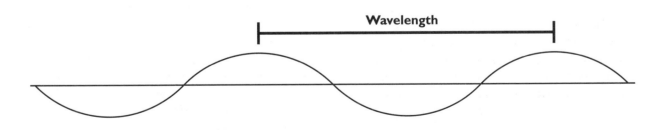

Figure 3.1—Wavelength

distance is the wavelength (Fig. 3.1). For electromagnetic waves, we can't see the peaks and troughs, but sensitive instruments can detect them as they move by the detector.

Typical water waves, like those on a lake, have wavelengths of 1 to 100 feet (ft). Ocean waves, caused by the wind moving across the surface of the ocean, have even longer wavelengths— from 100 ft up to 1000 ft. Electromagnetic radiation has an even larger range of wave-lengths. The longest electromagnetic radiation we can detect has wavelengths of 30,000 ft or more, whereas the shortest wavelength electromagnetic radiation is only 0.0000000000003 ft or even smaller. This entire range of wavelengths is known as the *electromagnetic spectrum*. Because of the wide range of wavelengths, charts of this spectrum usually give the wavelengths in powers of ten instead of writing out the actual size in inches or feet.

SIGHT

Sight is one of the most amazing properties of animals and humans alike. The fact that we can receive electromagnetic radiation with our eyes, form images, and detect colors is one of the happy miracles of life here on Earth. But how do we really see? The eye is basically a simple telescopic system. The lens of our eye, which can be partially blocked by the iris to limit the amount of light that enters the eye, focuses the light on the back portion of the eye, called the retina. The *iris* expands or con-tracts to limit the amount of light that enters the eye, and the *retina* is the back portion of the eye that is composed of cells that are sensitive to light and convert the incoming light waves to electrical signals that are sent to the brain along the optic nerve (Fig. 3.2).

Everyone has a blind spot. The *blind spot*, different for each person and each eye, is the portion of the retina where the optic nerve attaches, preventing the reception of light. There are no light-sensitive cells at the loca-tion where the nerve attaches. Happily, we hardly ever notice our blind spots, because the brain quickly interprets the signals from both eyes and uses the visual signal from one eye to cover up the blind spot in the other eye.

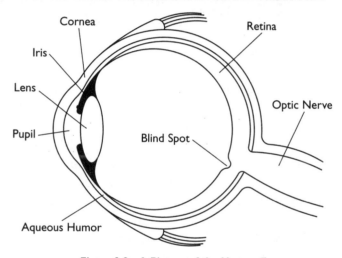

Figure 3.2—A Picture of the Human Eye

When we see color, our brain is really telling us about the wavelength of the light that the eye is seeing. Red light has longer wavelengths and blue light has shorter wavelengths. There are three different kinds of retinal cells that react differently to different wavelengths and send different signals to the brain based on the wavelength of light we are seeing. Color blindness can take place when the electrical signals from retinal cells are the same for different wavelengths of light or when one kind of retinal cell doesn't work.

The light we see with our eyes has very small wavelengths. Scientists use a convenient unit for these small wavelengths called the nanometer. A *nanometer* (nm) is a unit of distance equal to 0.000000001 m, or about 0.00000004 inches (in.). Visible light begins at about 700 nm, and we can't see waves much shorter than 450 nm. Our eyes don't actually "see" the waves as they come into our eye. Instead, the radiation interacts with molecules in our eye that stimulate small electrical impulses in our nervous system, and our brain interprets these signals to form our impression of the world around us.

Speed

The speed of light was always a puzzle to scientists, and a number of interesting experiments were developed to figure out just how fast it moved. When we turn off a light or open the refrigerator door, it seems that the light instantly leaves the room or lights up the goodies in the fridge. Galileo devised an experiment that he claimed he tried, where two people with lanterns start off close together and then slowly separate. By having one person uncover his or her lantern and the other person uncover his or her lantern when the light of the first lantern is visible, and slowly separating from each other, eventually a delay should be detected. Galileo tried it out to a separation of probably half a mile and couldn't see a time lag.

In 1667, Ole Römer (1644–1710), a Danish astronomer working in Paris, carefully studied the orbit of one of Jupiter's moons, Io, and found that at some points of the year it passed behind Jupiter a few minutes before it was predicted to, whereas at other times of the year it passed behind Jupiter a few minutes later than predicted. The maximum delay was about 8 minutes (min).

Because we see planets due to reflected sunlight and because part of the year we are closer to Jupiter than at other times, Römer reasoned that Io's changing times of eclipse behind Jupiter were due to the amount of time it took the light from Io and Jupiter to reach Earth. In other words, Io happily orbited around Jupiter at a smooth and regular rate, but because the distance between Earth and Jupiter slowly changed during the year, the light that arrives on Earth, allowing us to view the eclipses, shows up a bit earlier at some times and a bit later 6 months after. Newton mentions this discovery in *The Principia*. This observation proved that light traveled at a finite speed, but since the scale of the solar system was not yet accurately known, the actual speed of light remained out of reach. We have to have a distance and a time to determine a speed.

In the 1800s, two French scientists developed independent but similar methods for measuring the speed of light. They were Armand Hippolyte Louis Fizeau (1819–1896) and Jean-Bernard-Léon Foucault (1819–1868). Fizeau developed an experiment that used a focused light beam passing through a partially silvered mirror. Part of the beam passed through the mirror. The reflected part was then reflected off another mirror and then back through the partially silvered mirror. The direct and reflected beams could then be observed as a combined image by someone looking at the source through the mirror. The beam was turned on and off by rotating a circular disk with small, regularly spaced gaps that allowed the light to pass through the disk. By rotating the disk at a particular

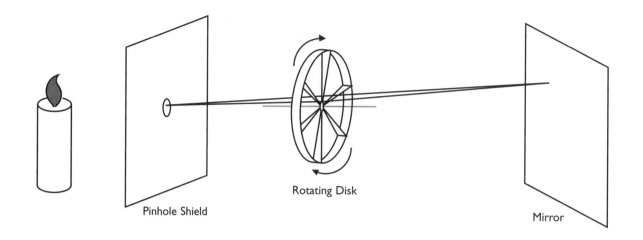

Figure 3.3—Diagram of Fizeau's Apparatus

speed, the reflected beam would be blocked by the disk. By knowing the speed of the wheel, the width of the gaps and the length of the reflected beam's path, Fizeau measured the speed of light at just over 310,000 kilometers per second (km/s), a good measurement, but just over 10,000 km/s faster than the true value. This value is within just a few percent of the true value. See Figure 3.3.

Foucault's apparatus (Fig. 3.4) was similar but used a rotating mirror in place of Fizeau's rotating disk. A beam of light was reflected off the surface of the rotating mirror onto a

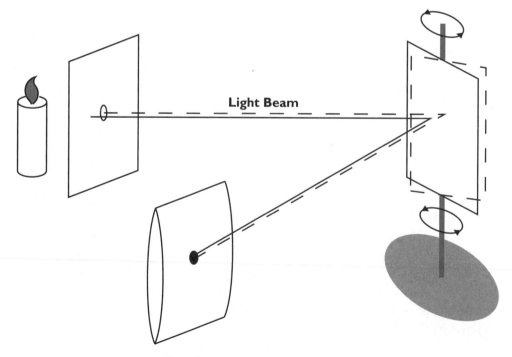

Figure 3.4—Diagram of Foucault's Apparatus

second mirror and then back to the rotating mirror. In the time that the beam was traveling from the rotating mirror and back, the mirror would have rotated slightly, so that the return beam would return to the source at a slightly different angle. From a measurement of this angle of deflection, Foucault was able to estimate the speed of light to within 1000 km/s of the actual value, better than Fizeau's measurement but still wide of the mark.

American scientist Albert Abraham Michelson (1852–1931) improved Foucault's experiment by increasing the distance the reflected beam traveled from 60 ft to 2000 ft and also by introducing lenses to help keep the beam focused as it traveled this larger distance. His measured value in 1879 was 186,329 mi/s, very close to the modern measured value of 186,282.397 mi/s. In the 1920s, he used the same basic experiment, but on a grander scale, in the mountains of California to measure the value at 186,285 mi/s, within just a few miles per second of the correct value.

The most amazing fact about the speed of light is that it is constant. Light emitted from the Sun moves at the same speed as light emitted from stars in distant galaxies. We don't know why light has a constant speed, but it is a property of our universe that we have now measured very accurately. This is a strange property: It does not have to be constant; one could imagine a universe where it was not, but in our universe, light moves at a constant speed.

Direction

Light also has a direction. Just as the ancient Arabic astronomer Alhazen hypothesized, light can be thought of as traveling in rays or straight lines. Light doesn't travel in curved lines or make funny looping paths as it moves along. It begins somewhere and moves straight until it is reflected or absorbed by some intervening object. This fact is very important in the design of telescopes and in understanding how light can be gathered and focused using mirrors or lenses.

Frequency

Because light has a constant speed, the number of peaks or troughs that move past us in a given amount of time is related to the wavelength of the light. In a given amount of time, we will see more troughs move past us for light of a short wavelength than of longer wavelengths. This means that the frequency and the wavelength are inversely related. As one increases, the other has to decrease. Mathematically, the two can be related in the following way (where lambda [λ] stands for the wavelength, nu [υ] stands for the frequency, and c for the speed of light):

$$\lambda \times \upsilon = c$$

The frequency of light is given in units of hertz (Hz), or cycles per second. It is simply a measure of the number of peaks that pass by an observer in 1 s. A frequency of 1 Hz means that one peak passes by each second.

Astronomers sometimes like to refer to the frequency of light instead of the wavelength. This is especially true for light used to broadcast radio signals. The signals our radios pick up are not sound waves, but electromagnetic waves about 3 ft or so in size. On a typical radio, you may find the frequencies printed right on the dial. AM radio begins around 55 kilohertz (kHz) and ends around 160 kHz. FM radio begins around 85 megahertz (MHz) and ends about 110 MHz. The prefixes kilo- and mega- represent metric scalings of the hertz unit. (Kilo- means multiply by 1000, whereas mega- means multiply by 1,000,000.) If we could see FM radio waves, we would see 100,000,000 peaks of the electromagnetic waves moving past us each second. That is a lot of peaks! But optical light has even higher frequencies, so high that it would be hard to write out all the zeros.

Polarization

You have probably heard about polarization even though you may not know exactly what it is. For example, you can buy special polarized sunglasses (see the sidebar) that are supposed to help you see better in certain conditions. What exactly is polarization?

We learned earlier that light travels as a pair of waves, one an electric field and the other, a magnetic field. Polarized light contains waves that vibrate in only one plane, just like the diagrams we showed earlier. The light we see is typically a bit more complicated. This unpolarized light contains waves vibrating in many different planes (see Fig. 3.5).

If we could see a polarized light wave moving toward us, we would see the electric field vibrating up and down along one axis and the magnetic field vibrating perpendicular to it, side to side. Unpolarized light waves coming toward us would have vibrations at all possible angles.

Light from an object like the Sun or an electric light is formed by the rapid and random motions of charged particles, which generate electromagnetic waves. Because the initial motions are random, the resulting light is unpolarized. *Unpolarized light* has no favored plane of vibration for the electric or magnetic fields that make up the traveling electromagnetic wave.

If somehow we funnel the motion into a single line, we get *polarized light*, which is light that exhibits a favored plane of vibration for the electric and magnetic fields of the traveling electromagnetic wave. Radio stations, which emit light by rapidly moving electric charges up and down in an antenna, emit polarized light. The electric field vibrates up and down, perpendicular to Earth. You may notice that

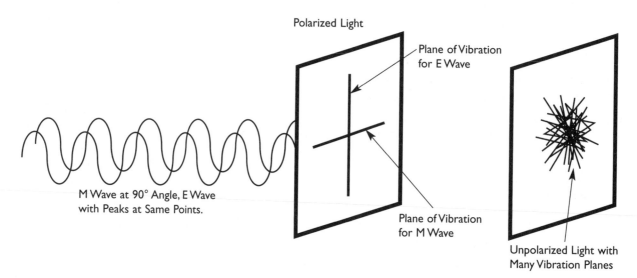

Figure 3.5—Diagram of Unpolarized Light

most car antennas are simply vertical pieces of metal or wire. This is the best alignment for picking up the polarized radio signals from broadcasting stations. If you rotate the antenna 90°, the signal will decrease in strength, because your antenna is not picking up as much light from the station.

POLARIZED SUNGLASSES

Filters can be designed that allow only one (or a small range of) polarization to pass through. Opticians have made sunglasses using this kind of material. Reflected light bouncing off water, snow or windshields is often highly polarized. Polarized sunglasses block these reflections, which allows us to see better when we drive, for example; it also helps people who are fishing to see into the water. Polarized sunglasses can be likened to a picket fence. If a stick is thrown at a picket fence so that it rotates exactly up and down, there is a chance that the stick will make it through the fence. However, if the stick is thrown so it rotates horizontally, there is no way it will make it through. This is exactly how polarized filters work. They let only light that is vibrating in a certain direction through and either reflect or absorb the others, depending on the type of filter.

WHAT LIGHT DOES

So, light is a traveling electromagnetic wave. It has a wavelength and a definite speed and direction, and it can even exhibit polarization. These properties alone can tell us much about where the light came from and about what it encountered on the way to Earth. But on its passage to us from its source, light certainly encounters matter. For example, when entering our atmosphere, it must interact in some

way with air. As light leaves a star, it must encounter hot gas that surrounds the star or the large quantities of dust we know float between the stars. But how does light interact with matter, and can we learn about the matter itself by studying the light we receive here on Earth? Yes, but we need to understand the basic ways light interacts with matter before we can interpret the messages delivered by the light we receive from distant cosmic objects.

Reflection

The most basic way that light interacts with matter is called reflection. *Reflection* is simply the redirection of light by a given material. Materials that are good at reflecting light are called reflective; we have used such materials in many different ways, from making mirrors to decorating our homes.

Reflection follows a simple law. An incoming light wave is reflected off a surface at an angle equivalent to that of the reflected wave leaving the surface. In other words, angle in equals angle out. Sometimes this is written as: angle of incidence equals angle of reflectance (Fig. 3.6).

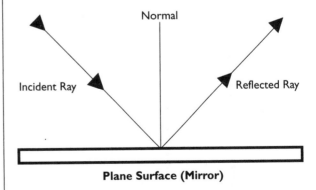

Plane Surface (Mirror)

Figure 3.6—The Law of Reflection

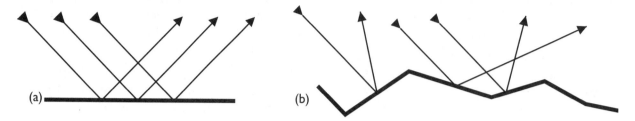

Figure 3.7—Reflection with Even and Uneven Materials

Refraction

Refraction is the bending of light by a material (Fig. 3.7). The amount of bending depends on a property of the material known as the *index of refraction*, which is the ratio of the speed of light in a vacuum to the speed of light in a given material. This number measures how much the material bends a light ray and differs for different materials.

The speed of light is constant in any given material, but it is different from material to material. It is fastest in a perfect vacuum, where it cannot interact with any matter. Because different materials interact with light in slightly different ways, each material has its own unique index of refraction.

When light moves from one material into another, it is bent, or refracted. The index of refraction in air is different than that of water. This is easily seen when looking into a pond of water. As the light bouncing off, say, a fish in the water enters the air, it is bent. This means that when someone on the shore looks at the water, where he or she sees the fish is not where the fish actually is. Experienced spear fishers know this well and compensate by throwing at where the fish actually are, not where they see the fish (Fig. 3.8).

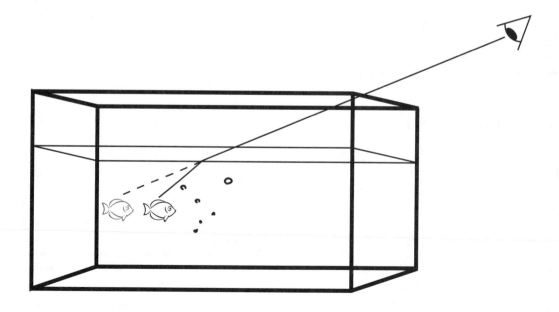

Figure 3.8—An Observed Fish and an Actual Fish in Water

LENSES

Lenses have been with us for a very long time, and the original inventor is lost to history. There are passages in Roman writings of "burning glasses" and "magnifying glasses," which are obviously primitive lenses used to concentrate the Sun's light to set things on fire and to enlarge things. By about 1200, lenses became widespread among scientists in Europe, mainly due to the superior ability of the glassmakers of Venice. With clear, bubble-free glass available and good polishing tools, lenses came into widespread use, especially as eyeglasses.

There are two basic kinds of lenses, convex and concave. *Concave lenses* (Fig. 3.9) are curved like the inner surface of a sphere, with thin centers and thicker outer portions. They spread incoming light, forming images on the front side of the lens. Images formed on the front side of the lens are known as *virtual images. Convex* lenses (Fig. 3.10) are curved like the exterior surface of a sphere; they focus light and are thicker in the center and thinnest at the edges. They are often called converging lenses, because they focus light to a point. They form images that appear to be on the opposite side of the lens. Images formed on the opposite side of the lens are known as *real images.* Most people have only encountered lenses that form real images, usually in the form of a magnifying glass, microscope, or telescope.

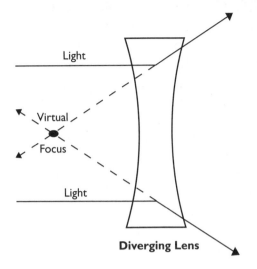

Figure 3.9—A Concave Lens

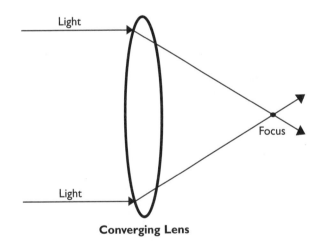

Figure 3.10—A Convex Lens

Light as a Tool

Light is an amazing tool. Originating in the vibrations of distant atoms, traveling at amazing speed through space, interacting with matter, perhaps reflecting off of a mirror or being bent by our atmosphere, it arrives on Earth. By studying light carefully, observing its polarization, wavelength, and direction, we can piece together an understanding of where it came from and some of the properties of the object that brought it forth into the universe. The next chapter explains just how astronomers do this.

SUMMARY

Light is a traveling electromagnetic wave known as electromagnetic radiation. Light is characterized by its wavelength, which we see as a color for light in the visible portion of the electromagnetic spectrum. Very long wavelength light is used to transmit radio signals. Very short wavelength light is used in medicine as X-rays. Shorter and longer wavelength light exists. The wavelength is related to the frequency, or how many cycles of the wave pass by a certain spot in a given length of time. The speed of light is constant in a vacuum, but it is slower in other materials like water or air.

Light can reflect off of surfaces, can be bent or refracted, and can be scattered or polarized. Reflections off a flat surface result in an outgoing ray of light traveling at the same angle as the incoming ray. Refracted light is bent in different ways, based on the material. Polarized light is formed when light is reflected or interacts in other ways with matter. It can sometimes indicate the presence of magnetic fields.

The various properties of light can be used to study both astronomical objects and the material between the distant astronomical object and Earth.

THE BIRTH OF ASTROPHYSICS

All substances can absorb and emit light of
one wavelength or another. Astronomers try to
understand the universe and the objects within
it by studying light from distant cosmic objects
received by telescopes on Earth. Of particular
importance to astronomers is how this light is
affected on its journey by matter that gets in
its way. To understand how matter interacts
with light it is necessary to understand what
matter itself is made of. This leads us to a
consideration of chemistry, physics, and,
ultimately, astrophysics.

ATOMS AND LIGHT

Matter is the stuff of which everything is made.
Clouds, air, water, rocks, birds, slugs, and even
the Moon are all made of matter. But what is
matter? Matter is composed of a finite number
of substances known as *element*s, which are
substances that cannot be broken down into
other substances, although they can interact
chemically with each other to form more
complicated substances. Iron is an element.
Iron oxide, or rust, is a more complicated
substance, a molecule, formed by a chemical
reaction between the element iron with the
element oxygen. A *molecule* is a group of two
or more atoms held together by electric forces.

There are 92 naturally occurring chemical
elements and 20 or so elements that have
been temporarily formed by physicists using
advanced tools known as accelerators, which
smash tiny particles together at great speeds.
That scientists have made new elements is
one of the triumphs of physics.

And what are these tiny particles? Imagine a
bucket full of a pure element such as sulfur.
We dump out half of the bucket, then dump
out half of what is left, and keep repeating
the process. Eventually, we end up with one
tiny piece of sulfur. This fundamental unit is
known as an atom. An *atom* is the smallest
unit of matter that still retains the properties
of a given element. Atoms are the pieces of
matter that interact, for example, binding
together to make new substances. The ancient
Greeks first developed the concept of atoms.
Of course, they didn't have the tools to study
atoms firsthand. They weren't able to pick
one up and look at it. (In fact, we still can't
directly look at atoms, but we have tools that
allow us to see them.) They developed the
concept after thinking about what they saw
in the world around them. Because boulders
can be broken into smaller pieces and those
pieces can be broken down into yet smaller
chunks, it made sense to them that there was
a fundamental piece of matter that cannot be
broken apart further. Their idea has withstood
the test of time and forms the basis of modern
science.

An Atomic Model

The modern model, or understanding, of the atom was first developed in the early 1900s and synthesized by the Danish physicist Niels Bohr (1885–1962), who was the first to put together a cohesive picture based on the ideas of other physicists. In his model, any given atom is made of three types of smaller particles. *Protons* (positively charged particles) and *neutrons* (particles having neither a negative nor positive charge) make up a central core, or *nucleus*, of the atom, and *electrons* (negatively charged particles) move around the nucleus. Although this model is not exactly how nature works, it's a good model and allows us to think about matter and how it interacts with light.

Protons and neutrons have roughly the same mass, about 1.676×10^{-30} grams (g). Even though this is a very small mass, the protons and neutrons represent almost all the mass in an atom. Protons also have a positive electric charge, whereas neutrons are neutral, having no charge at all. Because like electric charges repel, there must be some force holding the protons together in the nuclei. If there were no such force, a nucleus would fly apart due to the repulsive electric force between protons. This attractive force between protons and neutrons that holds the atoms together is known as the *strong nuclear force*, because it is able to overcome the electric force and hold the nucleus together.

Electrons have very little mass—about 1000 times less than protons and neutrons—and have a negative electric charge. Electrons are responsible for all the interactions between atoms. Through the sharing of electrons, atoms can stick together to form molecules. Chemical reactions take place when atoms and molecules interact, swapping electrons and finally settling down to form new molecules or breaking apart

BUT WHAT ARE PROTONS AND NEUTRONS MADE OF?

Somewhat unbelievably, given the microscopic scale of the atom, protons and neutrons are made up of even smaller particles known as *quarks*. Quarks don't interact with light or play a major role in normal astronomical situations, but the simple fact that an atomic building block as small and basic as a proton is made up of something even smaller is in itself remarkable. It takes tremendous energy to break up protons and neutrons into their constituent quarks, energy not normally available in the universe now but present at the time of its origin, an event known as the Big Bang. To study such particles today, physicists use accelerators to slam atoms together at very fast speeds and watch the results with high-speed cameras and other types of detectors. They have found many different kinds of subatomic particles and given them some fanciful names. Quarks, which come in three different colors (red, green, and blue), come in three kinds of pairs: up and down, top and bottom, charm and strange. The colors are akin to electric charge; they aren't really a given color, it is just a way of naming a common property. Studying subatomic particles is becoming harder and harder because progress can be made only by building bigger and more powerful accelerators, which are now so costly that it takes the resources of many countries to construct them. New discoveries are likely to come through studies of objects elsewhere in the universe that accelerate particles themselves.

into their constituent atoms. Protons and neutrons, concentrated in the terrifically small nucleus, take no part in chemical reactions. The electrons alone are responsible for the great diversity of molecules we see around us. They are the glue that holds atoms together in the millions of diverse combinations that make up the material we see around us.

THE SIZE OF THE NUCLEUS

It is difficult to understand the small scale of the atomic world. Here's a real-world comparison: if you had a fruit bowl with some oranges in it, representing the protons and neutrons of an atom's nucleus, the electrons of the atom would be located about 5 mi away. The nucleus is tremendously small relative to the size of the whole atom. In fact, there is a huge gap between the nucleus and the innermost electron of a given atom. This almost invisible space is a gigantic void at atomic scales—similar to, but larger in scale than, the tremendous distances between the planets. One way to think about these distances is to compare ratios of size and distance. The typical diameter of a nucleus is about 5×10^{-15} m and the innermost electron is typically 1×10^{-10} m away from the nucleus. Taking the ratio of the separation distance to the diameter, (1×10^{-10}) 4 (5×10^{-15}), we get 20,000. The diameter of the Sun is 870,000 mi and the distance from the Sun to Earth is 93 million miles. Taking the same ratio, 93 million 870,000, we get about 111. Comparing these two numbers, the atomic system is 180 times more spacious than the Earth-Sun system. You would have to move Earth about three times further than the most distant planet from the Sun, Pluto, to make the Earth-Sun spacing comparable to the atomic spacing. You can begin to understand just how small the nucleus is compared to the size of the atom and the tremendous emptiness contained in each and every atom.

Absorption and Emission of Light by Atoms

It would be a pretty boring universe if there were just atoms flying about forming and reforming into molecules through chemical reactions. Luckily, electromagnetic radiation (light) can interact with the electrons surrounding atoms and molecules. In Bohr's model of the atom, electrons reside in complex shells, or orbits, around the nucleus, with the lowest-energy orbits being closest to the nucleus and higher-energy orbits being further out. One way to think of this model is as a tiny solar system, with the Sun as the nucleus and the planets as the orbiting electrons. This is *not* what is actually going on—the electrons don't orbit in a plane, for example—but it helps us visualize some important points.

As scientists were uncovering the inner workings of the atom in the early 1900s, they ran into a problem with their understanding of light. Suddenly, light didn't always act like a wave. When experiments were set up using particular kinds of detectors, it seemed that light was actually composed of particles. With the right kind of detector, individual "pieces of light" could be counted. These particles were called *photons*, or packets of energy that have characteristic wavelengths and energy. They could be counted individually and had a particular energy, which was found to be related to the wavelength of the light. This odd situation, called the wave-particle duality, is just how the universe appears to be. Sometimes light acts like a wave, sometimes like a particle. Scientists have different tools and formulas that they use interchangeably to describe light given varying situations.

When a photon comes near an atom, it can interact with an electron. If the electron takes energy from the light, it changes its orbit from a lower-energy-level orbit to a higher-energy-level orbit. The orbits basically get larger as their energy level increases. Higher-energy orbits are further away from the nucleus. If the light is particularly energetic, say, some short-wavelength ultraviolet light, the electron can take up so much energy that it escapes from the atom. Interestingly, if an atom with an electron in a high-energy level is left alone, over time the electron will spontaneously move to a lower-energy level and give off energy in the form of light.

Electron energy levels are distinct, like floors in an elevator building. When riding in an elevator, you can get off only where a floor exists; you can't get off halfway between two floors. Similarly, electrons can exist only in particular orbits or energy levels, not in between. Each atom has its own set of electronic energy levels. Those of hydrogen are different from sulfur and every other element.

This property leads to a key phenomenon for astronomy: atoms can absorb or emit only light of particular energies. This energy is the exact amount needed to move an electron from one energy level to another. Because each atom's energy levels are unique and the energy (or color) of light absorbed or emitted by the atom is dictated by the energy levels, each atom has a unique color-based fingerprint. It should be possible to carefully measure the light absorbed or emitted by each element in the laboratory and write down all the wavelengths unique to that particular element. This information can then be used to identify mixtures of elements. This technique is utilized in all the sciences but is a key method of investigation for astronomers. By carefully studying the light from celestial objects, astronomers can identify what they are made of. From the most distant galaxy to comets in our own solar system, we know what they contain due to the small-scale interactions of light with electrons.

SPECTROSCOPY

The study of light by separating it by color and studying its particular interactions with matter is the science of *spectroscopy*. It is fundamental to both physics and astronomy and has led to much of our knowledge about the objects in the universe and the physical laws that govern the interaction of matter and light.

SPECTROSCOPES

A *spectroscope* is a device that collects and then disperses light, so that its constituent colors can be identified. There are many different types of spectroscopes, but they all share the same basic function. Light is directed through a small slit and then dispersed with either a prism or a device known as a grating. The light is then directed to a camera or an electronic recording device or projected onto a screen. Instead of just looking at the light and writing down the visible colors, a kind of scale like a ruler is used to measure the wavelength of the light; for example, green light has a wavelength of about 450 nm. Because the light entering the device came in through a small slit, the image projected onto the scale is in the shape of a line. This linear image makes it easy to measure the wavelength of the light. If the slit were circular, like a small pinhole, the image projected on the scale would be round, and it would be much harder to measure the light's exact wavelength.

Because atoms absorb and emit only particular wavelengths, or colors, we see lines of color when using a spectroscope. This led scientists to use the name *spectral lines* to describe the particular colors of light seen from atoms using a spectroscope. It is important to remember that this term refers to a specific color-based signature, not that the light coming from atoms (or being absorbed by them) has the physical appearance of a line. Spectroscopes produce images that are lines by design, so it is easier to measure their wavelength.

Astronomers found that some objects, usually hot, dense objects like the Sun, give off a continuous range of colors. This *continuous spectrum* is best known by most people as the colors seen in a rainbow. Sometimes particular colors were found to be missing or highly dimmed relative to the rest of the colors. Because they were viewed through a spectroscope, they appeared as dark lines across the otherwise bright continuous spectrum. Because light was missing, apparently absorbed by something, these were called absorption lines. *Absorption* is the process of matter absorbing light. When astronomers pointed their spectroscopes at interstellar gas clouds, or at hot gases in the laboratory, isolated colors were seen, without a continuous spectrum. These became known as emission lines, where emission is the release of energy from atoms or molecules in the form of light. (Again, remember that they are called lines only because of their appearance when seen through a spectroscope; a particular line is simply light of a particular wavelength or color.)

Kirchhoff's Laws

The German physicist Gustav Kirchhoff (1824–1887) developed several rules that enabled scientists to predict the type of spectrum that would result in certain situations. Like Kepler's laws, which tell us how the planets move but not why, Kirchhoff's laws predict the type of spectrum but do not provide an explanation of how the spectrum is made. A complete understanding of the source of spectra and the details of how light and matter interact to form spectra was not developed until the early 1900s.

Kirchhoff's laws are:

1. Hot, opaque objects, whether they are solids, liquids, or gases, will produce a continuous spectrum. An example of an object that produces a continuous spectrum is the glowing tip of a hot fireplace poker.

2. A hot, transparent gas produces a spectrum with only certain colors. The number of colors and their intensity varies for different gases. Neon signs, which are filled with neon gas, are good examples of this kind of spectrum.

3. If the light from a hot, opaque object passes through a cooler gas, then certain colors in the continuous spectrum will be missing or reduced significantly. The amount of reduction and the exact colors missing depend on the gas between the observer and the hot, opaque object.

When we view the Sun's light with a spectroscope, we see a continuous spectrum with absorption lines. Using Kirchhoff's laws, we know that we must be looking at a hot, opaque object (the Sun) with a cooler gas somewhere between us here on Earth and the Sun itself. There is Earth's own atmosphere, but most of the absorption comes from cooler gas located around the Sun. We know that it is the gas around the Sun because the absorption lines look very different than those created by the air in our earth-bound laboratory. This is because the gas near the Sun is at a higher temperature than the air in our laboratory and is made of different elements as well.

Kinetic Theory

The *kinetic theory of gases* is the study of the microscopic behavior of atoms and molecules and the interactions that lead to larger-scale phenomena observable with spectroscopy or other means. Although the complete concepts of the kinetic theory are too complex for this book (and are not needed to understand most astronomy results), there are a few aspects of the theory that we need to cover.

The temperature of a gas is the measure of how fast the gas particles (either atoms or molecules) are moving. A higher temperature means that more of the gas particles are moving faster than are the gas particles in a cooler gas. Also, the range of gas particle speeds becomes larger as the temperature goes up. Not all the gas particles are moving at exactly the same speed; some are fast, some are slow. At very low temperatures, the spread in speeds is pretty small, with most particles moving quite slowly. Even in the hottest gas there are some particles that are not moving very fast, but in the hotter gas there are particles moving very fast indeed, and the spread, or distribution, of the speeds is larger. This spread in speeds affects the light that a given gas emits through a phenomenon known as the Doppler effect.

The Doppler Effect

When an ambulance passes by, we can hear a change in the tone of the siren. As it approaches we hear a certain pitch, and as the ambulance rushes past, the pitch decreases. Of course, the tone of the siren doesn't change for the ambulance driver, and the pitch of the siren doesn't, in fact, change at all. The apparent change is simply due to the motion of the ambulance relative to the listener. This effect happens not just with sound, but also with light. When a light-emitting object moves toward us, the color of the light it emits is shifted slightly toward the blue end of the spectrum (shorter wavelengths), and if it is moving away, the color is shifted toward the red (longer wavelengths). These color shifts are exactly parallel to the changes in pitch of an ambulance siren we hear as it approaches us and drives past. First described by Christian J. Doppler (1803–1853), who noticed the effect on sound waves, the Doppler effect was found to influence the color of light by Armand Hippolyte Fizeau, who developed an innovative way to measure the speed of light and whom we first met in Chapter 3.

How is the Doppler effect important in astronomy? First, because the amount of color shift depends on the velocity of an object (and also the observer, but let's pretend we are at complete rest for right now), by measuring the shift we can determine the speed of the object emitting the light. Second, we know from the kinetic theory of gases that hot gases have some atoms moving toward us and others moving away and that the spread in the speed of the gases goes up as the temperature increases. Taking into account the Doppler effect, the atoms moving toward us will emit blueshifted light, and atoms moving away will emit redshifted light. Because the spread of velocities increases as the temperature goes up, the spread of colors given off by the gas will increase as well. This means that if we observe a spectral line from a hot gas, the line will be spread out more than if the gas were cold. This is one of the reasons we know that the absorption lines seen in the Sun's spectrum come from gas around the Sun and not Earth: they are more spread out in color than the same lines generated by gas at Earth temperatures.

MOLECULAR INTERACTION WITH LIGHT

The universe isn't made up only of unattached atoms. Many of the objects astronomers observe contain mixtures of simple elements and more complex molecules. Happily, molecules, too, interact with light. Like atoms, they have electrons, and these electrons can absorb and emit light just like the electrons around single atoms. Molecules can also vibrate and rotate. Just as electrons in atoms have particular energy levels at which they must exist, molecules can vibrate and rotate only in particular ways and with particular energies. Because vibration and rotation take less energy than moving electrons up and down in levels, the wavelengths that are emitted or absorbed by molecules that change their vibration or rotation are of lower energy than the visible light given off by electrons. In fact, the rotational energies are so low that the light emitted or absorbed is similar in size to the wavelengths of light used to broadcast music to radios. Vibrating molecules are a bit more energetic, and the light emitted or absorbed by changes in the vibrational state of a molecule is less than a millimeter in length, longer than optical light by a fair bit but also much shorter than the radio wavelength energies of the rotational changes.

One of the biggest international astronomy projects ever undertaken is a radio telescope optimized to study the light emitted by molecules. The United States, several countries in Europe and South America, and also Japan are pooling resources to build this large device. The Atacama Large Millimeter Array being built in the high, dry desert of northern Chile will have at least 60 individual radio telescopes; these will work together to study light from molecules in objects both nearby, such as comets, and far away, such as those in the most distant galaxies. Although the exact completion date of the telescope is uncertain, by 2010 this exciting instrument should regularly be producing results that will no doubt appear on the front pages of newspapers worldwide. More information about this telescope and others is provided in Appendix 1.

SUMMARY

The birth of astrophysics came with the application of physical laws governing light and its interaction with matter to celestial objects and the light we receive from them. Atoms absorb and emit light. The atomic model tells us how light interacts with matter through the changing energy state of electrons, which orbit the atomic nucleus, which is composed of neutrons and protons.

Spectroscopy is the detailed study of the wavelength of light we receive from celestial objects. Kirchhoff's laws state that light from certain situations should have certain spectroscopic characteristics. Light from a hot object should be continuous. Light from a hot gas, with nothing behind it, should be composed of individual colors, and light from a hot object that passes through a cooler gas will have certain colors missing. These effects are caused by the interaction of light with atoms. The Doppler effect is the change in wavelength, or color, of light emitted from a moving object. The Doppler effect can be used to measure the speed of celestial objects either toward or away from Earth. Molecules interact with light in much the same way as atoms, with the additional possibility of both vibrational and rotational energy transitions, which usually produce light in the radio, or infrared, portion of the electromagnetic spectrum.

THE NEW ASTRONOMY

As physicists developed an understanding of atoms and light, it was quickly adopted by astronomers to explain phenomena they observed. Astronomers began to think of themselves as *astrophysicists*, or scientists who apply the laws of physics to objects in the universe. Classical astronomy, the measuring of positions of the stars and planets and making accurate star charts, became less interesting. Attempting to understand exactly how some odd object in space actually works—why it is bright or why it has an odd shape—was just much more satisfying to most scientists. The old research continued, but most twentieth-century astronomers began to pursue research in this field, called *astrophysics*, which is the study of objects in the universe using the laws of physics. This chapter summarizes some of the physical laws developed by physicists and their importance to the new astronomy of the modern era.

RELATIVITY

It is easy to assume that the laws of physics work the same everywhere in the universe. Somehow it just seems right. If magnets work here, they should work in my neighbor's yard and at my aunt's house in California and on Mars and even in another galaxy. One of the greatest discoveries in physics was that, in fact, the laws of physics are relative; that is, the same event can appear different to observers in different locations. Newton stated that all laws worked the same everywhere. We now know that he was wrong.

How Newton Was Wrong

Newton's ideas about motion and forces work very well in our immediate cosmic neighborhood. The motion of the Moon around Earth could be predicted and understood using Newton's laws. Cannonball trajectories on Earth could be worked out accurately and a number of complex phenomena—for example, centrifugal force—could be explained using Newton's basic principles of motion. However, as physics began to expand in the early 1900s, new ideas were developed, not because of any experiment that was not explainable, but simply through creative exploration of the basic ideas of physics. The old ideas were tested and thought about, and sometimes new ideas resulted. As sometimes happens in science, a single individual, working more or less in isolation, produced ideas that would change our understanding of the world we live in. In this case, the individual was Albert Einstein (1879–1955).

Einstein's Ideas

After high school, Einstein failed the exams necessary for entrance to the technical school where he hoped to train to be an electrical engineer. After teaching mathematics in a few schools in Germany, he ultimately got a job in the patent office in Bern, Switzerland, working there from 1902 to 1909. Reviewing new inventions and performing research to see if a new patent should be issued or not required creative and quick thinking, helping to sharpen his mind. Many scientists would not like this kind of job (although many work as patent reviewers today) because it does not allow independent research, but when the workday was over, Einstein's time was his own. He read scientific journals and was fascinated by some of the new experimental results being published. He was also bothered by the fact that Newton's laws of gravitation were simply predictive tools and did not provide a coherent explanation of *how* the force of gravity arose. Just why were objects attracted to one another? Working alone, he was not too intimidated to question Newton's basic assumptions. Had he been working in a university department or had he chosen to share his thoughts with academics, it is likely someone would have called his ideas crazy and dismissed them.

Newton's first law defines *natural motion*: either something is at rest, or it is moving in a straight line at constant velocity. But is this natural motion? Einstein wasn't sure. Newton assumed that the geometry of our universe was Euclidian. This is the geometry familiar to us from high school, in which the angles of a triangle add up to be 180°. Einstein didn't see why this had to be assumed. He felt it should be tested or at least measured. Newton's laws explain that accelerated motion is caused by a force—in the case of the Moon orbiting Earth or a stone falling to the ground, the force of gravity. Einstein questioned this assumption. How could a force be felt instantly across the

vast reaches of space? It just didn't make sense to him and had long been a problem for many physicists. He set out to develop a new way of looking at the universe.

In his first major paper, published in 1905, on what has become known as the special theory of relativity, Einstein tried to establish the laws of physics without Newton's basic assumptions for observers undergoing natural motion (either at rest or moving at constant velocity in a straight line). He came up with a different way of looking at the world by reconsidering the classical notion that the laws of physics have to work the same way no matter where we are. From any frame of reference, we should be able to use basic physical formulas to predict motions and forces and so on. Taking this as his starting point and including James Clerk Maxwell's result (discussed in Chapter 2) that the speed of electromagnetic waves, or light, was a constant, Einstein developed his most famous equation, $E = mc^2$. This equation states that energy (E) and mass (m) are equivalent, or, more importantly, that matter can be converted to energy, and vice versa. This *equivalency principle* was an unexpected result and ultimately led to the development of nuclear weapons, whose immense destructive power comes from the conversion of a small amount of matter into energy.

This special theory of relativity also established a new, fundamental concept of space and time. When something happens in the world, Einstein said, it takes place both in space and at a particular time, and the laws of physics had to take into account both the spatial location and the time of an event. Scientists had traditionally considered these to be separate concepts. Einstein developed the concept of *space-time*, the joining of the three dimensions of space and the single dimension of time. Although Einstein's special theory of relativity established fundamental connections between space and time and made plain the equivalence of mass and energy, his general theory of relativity used these connections and the constant speed of light to understand the laws of physics as seen by observers undergoing accelerated motion. This special theory dealt only with stationary observers or observers moving at a constant speed.

Einstein's general theory states that it is impossible to tell the difference between accelerations caused by gravity and those caused by other forces. In other words, the *general theory of relativity* states that all accelerations are equivalent. Take a rocket ship here on Earth and one in space, both with no windows. If we are in the rocket ship here on Earth when we drop a marble and measure its acceleration, we find it accelerates at the rate of 9.8 m/s^2. In other words, every second, the marble's velocity increases by 9.8 m/s. After 1 s of falling, it is moving at a speed of 9.8 m/s, and after 2 s it is moving at 19.6 m/s. Now, turn on the engine of the rocket ship in space. Accelerate the rocket at 9.8 m/s^2. If we are in the rocket and drop a marble, it will accelerate in a direction opposite to the spaceship's motion, and we will see it acting exactly the same as when we are on Earth. The acceleration caused by the force of the rocket ship's engines and the acceleration caused by gravity are indistinguishable. If we could somehow teleport back and forth between the two ships, we would never be able to tell whether we were moving through space or standing still on Earth.

THOUGHT EXPERIMENTS

Einstein made use of a powerful tool that scientists often employ when trying to understand some particularly knotty phenomena or situation. He would imagine a physical situation one way and then try to think of the best possible explanation for the given result. A scientist might imagine being a very small observer watching a physical phenomenon up close, such as an electron absorbing light. Other times, such thought experiments might take the form of estimation exercises. For example, a scientist might speculate how much extra coal needs to be mined because of the invention of hair dryers. By making educated guesses, surprisingly accurate answers can be determined. Italian-American physicist Enrico Fermi (1901–1954) was famous for these kinds of estimation problems. Einstein didn't arrive at his brilliant insight into how our world works because of observations or measurements he made in a lab. His revolutionary result came from looking at the world, rejecting the accepted explanations for how it worked, and developing an alternative explanation. Thoughts alone can bring great insight, though only rarely as revolutionary as Einstein's.

What about weightlessness? Far away from any massive object, we would experience no force of gravity, but astronauts orbiting Earth only a few hundred miles above the Earth also experience weightlessness. Astronauts in orbit are falling toward Earth, but due to their forward motion they never hit the surface, just keep on falling around it. By falling, the force of gravity appears to disappear. How can this be?

Einstein's theory stated that space-time was curved by the presence of matter and that there was no force of gravity; objects simply moved in response to the curve of space-time. Accelerations were not caused by forces but represented the modified natural motion of an object when it was near an object of greater mass. Far from any massive object that curves space-time, a rocket ship with its motor turned off cruises along at constant velocity, and the occupants experience weightlessness. As the ship approaches a massive planet, it begins to accelerate. In Newton's view, the force of gravity from the massive planet is drawing the ship toward the planet's surface. In Einstein's view, the planet is bending space-time, and the rocket's natural motion in a straight line is deflected. It appears to follow a curved path and experience an acceleration, but this is just our point of view. Really, the rocket's motion continues in a straight line, but space itself is curved, generating the apparent curved trajectory. Newton's laws no longer apply, at least out in space. There is no need for mysterious forces acting instantly across the reaches of the universe; natural motion in our universe is governed by the local geometry of space-time.

VISUALIZING CURVED SPACE-TIME

The easiest way to visualize curved space-time is to take away one of the three spatial dimensions with which we are familiar. Imagine a large rubber sheet stretched tightly and mounted in a frame. Place a bowling ball on the sheet. It makes a depression in the center of the sheet and causes the rubber to curve across the whole surface, not just in one place. Now place a smaller ball, such as a baseball, onto the sheet. It will begin to move, accelerated by the curvature of the rubber sheet caused by the bowling ball. No forces are necessary for it to undertake its natural motion, just curved space. Our universe is just like this rubber sheet, but with a third dimension, which is nearly impossible to visualize (although some bright people claim they can). Thankfully, the taut rubber sheet can be used to represent how our universe appears to work.

Tests of Einstein's Theory

Theories are useless unless they make predictions of some sort, and Einstein's theory of general relativity makes a number of testable predictions. Two can be tested right here in our solar system, and astronomers have carried them out. As far as we can tell, Einstein was right on the money.

The first prediction is that light can be bent by curved space-time. Because space-time is curved by the presence of a large mass, the Sun itself should cause light from background objects to be bent slightly as it makes its way toward us. Einstein's theory predicted both that the bending should take place and the exact amount of bending that would occur.

Using very accurate measuring techniques, astronomers went out and measured the positions of objects in the sky and then, when the Sun moved closer to these objects, re-measured their positions. Sure enough, the objects appear to be displaced ever so slightly by the presence of the Sun, and the amount of the displacement was exactly that predicted by Einstein's theory. When the first results of these experiments were made public in 1919, after a British expedition made the measurements during a total solar eclipse, the London Times ran this headline: "Revolution in science—New theory of the Universe—all accelerations are equivalent. Newtonian ideas overthrown."

The second prediction has to do with the change in the point of closest approach of Mercury to the Sun. Astronomers calculating the orbit of Mercury compensated for the gravitational tugs of all the other planets and still found that they could not predict the exact location of closest approach. The point rotated slowly about the Sun, advancing by about 41 arcsec each 100 years (an *arcsecond* is 1/3600 of a degree). However, Einstein's theory predicts that a motion of roughly this scale should take place due to the curved space-time near the Sun. Working through the equations, Einstein predicted a shift of 43 arcsec per century for Mercury and also smaller shifts for the other planets. This very near agreement of Einstein's calculation to the observed drift has since been proved even more precisely by studying the orbits of some extreme objects elsewhere in the Universe.

Impact on Cosmology

Einstein began working on his theories trying to understand how gravity worked. They ended up affecting our understanding of the whole universe.

Cosmology, the study of the origin and change over time of the entire universe, was understandably altered by his discoveries. The idea that space itself was warped by the presence of mass and that it might have a non-Euclidian geometry opened the door to a golden age of cosmology research, an age we are still in today. It is odd that the geometry of the universe could affect it in any significant way, but in fact its ultimate fate is intimately tied to its shape. There are several possible fates:

the universe could expand forever, with stars and galaxies slowly cooling down over time and getting further and further away from each other; the universe could expand over time, ultimately slowing down and stopping; or the universe could expand, grow, and then recollapse. These possible end states are dictated in part by the shape, or geometry, of the universe, and this is why cosmologists are obsessed with observations that may tell us just what geometry holds sway. Einstein's theory of general relativity applies not just to local situations, but the whole universe. Attempting to figure out the geometry of the universe and its ultimate fate began soon after Einstein's theories were published.

Three basic geometries are possible under Einstein's theory, flat (Euclidian), spherical, or hyperbolic. In a flat, or Euclidian geometry, the sum of the angles in a triangle is equal to exactly 180°, and parallel lines stay a constant distant apart. In a spherical universe, the sum of the angles in a triangle is always greater than 180°, and parallel lines converge (similar to what happens here on Earth, because lines of longitude converge at the poles). In a hyperbolic universe, the sum of the angles in a triangle is always less than 180°, and parallel lines diverge. Spheres are closed structures, and a universe with a spherical geometry is said to be closed; it ultimately

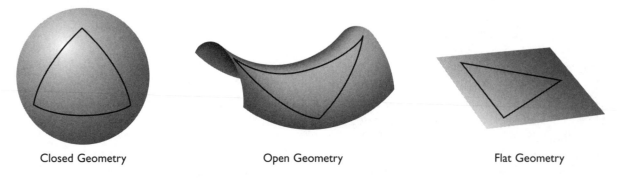

Closed Geometry   Open Geometry   Flat Geometry

Figure 5.1—The Various Possible Geometries of the Universe

curves back onto itself. A hyperbolic universe does not close back on itself and is called an open universe. It is relatively easy to think about the two-dimensional versions of these universes (see Fig. 5.1).

THE EXPANDING, ACCELERATING UNIVERSE

In 1920, American astronomer Edwin Hubble (1889–1953) discovered that the universe was expanding. With data from the 200-in. Palomar telescope in California, he used a spectroscope to measure the Doppler shift of distant galaxies. He found that the more distant a galaxy appeared to be, the greater its Doppler shift. Because all the shifts were toward the red, or redshifts, this meant that more distant galaxies were moving away from us at greater speed. He plotted a straight line over the data points, assuming that the universe must be expanding at a constant rate. The slope of the line has become known as the Hubble constant, and the determination of this number was long the holy grail of observational cosmology. The scientific community took Hubble's observations as evidence for an expanding universe and a confirmation that Einstein's cosmological constant was not necessary. However, the universe is more complicated than these early results seemed to indicate. Recent observations by multiple international teams of astronomers have shown that not only are distant galaxies moving away from us at great speed, it appears that they are accelerating. This means that the universe is not simply expanding at a constant rate, but it is growing more quickly now than it did in the past. We describe some of the details of these new observations in more detail in Chapter 15. Einstein's cosmological constant is required after all to explain this acceleration. Einstein, were he alive today, would likely be pleased to know that his biggest blunder wasn't a blunder after all.

Newton imagined that the universe was infinite. Einstein's theories led to the possibility that the universe was closed. Einstein's theory also indicated that the universe was likely to be either expanding or contracting. Einstein felt that, even though his basic theory predicted it, a universe that changed in size over time could not be correct and introduced an extra variable into his equations that would keep the universe from expanding or contracting, yielding a static universe. A few years after he did so, astronomers discovered that in fact the universe was expanding. Einstein subsequently called his decision to include the extra variable his biggest blunder.

SUMMARY

The basic understanding of the universe in place by 1900 was modified by Einstein's theories and the development of quantum mechanics. Einstein's special theory of relativity showed that gravity could be thought of as a modification of space by the presence of mass; his general theory explained physics in accelerated situations. Various tests of Einstein's theories have shown his ideas to be correct. Newton's basic ideas work in the everyday world we know and experience, but in more extreme situations, such as when things move very quickly or particularly strong gravity is around, Einstein's theories must be used. Einstein's theories have an impact on cosmology, the study of the whole universe, by predicting several geometries, open, closed, or flat.

THE TOOLS OF ASTRONOMY

KEY TERMS

resolution, light-gathering power, magnification, photoelectric effect, refracting telescope, reflecting telescope, scattering, distortion

Light comes to us from a variety of celestial objects and is created in many different ways. Astronomers use *telescopes* to study objects by gathering and analyzing the light from distant objects. Ancient astronomers just used their eyes and made rough diagrams of the events they saw in the sky. After the invention of the telescope, astronomers made detailed sketches of what they saw. Once photography was invented in the mid-1800s, telescopes were one of the first tools to incorporate this practical application of chemistry, capturing the light from the stars for future study. Modern astronomers now use electronic equipment to gather and analyze the light they gather.

This chapter explores how telescopes work and how astronomers use the information their telescopes receive to make sense of what's going on in the universe, both locally and in the most distant galaxies.

TELESCOPES

Telescopes come in a variety of different sizes and types, with the common goal of gathering and magnifying light from distant objects. The human eye is actually a simple telescope itself, although it is limited for a number of reasons, most importantly, its very small size. Our eyes

have evolved to perform under a variety of conditions, such as bright light, dim light, moonlight, and even pitch darkness, with varying degrees of performance. However, our eyes are not well suited to studying distant and faint objects.

Luckily, astronomers have been able to overcome the limitations of the eye by constructing telescopes. Before looking at the different types in detail, we need to understand a few basics.

Telescope Basics

Galileo was the first to point a telescope at the heavens and to tell others what he saw there (Fig. 6.1). The sight of Jupiter, even through his small, handmade telescope, was to him truly fantastic. He saw and tracked the movement of Jupiter's moons as they orbited their host planet. He was initially accused of making the story up or of having built an elaborate parlor trick out of a brass tube and glass, but others soon built and pointed their own telescopes toward Jupiter and saw the same celestial dance that Galileo saw.

Galileo initially had a telescope with a primary lens of only a half an inch in diameter and was able to increase the apparent size of distant objects by a factor of three. (The magnifying power or magnification of telescopes is often noted by a number followed by an ×. For Galileo's initial telescope, we would write 3× to indicate a threefold increase in the apparent

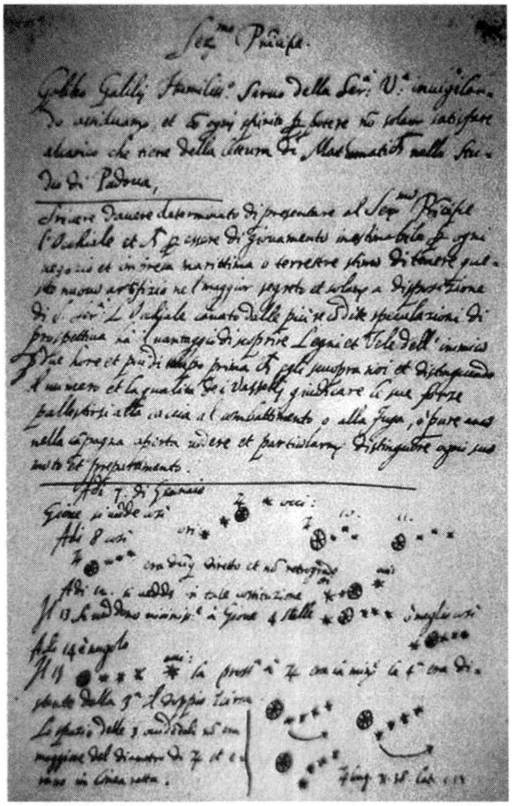

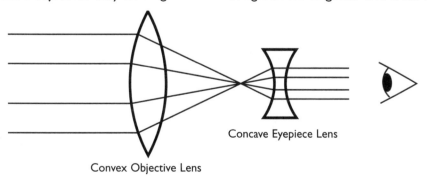

Photo courtesy of Biblioteca Nazionale Centrale–Florence

**Figure 6.1—A Page From Galileo's Notebook
(From the Galileo Project Pages, Rice University)**

size of distant objects.) Ultimately, Galileo built larger telescopes with a primary lens diameter of about 1 in. and 20× magnification. Making lenses is a difficult and labor-intensive process, and making lenses with diameters greater than 1 in. was a great challenge then. It took about 6 months after his book *Sidereus Nuncius* was published in March 1610 before others had built telescopes of similar size and magnification to allow confirmation of his observations. He was soon outstripped in new discoveries by other instrument builders, such as Thomas Hariot (1560–1621), David (1564–1617) and Johannes (1587–1616) Fabricius (father and son), and Christoph Scheiner (1573–1650), who all studied the dark spots, called sunspots, on the Sun. The race to create even larger telescopes, in order to make ever more startling discoveries, continues today.

Why would Galileo (or anybody, for that matter) want to spend so much time and effort to make a larger lens? The larger the

BUILDING A SIMPLE TELESCOPE

By combining a concave lens with a convex lens (discussed in Chapter 4), we can make distant objects appear larger (Fig. 6.2). The convex lens gathers the light and focuses it, whereas the concave eyepiece forms a larger image of the distant object for easy viewing.

This is the basic idea that led to the development of the telescope. Subsequent telescopes used two concave lenses, which increased the amount of magnification possible. Today's telescopes often don't have any lenses at all, instead using mirrors to gather and focus the light.

Concave Eyepiece Lens

Convex Objective Lens

Figure 6.2—A Basic Telescope

diameter of the primary lens or mirror of a telescope, the more light it gathers and the more resolving power it has. Since more light means more information from fainter and more distant objects, astronomers will always be interested in the largest possible lens. Let's look at light-gathering power and resolving power in more detail.

Light-Gathering Power

The *light-gathering power*, or ability of a telescope to gather light, of an optical telescope is an important characteristic for both amateur and professional astronomers. Only by increasing the size of a telescope can its light-gathering power be increased. Because the amount of light that a telescope can gather is directly related to the area of the primary lens or mirror (otherwise known as the *objective*), it is ultimately related to the radius of the objective through the simple formula for the area of a circle: $A = \pi r^2$. As the radius (r) increases, the total area (A) available to gather light increases quite quickly. This again is why astronomers always want the biggest telescopes possible, so they can see faint objects well by gathering as much light as possible from them.

Resolution

As telescopes get larger, their resolving power, or resolution, increases. *Resolving power* is the ability of a telescope to separate two closely spaced objects. It is not the same thing as *magnification*, which is simply the increase of apparent size of an image seen through a telescope or microscope. Good magnification is important, but magnifying a poorly resolved image just means you have a bigger image, not a clearer one.

Imagine a line of telephone poles set up across a large, flat desert. If we walk directly away from the line of poles so that your back is to the line, we can, on turning around after a few hundred yards, clearly separate one from the other. But as we get further away, say, a few miles, they grow closer and closer together, finally becoming so close that we can't differentiate one from another. This is an example of not being able to resolve the telephone poles. Magnifying the image we see with our eye will show only a larger, undifferentiated image; using a telescope with a greater resolving power than our eye will show us separate telephone poles.

The resolution is related to the diameter of the primary objective and the wavelength of light we are observing. The resolution is governed by the formula $R = 1.22 \times \lambda \div D$, where R is the resolution (a smaller number means you can make out smaller details), λ is the wavelength, and D is the diameter of the objective. Shorter wavelengths (smaller λ) observed through the same telescope provide greater resolving power. This formula gives the resolution, R, in arcseconds. Bigger telescopes (bigger D) provide more resolving power. The formula tells us exactly what drives astronomers to build large telescopes.

Recording the Sky: From Sketches to CCD Cameras

Early astronomers recorded the positions and brightnesses of objects in the sky simply by observing them with their eyes. This method works well for the brightest stars and planets, but doesn't work well for objects too faint to be seen by the eye alone. Telescopes allowed astronomers to see fainter objects and see them in greater detail. But for hundreds of years, the only way to record what one saw through a telescope was by drawing what was observed. This method worked quite well and many astronomers became accomplished sketch artists.

Photography Comes to Astronomy

Sketches were still limited to relatively bright objects. The advent of photography, a chemical process that allowed images to be recorded permanently on paper or glass, in the early 1800s led to the use of photographic plates in telescopic observations. In fact, one of the earliest photographs, made by Louis-Jacques-Mandé Daguerre (1789–1851), the inventor of the daguerreotype (an early photographic process), was of the Moon, in 1838. The first public announcement of the daguerreotype process was made in January 1839 by the scientist-politician Francois Arago (1786–1853); months later. Arago saw the importance of this method for observing very faint objects with telescopes and using the method for scientific observations.

The first photograph of a nebula, or region of bright gas in interstellar space (which we discuss in greater detail in Chapter 12), was made in 1880 by the American amateur scientist Henry Draper (1837–1882) using an 11-in. telescope designed for photography. Exposing the plate for 137 min, Draper captured the well-known Orion nebula, located in the sword of Orion.

Methods were developed to take images of the spectra of astronomical objects (spectroscopy was discussed in Chapter 4). The first spectral image was made by English amateur astronomer William Huggins (1824–1910) in March 1882, a 45 min exposure of Orion. Five emission lines were recorded and one was shown to come from the ultraviolet range, previously unknown. The first photograph of another galaxy was made in 1884 of the Andromeda galaxy, located 2.2 million light-years away, using a 36 in. telescope. In 1899, the spectrum of Andromeda was shown to have no emission lines and to resemble typical stellar spectra. This result strongly hinted that galaxies were made of stars, a fact not proven until 20 years later when actual stars were resolved in photographs made using the 100 in. Mt. Wilson telescope. This first galactic spectrum was made by German astronomer Julius Scheiner (1858–1913) at the Potsdam Observatory near Berlin, Germany.

Thus, before 1900, much of the future work for astronomy was already established by astronomers using photographic plates. Slow but steady improvements in photographic emulsions increased the sensitivity of the photographic plates and spurred the continuing quest for larger telescopes. The early spectroscopic results also showed that telescopes could be used to do more than make pretty pictures. Information was available in all wavelengths of light from distant objects. One needed only the right instrument and a large telescope to decipher the message.

Electronics Comes to Telescopes

With the rise of electronic technology in the 1950s, a wide range of new detectors became available for use on telescopes. Some were designed to work in a particular wavelength (infrared), and others were sensitive over wider wavelength ranges. There are two broad classes of detectors. The first class uses the fact that light falling onto a material changes some property of the material (such as resistance) to produce an electrical signal or other measurable effect. Solar panels are a good example of this. Light falling on these panels creates an electrical current, typically used to power homes and cars. Such panels could also be used to detect light from distant stars, turning the incoming light not into usable electricity, but some kind of measurable signal. The other class of detector counts the amount of light falling on the material. A now common example of this type of detector is the charge-coupled device, or CCD, now an integral part of today's digital video and still cameras. Many of the detectors rely on a fundamental property of matter discovered by Einstein, called the photoelectric effect. Light, when hitting the material, can liberate electrons if the frequency of the light is above a certain threshold value. Increasing the amount of light hitting the surface increases the number of electrons liberated. Einstein ultimately won the Nobel prize for this work, not his work on relativity.

The Photoelectric Effect

One popular way to play with marbles is to gather some into a group and then use a special marble, the shooter, to knock marbles out of the group. When one of the marbles gets knocked out of the ring, you get to keep it. When electrons hit just about any material, they act in a very similar way, knocking off other electrons in the process. This effect, the photoelectric effect, states that light delivers energy to any absorbing surface in packets of energy or photons, which can knock loose electrons from the material itself, but it does so in proportion to the intensity and frequency of the light. The more photons that hit the material, the more electrons are liberated.

Also, since the amount of energy in each photon is proportional to the frequency of the light (and inversely proportional to the wavelength)—with higher-frequency (shorter wavelength) light delivering more energy and lower-frequency (longer wavelength) light delivering less energy—then the number of electrons liberated is also proportional to the frequency. If the frequency goes below a certain threshold value, no electrons will be liberated. This is because they tend to stay with their atom unless kicked hard enough by an energetic photon.

This physical effect can be used to build instruments to measure the amount of light arriving at the detector. The most common of these devices is known as a phototube and is sometimes still used today. The more modern version of this kind of detector is the CCD. The CCD was originally developed at Bell Labs in the 1970s, and took advantage of silicon's ability to gather electrons knocked loose by impinging light, converting them to an electronic signal. CCDs can be thought of as a grid of light-catching buckets. The buckets catch photons, and we simply count up how many photons were caught in each bucket to produce an image.

All this is good news for modern astronomers. Sketching just doesn't work as well or as reliably as photography and electronics. These tools allow us to observe very faint objects that are otherwise totally invisible to our eyes, even when we stare through the largest telescopes. The future will no doubt bring advances that will improve how we record light from celestial objects, but the ultimate goal will remain the same: to gather and record the light coming from the objects under study.

OPTICAL, ULTRAVIOLET, AND INFRARED TELESCOPES

The light we see with our eyes is known by astronomers as the optical, or visible, part of the electromagnetic spectrum. This visible region naturally formed the core portion of astronomy for many years. In 1800, British astronomer William Herschel (1738–1822) performed an experiment that confirmed the existence of light beyond the wavelength region we see with our eyes. Wondering about the temperature of light as a function of wavelength, Herschel directed sunlight through a prism, spreading the light into the familiar rainbow pattern. Moving a thermometer through each color zone, he found that the temperature increased as he moved toward the red and was even higher when the thermometer was placed beyond the red portion of the spectrum, where there was apparently no light at all.

He subsequently performed additional experiments showing that this "infrared" light (which he originally named calorific rays, to imply that they carried heat energy) could be focused and reflected. He had discovered a kind of light that could not be seen but that carried energy. This discovery began an ongoing revolution in astronomy: the observation of objects using every wavelength of light, visible or not.

So many optical telescopes have been built that it is impossible to describe them all. But we can discuss the two basic kinds, *refracting telescopes* and reflecting telescopes. *Refracting telescopes* use lenses to gather and focus light. Reflecting telescopes use mirrors to gather and focus light. Reflecting telescopes are so efficient at gathering light that they are by far the most popular telescopes used by astronomers.

Many different designs exist, but one recent one deserves special mention, the segmented mirror design. A segmented mirror consists of small mirrors that are carefully shaped and then mounted into a framework that allows them to work together as a single mirror. The largest optical telescopes now in existence, the Keck I and II telescopes on top of the extinct Mauna Kea volcano in Hawaii, were built using this design. They are both about 10 m, or 34 ft, across. Imagine a very large backyard swimming pool. Now imagine six of them clumped together. This is about the size of the Keck mirrors.

Future Optical Telescopes

With the triumph of the Keck telescopes' segmented mirror design, many organizations are copying this basic plan to build similarly sized instruments. However, two size ranges remain in the far future: 20-40 m-sized telescopes and, very far in the future, 100 m behemoths.

In the 20-40 m class, there are currently several groups actively developing designs. They are the Giant Segmented Mirror telescope; the Extremely Large Telescope (XLT), to be built as a replacement for the Canada-France-Hawaii Telescope; the California Extremely Large Telescope (CELT); and the Euro50. These telescopes all are in the 30 m size range, except for the Euro50, which is planned to be 50 m in diameter.

The Overwhelmingly Large Telescope, a design effort from the European Southern Observatory, is planned to be a 100-m diameter optical telescope. Such a behemoth will have to be built close to the ground, in fact, partially into the ground, in order to minimize the size of the support structures. This design limits how much of the sky it could see without blockage. It would operate in the open air, as any enclosure would have to have a 100 m opening to allow the telescope to see out, hardly helping to block any distorting wind at all.

The cost to build these large telescopes continues to drop as new materials and building methods develop, but it is estimated that a telescope like the OWL will cost well in excess of $1 billion. That is not cheap, by any means, but it is not terribly expensive relative to, say, defense spending or Medicare. Such an instrument will have to be built by a multitude of countries because no nation has spent such a large amount on any ground-based instrument before and is not likely to do so in the future.

These large instruments face a number of hurdles, the primary one being the difficulty of correcting for atmospheric distortion of the light using *adaptive optics*, which are any of a number of devices used on ground-based telescopes to compensate for the effects of astronomical errors. Adaptive optics, originally developed for military applications and, somewhat in parallel, by astronomers, uses small mirrors that can be adjusted in alignment and in shape very quickly. Using fast computer control, the mirrors themselves can be repositioned and bent to compensate for the distortions introduced by the atmosphere. Current systems work well for the 8-10 m telescopes but induce constraints on the type of observing that can be done. Telescopes beyond this size will require significant design and investment in improving and extending the adaptive optics technology.

Radio Telescopes

Despite the fact that radios in our car and home produce sound, radio waves are a form of light that can move through our atmosphere with a minimum of absorption. Radios pick up radio waves produced by broadcasting antennas hundreds or thousands of miles away and change the received light into sound for our ears to hear. Interestingly, objects in space emit a range of light, including radio waves, not just light we can see with our eyes. Remember that radio waves have the longest wavelengths, from tens of meters in length to just less than a millimeter. Radio astronomy got its start shortly before and during World War II, when radar was invented and experiments were made using radio antennas. Karl Jansky was the first to positively observe radio signals from space when in the course of an experiment at Bell Labs studying the effect of distant thunderstorms on radio reception, he discovered radio waves emitted by the Milky Way galaxy itself. But radio astronomy really took hold when a curious American amateur astronomer, Grote Reber (1911–2002), built a parabolic dish antenna in his Wheaton, Illinois, back yard and made detailed maps of emissions from the Galaxy (Fig. 6.3).

Single-Dish Telescopes

Single-dish radio telescopes work much the same as reflecting telescopes that are used to observe visible light. They are usually formed of wire mesh or metallic panels that are formed into a parabolic shape to focus the incoming radio light. Some bring the light to a focus in front of the dish, but most modern radio telescopes have a secondary reflective surface mounted on support legs in front of the dish that bounces the light back through a small hole in the center of the dish, where the light reaches a focal point or focus. Sometimes the receivers are actually mounted on the dish surface instead of behind the dish.

Instead of an eyepiece or a camera, astronomers place sensitive receivers at the focus to pick up

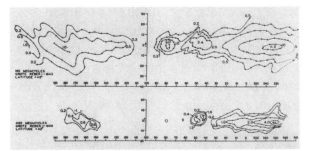

Photo courtesy of NRAO

Photo courtesy of NRAO

Figure 6.3—Reber's Telescope and Map of the Milky Way

Photo courtesy of NRAO

Figure 6.4—A Single Dish Telescope at the Green Bank Radio Observatory

incoming radio light and amplify the signal before sampling the signal and storing it digitally. Because radio telescopes don't use film, they usually make images by scanning across a region of sky and recording the intensity of the received signals. An image can then be built up over time that shows the intensity of the radio light across the sky. Such an image can be very useful to astronomers trying to understand the overall structure of a given region.

New electronics have enabled some telescopes to observe very short wavelength radio waves, 1 mm or so, by mimicking the concept of the CCD camera and placing arrays of receivers in the focal plane of the telescope instead of just a single receiver. This allows the telescope to quickly make an image instead of having to scan the sky (Fig. 6.4).

Interferometers

Radio telescopes have to have large diameters because the light they gather has long wavelengths. To increase the resolution, astronomers must build larger and larger radio telescopes (remember the formula for resolving power from earlier in this chapter). However, their physical size is ultimately constrained by price and practicality. Telescopes like the Green Bank telescope (GBT) in West Virginia and the

Effelsberg telescope outside of Bonn, Germany, will likely be the largest single-dish telescopes constructed on Earth. They are both about 100 m in diameter, or almost 330 ft.

But the quest for resolution has driven radio astronomers to develop a method to increase the resolution they can achieve without the extreme expense of very large telescopes. This method, known as interferometry, is one of the major triumphs of modern astronomy. An *interferometer* is a telescope composed of multiple smaller telescopes that generates the same resolution as a large telescope with a diameter equal to the maximum small-telescope separation.

Interferometry is a technique for combining the signals of many telescopes that generates the same resolution as a large telescope with a diameter equal to the maximum small-telescope separation. Taken together, these telescopes produce images with far greater resolution than single telescopes. The further the telescopes are separated, the greater the resolution. Very Long Baseline Interferometry (VLBI) uses radio telescopes spread across the whole surface of Earth to observe at the highest resolutions currently obtainable by any method. Some say that if an astronaut's fingernails were observable using VLBI (they aren't, because fingernails don't give off detectable levels of radio waves) then we could watch them grow from Earth. This is not too far from the truth (although the astronaut would have to stand really still!). Resolutions can approach 10 microarcseconds. To put this in perspective, the moon is 30 arcminutes in size, each arcminute being made of 60 arcseconds. Each arcsecond is composed of 1,000,000 microarcseconds, so the moon is 1,800,000,000 microarcseconds in size. Another way to comprehend this amazing resolution is that the

Hubble Space Telescope's ultimate resolution approaches 1 milliarcseconds. VLBI can reliably provide resolutions 100 times better than this. However, VLBI has its limits. Only very bright and compact sources can be observed with this extreme technique.

The Very Large Array, made famous in the movie *Contact*, is composed of 27 radio dishes, each 25 m in size arrayed in a Y-shaped pattern in the high desert of New Mexico. The VLA is the largest radio interferometer currently operating. This telescope is tremendously flexible and moves regularly through four configurations that provide a range of resolutions for astronomers to use. There are plans afoot to increase its capability. The array can be expanded by placing other telescopes at greater distances from the main array and enabling it to observe light of shorter wavelengths.

Future Radio Telescopes

A new telescope that will see first light in 2006 or 2007 is to be located in the high plains of the Chilean highlands. The Atacama Large Millimeter Array, or ALMA, will be a specialized interferometer designed to receive radio light in the millimeter wavelength range. This particular region of the electromagnetic spectrum will allow astronomers to peer into regions of star formation both in our own galaxy and in far-away galaxies, as well as emissions from a whole range of molecules from carbon monoxide to acetic acid to even more complex organic molecules—the building blocks of life. ALMA builds on the successful construction and operation of several millimeter arrays built in Spain, California, and Japan.

Sometime before 2020, a truly huge ground-based radio telescope will be built. Known as the Square Kilometer Array (SKA)—its total collecting area will be 1 square kilometer (km²)—and taking advantage of the rapid increases in computing speed and innovative antenna designs, this machine will be the most sensitive radio telescope ever built. However, it will be expensive and will require international partnerships to reduce the cost to any single country. Why build such a large telescope? In radio astronomy, the receivers are already as sensitive as can be made. They no longer limit the observations. To see fainter and fainter objects, astronomers must gather more and more light; thus the move to larger telescopes like the SKA is necessary.

PROBLEMS CAUSED BY THE ATMOSPHERE

The proliferation in the number and type of telescopes and the push to place them in orbit has a very simple explanation: we live at the bottom of a seething, cloudy, dusty, absorbing, and disruptive atmosphere. Living at the bottom of this soup of tumultuous vapor makes being an astronomer difficult. Early astronomers were constantly frustrated by clouds. Waiting for weeks, months or even years for a particular celestial event, only to have a thin layer of water vapor block it from sight, has been a frustration for astronomers since Babylonian times.

Modern astronomers share this frustration. Observing nights can still be "clouded out." When clouds move over the observatory, blocking the light from celestial objects, work stops. On such cloudy nights, astronomers today usually work on stored data taken on clear nights (or just watch television). This is possible because most telescopes record data digitally. In the past, they shut the dome and went home to sleep or to plan their next observations.

The atmosphere does more to negatively impact astronomical observations than simply carry clouds over observatories. Our atmosphere, made of a mixture of gasses and particles that we call air, absorbs light, scatters light, disrupts the passage of light, and even emits light itself. With all these problems it is no wonder that astronomers have now launched telescopes into space, beyond the negative effects of our problematic (though life-giving) atmosphere. However, the cost of space flight limits the size of telescope that we can send into orbit. The atmosphere and its corrupting properties—absorption, scattering, distortion and emission—will always remain a fundamental frustration for Earth-based astronomers.

Absorption

As we learned in Chapter 5, any gas can absorb light. The wavelength of light that is absorbed depends simply on the atoms or molecules in the gas and on its temperature or motion.

Our atmosphere is similar to the gas clouds found between the stars, or *interstellar clouds*, that absorb light of various wavelengths from celestial objects as we look at them from here on Earth. The air above us can absorb and emit light, and both these processes can corrupt astronomical observations.

Absorption of certain wavelengths of light limits the information that astronomers can gather from the surface of Earth. For example, if an astronomer wanted to study the light emitted by water molecules on a distant planet (remember from Chapter 4 that all atoms and molecules can both absorb and emit light under the right conditions), some of the light from the planet would be absorbed by the

OZONE HOLE

Perhaps the most famous absorption by our atmosphere is the absorption of ultraviolet light by *ozone*, a gas made of molecules composed of three oxygen atoms. Ozone is found in the upper regions of our atmosphere and absorbs ultraviolet light. When this molecule interacts with ultraviolet light, the ultraviolet photon is absorbed and does not continue on its journey to the surface of Earth. Ozone is constantly replenished though chemical reactions, so the absorption is a nearly constant effect on Earth, even though some ozone is destroyed normally. Ozone absorbs the ultraviolet light, is broken apart, and then more ozone is made.

Thankfully for us, this cycle keeps us protected, because ozone limits the burning of our skin by ultraviolet light. But in the 1970s, scientists determined that more ultraviolet light was penetrating the atmosphere over the South Pole and found that this was caused by a depletion of atmospheric ozone, a condition that became known as the ozone hole.

The depletion of ozone was shown to be directly caused by the release into the atmosphere of certain complex molecules known as chlorofluorocarbons (molecules with chlorine, fluorine, carbon, and other atoms and commonly referred to as CFCs) and temperature conditions in the upper atmosphere. These molecules, typically used in air conditioners and other industrial applications, were shown to destroy ozone through chemical reactions. When the CFCs reach the upper atmosphere, they break down in the presence of ultraviolet light, releasing chlorine atoms that are highly reactive and that destroy ozone. The rate of destruction is moderated by the temperature in the upper atmosphere.

Thoughtful application of laws in the industrialized nations limited the production and release of CFCs, and the ozone hole has since closed up, with ozone once again protecting Earth from ultraviolet light. However, CFCs are not easily destroyed in the atmosphere, and this problem may continue to haunt us for many years to come. In fact, in 2003, the ozone hole returned with a size similar to its largest size in 2000. Scientists now think the expansion is being caused by global warming and the temperature changes in the high altitude air. Whatever its cause and ultimate condition, it is clear we need further study of this puzzling phenomenon.

water vapor in our own atmosphere, perhaps spoiling the study. Only by launching a telescope beyond our atmosphere can certain wavelengths be studied. Figure 6.5 shows the wavelengths of light that are most strongly absorbed by our atmosphere. Notice that the light we see with our eyes can penetrate the atmosphere quite well, just like much of the radio region of the spectrum. The ultraviolet, infrared, X-ray, and gamma-ray portions are more strongly absorbed. To study these wavelengths, astronomers must launch telescopes into space.

Scattering

Molecules and particles in the atmosphere can also scatter light. Scattering of light is fairly complicated and can happen in a number of different ways. Basically, *scattering* is a change in direction and character of light by the interaction of light with matter. The most well known scattering of light is by molecules in our upper atmosphere that preferentially scatter blue light, causing the blue color of our sky. This scattering not only produces a blue sky, but it causes some of the scattered light to be polarized (defined in Chapter 3).

This polarization can be seen on very clear and dry days by looking in the sky about 90° away from the Sun with polarized sunglasses and tipping your head back and forth. Although passersby may gawk, you will be able to see that when you tip your head one way, a portion of the sky gets dark, and when you tip it the other way, the sky grows light. Because your sunglasses are blocking light of only one polarization, this is evidence that the blue light coming at you in the sky came from a scattering event that caused the light to be redirected and polarized.

Scattering acts mainly to reduce the amount of light we receive from celestial sources, but it can also change the color we see, because scattering acts differently at different wavelengths. Astronomers must carefully compensate for this effect by observing "standard stars" throughout their nightly observations. Standard stars have been carefully observed for many years, and their colors are known with great accuracy. Corrections can be determined by observing these stars and then applying the information to observations of other stars to correct for atmospheric scattering.

Distortion

The atmosphere is in constant motion, and this motion can seriously hinder astronomical observations. As clumps of air rise and fall due to differing temperatures or move about due to winds or turbulence caused by passage over mountains, the air itself can disrupt the path of the incoming light. This is because of changes in the index of refraction. This index is a measure in some sense of the amount of interaction a given material has with light. The blurring of an image by turbulent atmosphere is called *distortion*.

The index of refraction, n, is defined as the ratio of the speed of light in a vacuum, c, to the speed of light in the medium under consideration, v: $n = c/v$. In a complete vacuum, electromagnetic waves propagate without interacting with anything, but when entering a medium, such as our atmosphere, the light interacts with atoms or molecules, thereby slightly accelerating the available electrons and slowing down in the process. This change in speed results in a slight change in direction. Although the exact reasons for this change in direction are very complex and are tied

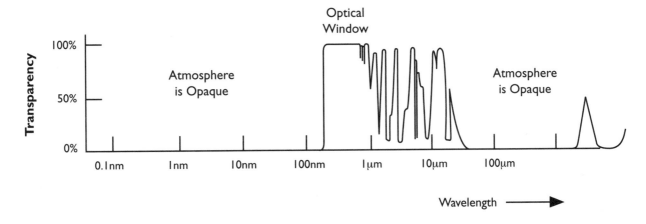

Figure 6.5—The Transparency of the Atmosphere in the Infrared, Optical, and Ultraviolet Portions of the Spectrum

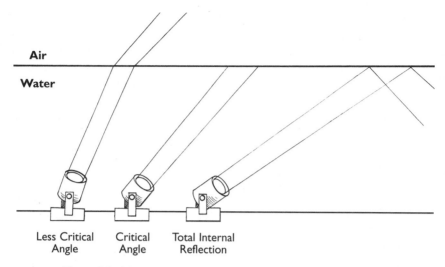

Figure 6.6—Light Entering Another Medium and Being Refracted

to quantum mechanics, an early empirical explanation was developed by French mathematician Pierre de Fermat (1601–1665).

Fermat's principle states that light always travels a path between two points that minimizes its time of travel. So, when light enters a medium with a different index of refraction, it changes direction to compensate for its reduced speed (Fig. 6.6).

The combined effect of air turbulence and temperature differences that causes blurred images for telescopes on Earth is often called *astronomical seeing*. When the seeing is good, astronomers can view astronomical objects more clearly, since the distortions are minimized. When the seeing is bad, the objects appear distorted.

Emission

After absorption, scattering, and distortion, a further difficulty is emission. Molecules in our atmosphere emit light that can negatively impact observations. Astronomers have detected this emission (in fact, scientists sometimes use this emission to study the atmosphere itself) and have developed methods to help

reduce its impact. However, this is not always easy or completely effective. Again, only by moving above the atmosphere can the effect be completely avoided.

GETTING ABOVE THE ATMOSPHERE

These four effects—absorption, scattering, distortion and emission—have led astronomers to move telescopes high onto mountains to get above as much of the atmosphere as possible (for example, the Keck telescopes in Hawaii, at 14,000 ft above sea level) or to launch telescopes into space, getting away from the atmosphere completely. The most famous of these space telescopes, the *Hubble Space Telescope*, has produced tremendous results and is the most referenced telescope in the professional astronomical literature.

The *Hubble* was designed to be serviced regularly by astronauts on the space shuttle. Since the terrible loss of the shuttle Columbia in 2003, future missions to repair the Hubble are doubtful. It is likely that the added costs to make flights to the *Hubble* safe for shuttle

Photo courtesy of NASA

Figure 6.7—HST in Orbit

astronauts will prove prohibitive, cutting *Hubble's* life short. It will just gradually break down. This is not a complete loss, because the telescope has already performed well beyond its design specification and longer than antici-pated. Still, to most astronomers, a working telescope in orbit above the hindering impact of the atmosphere is a great resource, and the eventual loss of the *Hubble* will be a tremen-dous blow to astronomy.

SUMMARY

Astronomers learn about the universe by gathering light and processing it with instruments. Telescopes are used to gather light. Two basic types are used in visual or optical astronomy, refracting telescopes and reflecting telescopes. Refracting telescopes use lenses to gather light and reflecting telescopes use mirrors. The larger a telescope is, the more light it can gather. The resolution of the telescope, or its ability to distinguish two closely spaced objects, also increases with diameter. The atmosphere ultimately limits the performance of optical telescopes by absorbing, distorting, and scattering the light we receive from distant objects.

Initially, sketches were used to record what objects looked like through telescopes. Once photography was invented, it found quick application in astronomy. Currently, electronic instruments are used to record the light gathered by telescopes.

Other types of telescopes are used to gather light outside the visual portion of the spectrum. Radio telescopes are used to gather longer-wavelength light that we cannot see with our eyes. Radio telescopes can be used together in teams to form interferometers, which greatly increase the resolving power available. Space telescopes are used to avoid the problems that the atmosphere causes for certain observing, but due to the higher cost of making, launching, operating, and servicing them, they are usually smaller than ground-based telescopes.

THE TERRESTRIAL PLANETS

When ancient Greek and Chinese people looked up at the sky, they could see that the planets had special motions, which we discussed in Chapter 1. The planets received special names because they were bright and did not follow the motion of the rest of the stars. In western cultures, descendants of Greek and Roman civilizations, they were named after the most important gods. Mercury, the winged messenger of Greek mythology, became the bright object visible close to the Sun and visible after sunset. They didn't know that a similar bright object seen near dawn was the same planet; they gave this planet a different name, Apollo. Venus, also visible near sunrise and sunset but visible well after the sky turns dark, was named after the Roman god of love. Mars, a bright red speck in the sky, was named for the Greek god of war. Jupiter, the brightest visible planet, was named for the king of the gods; Saturn was named for the god of time, due to its slow motion through the sky.

We know now that planets come in two basic types, small, dense planets mainly made of rock, and large, less dense planets composed mainly of gases like hydrogen. In this chapter we talk about the small, rocky planets; in Chapters 8 and 9 we talk about the gas giants and the most remote members of the solar system, such as Pluto.

MERCURY: THE WINGED MESSENGER

For a messenger, Mercury is hard to see. It is the planet closest to the Sun; as a result it is often blocked from our view by the light of the Sun itself. Because Mercury is very small and reflects light only from the Sun, it can be hard to see the planet when the Sun is above the horizon. But just after sunset or just before sunrise, Mercury can be seen by looking in the same region of the sky where the Sun is preparing to rise or has just set, Mercury appearing as a bright dot in the sky. When Mercury is furthest away from the Sun from our point of view, we say it is at greatest elongation. Elongation is the angular distance of a planet from the Sun, so *angular elongation* is the greatest angular distance of a planet from the Sun. Mercury's greatest elongation is 28°. We never see the planet more than 28° away from the Sun itself. This angle is determined by the average distance of Mercury from the Sun, a mere 960,000 mi, and its distance from the Earth, which varies from 129 and 57 million miles.

Fire and Ice: Mercury's Locked Orbit

Mercury orbits the Sun once every 88 days (on Earth this number is $365\frac{1}{4}$ days) and rotates once on its axis once every 58.6 days (on Earth this rotation defines 1 day). This odd situation, where the rotation period is about two-thirds the length of the year, causes an interesting effect: every 2 years, the Sun as seen from Mercury rises and sets exactly three times. Three days on Mercury is the same length of time as two Mercury years. This means that the sunlit side of Mercury has a long time to absorb the energy from the Sun, whereas the side not illuminated by the Sun has a long time to cool off. The surface facing the Sun is thought to have temperatures of almost 800°F, but the side facing away from the Sun is cold, about 300°F below freezing, a differential of roughly 1100°F. On Earth the range is only a few tens of degrees Fahrenheit, mainly due to the warming and heat-retaining properties of our atmosphere.

Exploration

Mercury is still very much a mystery. This is due partly to the fact that it is hard to observe with telescopes because it is never far from the Sun. The amount of time available for observation is limited, and observations must take place when the planet is low on the horizon, when, unfortunately, the most atmospheric distortion takes place. Astronomers can also use special filters to block the Sun's light.

It is also very hard to send a probe to Mercury. Arranging for an orbit that takes a space probe so close to the Sun is a great challenge. However, NASA scientists and engineers managed to get one near Mercury in the early 1970s. During 1973 and 1974, the *Mariner 10* probe managed to get close to Mercury three times and took some interesting pictures. To the surprise of scientists, the planet looked very much like our Moon. It had craters and other features similar to those on the Moon, such as broad plains, but there were no large lava basins as on the Moon. Unfortunately, not all of the planet was illuminated when the probe took its pictures, and we still do not

Photo courtesy of NASA

Figure 7.1—Image of the Surface of Mercury from the Mercury 10 Spacecraft

know what about half of the surface looks like. Mercury could still hold some surprises. See Figure 7.1.

NASA scientists are hoping to send another probe to Mercury soon. Called *Messenger*, the probe will arrive in orbit around Mercury sometime in 2009. *Messenger* will be equipped with imaging cameras, spectroscopes, magnetic field-measuring devices, and a laser altimeter to accurately measure the surface features of Mercury. This long-awaited mission will expand our knowledge of Mercury in all areas and should finally give us a picture of the whole planet, instead of just half.

Observation

Images of Mercury from Earth are not that great. At best, one can make out large, dark features, never sharp details. Mercury is just too small and too far away. In the 1960s astronomers began a serious study of Mercury using radar. By sending radio signals toward the planet and carefully measuring how and when they return, astronomers could map out the planet's surface features. In the end, all that could really be determined was that the planet did not always have one side facing the Sun, but it spun on its axis about once every 59 days.

A discovery in 1992 using radar showed that (frozen water) ice might actually exist near the poles of Mercury. How can ice exist on the planet closest to the Sun? Using radar and improved computers, scientists can make better sense of the reflected radar signals sent toward Mercury. They also have larger telescopes available and have used the Arecibo radio telescope in Puerto Rico, the Goldstone radio telescope in the Mojave Desert, and the Very Large Array in New Mexico. (More information on these telescopes is available in Appendix 1.) The radar signals leave Arecibo or Goldstone, travel for about 8 min (depending on where Mercury is in its orbit), and then finally hit Mercury. Some of the radio waves are reflected; some are absorbed (remember Chapter 4). The reflections travel back to Earth and are picked up about 8 min later (total trip: 16 min) by the Very Large Array. Reflections received from the polar regions were particularly strong, stronger than reflections expected from just rock. Using computer modeling of the reflected signals, astronomers can tell that the material reflecting so strongly is water ice and that the ice is in craterlike shapes. The ice is likely hidden from the direct light of the Sun in craters (preventing it from *sublimating*, or changing from a solid directly to a gas without becoming a liquid).

Atmospheres distribute warmth around a planet. Because Mercury has no atmosphere, anything in permanent shadow would be very cold, more than 150° below freezing. Unlike Venus, which has a thick atmosphere and a hot, almost uniform temperature, Mercury is hot only where the sunlight hits the surface, and it is very, very cold in the shadowed regions. It is truly a planet of fire and ice, the planet with the largest range in temperatures in the solar system.

Properties

Because Mercury is closer to the Sun than Earth, we see its phases. Sometimes, when Mercury is on the far side of the Sun from Earth, we see it as full; when it is on the same side of the Sun as Earth, we see it as a crescent. To the naked eye, it will always be just a bright dot in the sky seen just after sunset or just before sunrise, because it takes a telescope to show the actual phases.

The *Mariner 10* probe was able to roughly measure the mass of the planet. Because the probe moves in response to the gravity of the planet, scientists can use Newton's laws of gravitation to measure Mercury's mass. Mass is a unit of measure of an object's inertia. (The metric unit for mass is the gram.) Mercury is rather massive for its size. Another way of saying this is that Mercury has a large density. *Density* is a measure of the amount of mass contained in a given volume. Greater density implies more matter in a planet of a given size; smaller density implies less. The only way Mercury can have such a large density is if its core is composed mainly of iron.

Mariner 10 also detected a magnetic field, not as strong as Earth's, but more than was expected by scientists. Current theories predict planetary magnetic fields only when the core of the planet has some liquid metal, such as iron or nickel. Mercury's core was expected to be solid metal, not liquid, so the fact that it has a magnetic field is an ongoing mystery.

VENUS: EARTH'S MYSTERIOUS NEIGHBOR

Since its discovery in antiquity, Venus has been an object of mystery. Its surface features are veiled in clouds. This thick atmosphere has caused the surface temperatures on Venus to soar above the melting point of lead, about 621.5°F. However, in other respects, Venus is nearly Earth's twin, with close to the same mass and size. Scientists are still trying to understand why Venus is so different from Earth and how this difference came about, despite their similarities.

Clouds and the Greenhouse Effect

Despite Venus' clouds, which one might think would help keep the planet cool, the surface temperatures approach 900°F. How can such immense temperatures develop? We can understand Venus' immense temperature by looking at how greenhouses work. Greenhouses, used in colder climates during winter to grow warm-weather vegetables and plants, are buildings made mainly of glass or transparent plastic. Limited winter sunlight enters through the transparent glass or plastic and deposits its energy into the air, plants, soil, and other material in the greenhouse. The contents of the greenhouse warm up. Because plastic and glass are fairly good insulators, meaning they reflect infrared light, or heat, quite well, the heat inside the greenhouse stays inside. Even on freezing nights, greenhouses can retain enough of the Sun's energy to remain as warm as 50°F or more.

Venus works in much the same way. Its atmosphere is very thick and is composed mainly of carbon dioxide. Carbon dioxide, a molecule made up of one carbon atom and two oxygen atoms, is very good at absorbing infrared light and reradiating it in the same wavelength range. In other words, it absorbs heat energy, hangs onto it for a while, and then emits it back into its environment more or less unchanged. Because Venus' atmosphere is so thick and has so much carbon dioxide, it is very good at hanging onto heat. Although the high-altitude clouds in the atmosphere do limit the sunlight that can penetrate to the surface, the light that does ultimately make it to the surface heats up the rocks and dirt and is then retained by the large amounts of carbon dioxide gas.

This effect is called the greenhouse effect. To have a greenhouse effect, you need some carbon dioxide or other gas that retains heat well and some incoming sunlight. The amount of heating you get depends only on how much carbon dioxide gas you have. Venus has

CAN EARTH BECOME LIKE VENUS?

Once scientists figured out that some gases are efficient at retaining heat in atmospheres, and, like carbon dioxide, caused warming, more attention was paid to how much carbon dioxide Earth has in its own atmosphere. Ever since humans began to use fossil fuels such as coal and gasoline, which emit carbon dioxide when burned, the amount of carbon dioxide in our own atmosphere has been increasing. Since 1958, a small atmospheric sampling station on the Mauna Loa volcano in Hawaii has measured a significant increase in the amount of carbon dioxide in our atmosphere as well as a seasonal variation related to the life cycle of trees. In 1958 there were roughly 315 parts per million (or 0.0315%) carbon dioxide in our atmosphere. In 2003, there were roughly 375 parts per million. In just 45 years, the amount of carbon dioxide has increased by 19%. If this trend continues, the amount of carbon dioxide could be double what it was in 1958 in less than 100 years.

Everyone agrees that the carbon dioxide level in our atmosphere is increasing; what we don't know yet is if this dramatic increase is having a clearly measurable impact on Earth's long-term temperature stability. We do know that the global average temperatures are increasing. Many of Earth's glaciers have begun to shrink significantly, melting more quickly in the summer and not growing as fast in winter. In the summer of 2000, the ice at the North Pole was not even solid, an event nobody expected.

If permanent ice features such as glaciers and polar ice melt, sea levels will rise, posing grave challenges for those who live in coastal areas or on low-lying islands. Some Pacific islands will be completely covered if the sea level rises even 10 ft or so. Atmospheric scientists, geologists and other researchers are actively trying to trace the impact of increasing carbon dioxide levels. The issue has become politicized, because any fixes to the problem will be expensive. Our economy depends on fossil fuels. We need gas to run our engines and coal to produce our electricity. Stopping the carbon dioxide from getting into the atmosphere or figuring out ways to remove it from the atmosphere may be our only chance to keep our planet from becoming like Venus, a hot, barren place with no life. But with the positive changes recently in our attitudes toward the natural world, such an outcome is increasingly unlikely.

---

become the ultimate greenhouse, although the temperatures on the surface are so high any plants, dried leaves, or wood would catch fire if they were able to exist there at all. Even some metals, such as lead, would be molten on the surface. It would not be a pleasant place for us to be, and we do not expect any form of life as we know it to be found there.

Exploration

Venus has been visited by more probes than any other planet; nobody can resist a good mystery. The first to arrive was the *Mariner 2* probe in 1962. Only a flyby mission, it was able to send back confirmation that the surface was tremendously hot. Later *Mariner* probes found that the upper atmosphere had high-speed winds and a permanent cloud layer beginning about 18 mi above the surface and extending to an altitude of 50 mi or so. The clouds aren't made out of water droplets, as on Earth. They also contain sulfuric acid, which is a dangerous, highly corrosive chemical. Because these clouds cover the whole planet, you wouldn't see any interesting shapes were you to glance skyward from the Venusian surface, just a solid layer of clouds higher up than our cirrus clouds (usually about 4 mi above the surface).

Other missions, like the Russian *Venera* probes, actually landed on the surface of Venus, sending back images of the surface before they stopped functioning in the immense heat and atmospheric pressure. *Atmospheric pressure* is related to the weight of the air in the atmosphere per unit area. Thicker atmospheres have greater atmospheric pressure at the surface of the planet and thinner atmospheres have less pressure. The *Venera 9* probe, which landed on Venus in 1975, has the honor of being the first probe to land on another planet. The images sent back to Earth through the thick atmosphere showed a barren rocky surface. The probes (there were ten in all that landed successfully between 1975 and 1981) were able to survive the extreme conditions on the planet's surface for only about an hour, but they were able to measure the temperature, the amount of sunlight reaching the surface (about as much as on Earth during a heavily overcast day), the color of the surface (a darkish orange due to the reddening of the light coming from the Sun through the thick atmosphere), and the remarkable similarity of the surface in the multiple landing sites: medium to large rocks scattered over lava fields. It seems not to be an ideal travel destination (Fig. 7.2).

The *Magellan* probe in the early 1990s used radar to map almost the entire surface. Details as small as 300 m (1000 ft) were imaged; this is not fine enough to see small rocks, but it is good enough to map out major surface features. The range of altitudes on Venus is less than that on Earth, although the highest point is nearly a mile higher than Mt. Everest, relative to Venus' version of our sea level, which is the mean altitude on the planet. The lowest

Photo courtesy of NASA/JPL

Figure 7.2—The Surface of Venus

altitude on Venus is 1.8 mi, whereas the lowest point on the Earth is the Mariana trench, which is about 7 mi deep.

The *Magellan* project maintains a narrative Web site of the mission at http://pds.jpl.nasa. gov/mveg/guide.html, one of the many sites in the planetary data system, an archived network of planetary data obtained with NASA probes.

Observation

Observations of Venus have been limited due to its planetwide cloud cover. However, radio wavelength light can penetrate the clouds, hit the surface, and be reflected back to Earth or an orbiting spacecraft, such as *Magellan*. As with Mercury, astronomers began using radar systems to observe Venus remotely in the 1960s. These studies were able to accurately measure the distance to Venus at its closest approach to Earth (just shy of 26 million miles), an important measurement that helps us gauge the scale of the whole solar system. Subsequent experiments, including a radar experiment undertaken in 2001 involving the Green Bank telescope in West Virginia and the Arecibo telescope, have been able to map the surface in surprising detail. Although these methods are convenient and relatively inexpensive (once you have built the telescopes), the best images have come from the *Magellan* spacecraft and its radar. The *Messenger* spacecraft, mentioned earlier, will pass Venus on its way to Mercury and is planned to provide some new images of Venus.

Properties

The *Magellan* probe revealed that there are three main types of topography on Venus. The main features are volcanic uplands, which cover about 70% of the surface. Lowland plains cover about 20% of the surface, and mountainous highlands cover about 10%. The lowland plains are regions where lava has flowed across the surface, creating large, smooth expanses. Some ancient lava channels were found in these regions, showing that volcanism has played a major role in the development of the Venusian surface. The volcanic uplands are transition regions between the lowlands and highlands and represent a range of terrain from rugged mountainous zones to smooth lava outflow regions. Many volcanic domes can be found in these regions and provide some of the most interesting topography on the surface. The highlands are the source of much of the lava that flowed into the lowlands and contain the highest mountains on Venus (See Figs. 7.3 and 7.4).

The Magellan probe also found that, despite the dense atmosphere, there is very limited wind erosion or movement of sand or dust by atmospheric effects. Despite the similarity in size and mass, Venus is hardly Earth's twin.

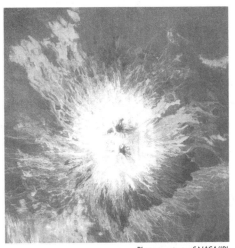

Photo courtesy of NASA/JPL

Figure 7.3—Sapas Mons

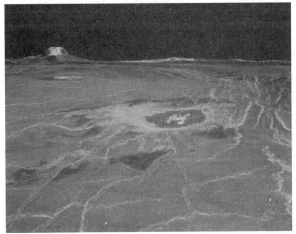

Photo courtesy of NASA/JPL

Figure 7.4—Estia Regio

EARTH: OUR HOME

It is our home, our shelter from the cold vastness of space and keeper of abundant life. But Earth is not entirely safe for us. Earthquakes make our buildings fall, and hurricanes and thunderstorms threaten us regularly. Lightning can wreak havoc on our electrical equipment, not to mention our bodies. Despite its regularly changing nature, Earth provides us with a relatively stable climate, with average temperatures above freezing, air to breathe, water to drink, plants and animals to enjoy, and resources to use. It is a good home.

But Earth is no less a planet than any other in the inner solar system. It has some unique characteristics, however, and these differences make it a good home for life. Let's get a handle on some of our home planet's basic characteristics.

Earth has a diameter of about 7930 mi and a circumference of almost 25,000 mi. We have clouds made of water droplets and water ice (depending on how high they are) that move about in an atmosphere made mostly of nitrogen and oxygen, with some carbon dioxide and other gasses. Weather takes place in the atmosphere, bringing wind and rain and sometimes snow to the surface. The surface of Earth is composed of large areas of land called continents and vast oceans of liquid water that cover about 70% of the planet. Ours is a water world, a planet almost entirely dominated by liquid water. Earth also has polar ice caps (which, we will see, Mars has as well). The continents have a great variety of landforms, from lush mountains to dry deserts. Rivers and streams guide water that falls as snow or rain back to the ocean basins, sculpting the land. Earth has a magnetic field, indicating that at least a portion of its core is made of liquid metal. We also find that our planet has volcanoes like those seen on Venus and, as we shall see, on other planets in the solar system. Finally, our planet has life, in the form of plants and animals that utilize the energy of the Sun and the chemical resources available on the surface and in the ocean to reproduce and interact with one another. Earth seems much more interesting than cratered Mercury or superhot Venus. Maybe this is because it is our home, but it is also so because there is simply more going on.

A Dynamic, Changing World

Earth has not stayed the same over time; its surface and climate have changed considerably. Through a variety of processes, the surface has been modified, added to, and destroyed, and the overall temperature has fluctuated. We are only now beginning to understand the history

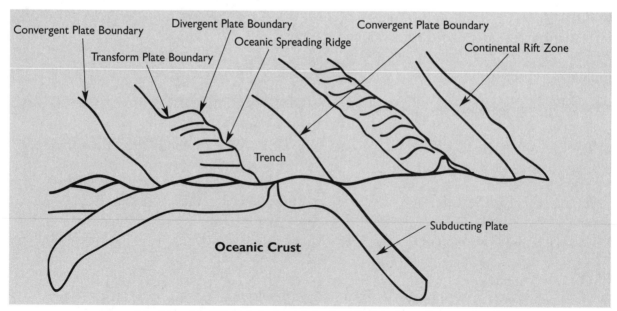

Figure 7.5—Diagram of Plate Tectonics, Subduction, Seafloor Spreading, and Volcanism

of long-term climatic change on Earth, but geologists have developed a deep understanding of how the planet's crust has changed over time.

Plate Tectonics

Our planet is apparently unique in the solar system in that it has shifting plates of solid material on its surface, known as *tectonic plates*, that move over time and dramatically affect the appearance of the surface. The plates are not uniform in composition. Some plates are made of less dense material than other plates. The continents, where there is dry land, are made of the less dense material and float on top of the denser plates, whereas the ocean basins are composed of even denser material and are therefore lower than the continental plates (See Fig. 7.5).

How do these plates form and how do they interact over time? Using deep-sea submarines beginning in the 1950s and continuing today, scientists have found zones of the ocean floor that are made of very new material. After looking closely, they found where the new material was coming from: volcanic spreading zones. In these zones, called *oceanic spreading ridges*, new molten rock comes up from the hotter regions under the crust and forms new crust material. The layer of Earth under the crust is called the *mantle*. Over time, the seafloor spreads away from these zones as the new material piles up, like a giant conveyor belt. Ultimately, the ocean crust bumps into one of the continents and, being heavier, begins to sink under the continental plate. This movement of the oceanic plates under the continental plates is known as *subduction*. The continental plates also build up over time through volcanic action. Volcanoes form and guide hot, molten material from either the mantle or regions where active subduction is

taking place to the surface of the continental plates, adding material to them.

A global cycle of formation of new crust from molten rock and volcanic eruptions, motion of the solidified crust over time, and the ultimate recycling of the crust through subduction would, if we could watch some time-lapse photography of these events, look very much like a complex dance. The continental plates would slowly move about on the surface, their motions dictated by the rate of spreading of the oceanic plates. Scientists have taken the positions of the current continents and, estimating average rates of seafloor spreading, made a kind of movie in reverse. We now think that at one point all the continents were part of one very large continent, which slowly broke up over time. Have you ever looked at a globe and noticed that South America looks as if it could fit into the notch of Africa? We now know that this actually is what happened. Geologists can match the rock types on the continents and show that all the continents were once together, more than 3 billion years ago.

Erosion

Plate tectonics is not the only force that has shaped our planet. *Erosion*, or the wearing away of rock through various processes, also plays a major role in modifying Earth's surface. The active weather of our planet produces strong winds. These winds can pick up dust and sand and move them from place to place. As the dust and sand are carried by the winds, they can rub against solid rock outcroppings, causing more dust and sand to be formed. This wind erosion takes place most often in desert regions where plants cannot grow over and protect rocks from this constant abrasion.

Rain and water can also erode rock. Just as rivers cut channels into the surface of Earth on their way to the sea, small flows of water from rain can slowly eat away at rock, carrying small pieces as they make their way to the rivers. Frozen water can also have devastating effect on rocks. When liquid water freezes, it expands slightly, exerting a force as it does. This process can cause rock to chip off and break away. Ocean waves, currents, and tides can all work to erode coastal rocks and shorelines. All these different forms of erosion slowly break down rocks and mountains over millions of years. Since Earth is about 4.5 billion years old, many mountains have had the chance to rise up and be eroded away. It is thought that the relatively low Appalachian Mountains in the eastern United States were once as large as the mighty Himalayas, home of Mt. Everest. Over time, wind, rain, streams, and rivers have taken them away piece by piece, slowly flattening them and making them small again. In the process, the water carries the sand and minerals from the rocks back to the oceans, forming a fundamental part of what's known as the hydrologic cycle.

The Hydrologic Cycle

Water is fundamental to life and plays an important role in shaping the surface of the Earth. The path that water takes through the Earth's various systems and life forms is known as the *hydrologic* cycle. Let's begin with the oceans. Earth's oceans, covering almost two-thirds of its surface, are salty. They have dissolved minerals and salts in them. These minerals and salts came from the continents. But how did the water get to the land? Heating from the Sun combined with Earth's active weather first evaporates liquid water to water vapor and then carries this vapor across Earth's surface, ultimately crossing a continent. Because the continents have mountains, the moving winds move up and over them, cool-

ing as they do so. Small water droplets condense from the water vapor as the temperature of the air drops and forms clouds. Clouds can also form without mountains. Anytime an air current moves upward and the temperature drops, condensation can take place. Water in the atmosphere is constantly condensing into small droplets and evaporating again into a gas as temperatures change and weather systems come and go.

Ultimately, the droplets can fall back to Earth's surface, either back to the oceans or onto the continents. If it falls onto the continents, it can be taken up by the soil and then into plant roots, which need water to produce energy from sunlight. Plants can't hold onto water, and as part of photosynthesis (their process of making energy), they release the water back to the air through small pores in their leaves. In other cases, rainwater is simply carried back to the ocean in streams and rivers, picking up sand or soil along the way and bringing this material back to the ocean. The water can also pick up salts and minerals in addition to the sand or soil, ultimately leading to salty oceans.

The hydrologic cycle is important because it provides a constant recycling of the water on Earth. The evaporation process leaves the salts and minerals in the oceans and deposits clean, fresh water on the continents. Life as we know it needs water without much salt in it, and although some life forms on the Earth can tolerate salt, it is certainly not good for us or the plants and animals that we use for food. The hydrologic cycle helps keep us alive, and it is directly linked to the physical properties of Earth, such as continents, weather, and ocean basins. There is a larger cycle, too, because life as we know it depends on Earth as a planet, and the planet is modified and changed by life.

The Moon

Earth is the only terrestrial planet in the solar system with a large moon. The Moon (capitalized to indicate that it is the Earth's moon) is about one-quarter the size of Earth and located about 230,000 mi away from us. It is much less dense than Earth, indicating that it doesn't have an iron core like Earth—and certainly not a liquid one, which is confirmed by its lack of a strong magnetic field.

Photo courtesy of NASA

Figure 7.6—Apollo 12 LEM Descending to the Lunar Surface

Americans have been to the Moon, gathered rocks and soil, and returned them to Earth (Fig. 7.6). This great effort was undertaken in an effort to understand its origin. We find that the rocks are similar to material here on Earth, especially the less dense material in the continental plates. Most scientists are now convinced that the Moon formed when a giant impact took place between the early Earth and another large object in the forming solar system. The dirt and rock left over after the impact, containing the material from the Earth and the giant impactor, gathered together to form the Moon. The denser material dredged up from the impact fell back to the Earth, whereas the less dense material formed the Moon.

Of course, such a large impact creates huge amounts of heat, and the material that came together to form the Moon should show evidence of melting. Careful analysis of the rocks gathered by Apollo astronauts back here on Earth shows that this is the case. All the material brought back appears to have melted at some time in the past and then solidified to make the Moon. Although we can't be certain that this is what made the Moon, all the evidence points to the giant impact theory as its source.

Besides being one of the dominant sights in our sky, the Moon has some characteristics of its own. It has no atmosphere, mainly because it is not that massive and its gravity cannot hold onto gas molecules for very long. Its surface is composed of mountain highlands, large flat basins known as seas, or *mare*, the Latin word for sea (though there is no water on the Moon!), and large numbers of craters. The craters are fascinating to look at through binoculars or a small telescope. You can see rays of brighter material coming out from some craters. These rays are actual material that was ejected from the crater when it was formed. One interesting fact about craters is that all of them look like they were formed by an object hitting the Moon straight on. This is impossible of course; there is no real reason why meteors hitting the Moon have to come straight at it, nor did most of them. In fact, since there is no atmosphere on the Moon to slow them down, the meteors actually plow deep into the surface of the Moon when they hit and cause an explosion of material up toward the surface.

The shortest distance to the surface is straight up, and this is why the craters all appear circular, with crater walls more or less perpendicular to the surface.

The photos taken by astronauts while they were on the Moon are truly amazing. The missions also had video cameras, so we can see movies of the astronauts bouncing around in the weaker gravity of the Moon, which makes them seem to weigh only one-sixth as much as they do on Earth.

MARS: THE RED PLANET

We have sent many probes to Mars, and President George W. Bush made sending humans to Mars a formal goal for NASA in 2004. Why are we so crazy about Mars? We are interested in Mars because it is probably the only other terrestrial planet in the solar system that we will ever be able to set foot upon. Mercury is both too hot and too cold to easily

LIVING ON MARS

Throughout human history, we have expanded into all possible places to live. From the northern Arctic to the most inhospitable desert, humans have moved into every possible niche on Earth. It is inevitable that we will ultimately free the bonds of gravity and our home world to explore outer space. Unfortunately, there aren't many places to go, and they aren't very hospitable. Mercury and Venus have such extreme conditions that there could be little benefit from traveling to them. The Moon does present one place we could live and work, but the material available there is substantially the same as the material here on Earth. Mars is more interesting—if only because it looks interesting, is nearly the size of Earth, and appears to have had water on its surface. The outer planets, discussed in the next chapter, have no surfaces, and their moons are inhospitable and cold.

So Mars is probably it, the only other body in the solar system onto which we can hope to expand as a species. What do we need to live there? Mainly electricity—power is needed to purify and concentrate the Martian atmosphere into a mix more nearly like our own atmosphere. We now suspect that there is frozen water just under the surface, which could be extracted and used for drinking. Greenhouses would have to be set up, but the light of the Sun would not heat them much above freezing, so extra heating from electricity would be needed to grow food. NASA is developing nuclear power systems for space probes that will travel far from the light of the Sun, where solar panels can be used to produce electricity; perhaps this technology development will allow a small nuclear reactor to be taken to the surface of Mars to make electricity for the first visitors or settlers. But what do we hope to gain by going to Mars? When astronauts landed on the Moon, they set up scientific experiments, took samples, inspected lunar rocks and even hit golf balls around. The cost of going to Mars and the great risk to the astronauts should cause us to ask why go to Mars at all? Robots can now perform much of the exploration and work that the Apollo astronauts performed. Only the glory of saying "we were there" is lacking from robotic explorations. Is this worth the cost and risk? Some say yes and some say no. Only time will tell if we ultimately land on Mars, whether for just a brief visit or a longer stay.

allow us to explore it, and it is also too close to the Sun to easily get there. Venus is a stupendously hot place with a crushing atmosphere, sulfuric acid clouds, and not a trace of oxygen. Mars is a bit more hospitable, and it is likely we will one day be able to visit Mars and perhaps even live there.

Percival Lowell and Life on Mars

In the late1800s, Mars made the news in a big way, mainly due to one man, Percival Lowell (1855–1916), an American amateur astronomer. Born to a wealthy New England family, Lowell had a wonderful education and became a diplomat, traveling widely in Asia. In the 1890s, he read a translation of a book written in 1877 by astronomer Giovanni Schiaparelli. Schiaparelli had made careful observations of the surface of Mars through a telescope. He subsequently published his maps, labeling the features he thought he could identify. Some long channel-like features he labeled "canali," which was translated in the English version of the book that Lowell read as "canals." This became the source of Lowell's lifelong passion—and lifelong confusion. He estimated that the reason Mars had canals was that there was a thriving population of Martians who lived on a desert world and made the canals to transport water from polar ice cap regions to equatorial areas, where farming could take place. He thought he could detect seasonal variations, which he took to show evidence of trees losing their leaves in winter and growing them back in summer. He spent considerable sums of money to build Lowell Observatory in Flagstaff, Arizona, to carefully observe Mars, ultimately publishing books describing his theories using sketches that he and observing assistants made. As larger telescopes became available and photographic techniques began

to be used with telescopes, most astronomers determined that there were no large canals on the surface—and no Martians either. Lowell Observatory became famous not for the observations made to support Lowell's mistranslated fantasy of Mars but for the discovery of the ninth and outermost planet in our solar system, Pluto.

Exploration

We have begun to seriously explore our nearby neighbor, Mars. In 2003, multiple probes landed on the surface, flew by the planet, or orbited it in order to gather enough data to make maps. The rovers *Spirit* and *Opportunity* bounced down on the surface in massive airbags and quickly began to explore the region of the planet where they landed. The early missions to Mars included the *Mariner* probes sent to Mars from 1965 to 1972, which flew by, took pictures, and made measurements. Temperature measurements indicate that on the Martian surface it rarely gets above freezing. It may get just above freezing near the equator in midsummer, but the poles were cold enough (about

Figure 7.7—First Panoramic Picture from the Surface of Mars, First Viking Lander

-200°F) for carbon dioxide to be frozen out of the atmosphere. The atmosphere is composed mainly of carbon dioxide, which explains why Mars is warmer than expected. The planet is being warmed by the greenhouse effect.

Subsequent probes include the *Viking* landers (Fig. 7.7), which touched down in 1976 on two different locations on Mars and which were designed using the knowledge gained from the earlier probes. These major missions were supposed to perform experiments that would provide evidence of any bacteria in the soil, indicating the presence of life, but the results were inconclusive, only adding to the mystery of the red planet. The missions did provide much more detailed analysis of the soil and atmospheric conditions, and more detailed images of the surface. We learned much about the planet, but with new knowledge came new questions. The surface was covered with rocks and dust, and occasionally the dust would be whipped up into great dust storms. But how did these storms begin? Why did they cover almost the entire surface? The red color of the Mars is from the commonly found material iron oxide, or rust, which is widespread on the planet.

Since the *Viking* missions, NASA has made a concerted effort to launch a constant stream of relatively inexpensive missions to Mars, some of which have been successful and some of which have been lost due to error or accident. A mission to Mars in 1997, the *Mars Global Surveyor*, mapped nearly the entire surface of the planet using high-resolution cameras from its orbit around Mars. It is now easier to get a high-resolution image of the Martian surface than Earth's. Due to the potential military use of high-quality pictures of the Earth's surface, it is hard to obtain pictures of just anywhere

Photo courtesy of NASA/JPL/Malin Space Science Systems

Figure 7.8—Mars Global Surveyor Images

on our home planet. The *Mars Global Surveyor* images are available online and provide some pretty striking detail, showing large boulders about the size of a small house (Fig. 7.8).

Results from the Mars *Global Surveyor* indicated that some structures on the surface could have been made only through the erosive process of liquid water flowing across the surface. Also, some craters showed features that could have been formed by liquid water flowing down the sides of the crater walls. If all these geologic features indicate water, where is it? The pressure of the Martian atmosphere and its temperature will not allow liquid water to last very long on the surface. If it did exist, it would quickly change to water vapor. However, in the past, the atmospheric conditions on Mars could have allowed liquid water to exist, which would explain the geologic features we see that seem to have been caused by rivers or floods.

WATER FOUND!

In early 2004, NASA announced that the rovers that landed on Mars had found evidence of water. One rover happened to land in a crater with exposed bedrock. This bedrock, upon inspection, revealed small spherical mineral deposits about 1 millimeter (mm) in size that were likely formed by water seeping out of the rock over time, evaporating and leaving behind the minerals it carried in solution. Additionally, by closely inspecting the exposed bedrock, one rover found evidence for standing water on the planet. Although these results need further interpretation and verification, it is looking very likely that early Mars had liquid water. Once we determine how long the water was around, we will have a better idea whether life could have formed on Mars or not. Stay tuned as NASA uncovers this vital mystery via the large number of missions planned through 2020.

THE FACE ON MARS

NASA makes all its images available for anyone to use; a few years ago, one of the images taken by the *Viking 1* orbiter made some news. This image, initially released by NASA's Jet Propulsion Laboratory, was of a region of the planet known to have buttes and mesas, similar to the American Southwest. The surface features in the photo resembled a face. Some members of the public immediately put forward the idea that the so-called face on Mars was actually made by intelligent beings and represented a monument or signpost for other intelligent beings to find. Figure 7.9 shows what the face looked like in the initial images.

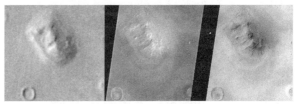

Photo courtesy of NASA/JPL

Figure 7.9—Mars Face Comparison Picture: Old Photo versus MGS

Although scientists explained that the lighting at the time could make the rock butte look like a face—and, in fact, other images taken at different times did not show a face—enthusiasts for life on Mars would not let the idea go. The *Mars Global Surveyor* took a high-resolution in view in April 1991. This zoomed-in view clearly shows that the so-called face is nothing but a rocky mesa. Lighting and our brains, so well tuned to finding patterns, see a face where none exists. Only a higher-resolution image can reveal the truth.

The rovers that landed in 2004 and other future missions have as their primary goal the discovery of water on the planet. With any luck, they may find signs of water ice or gouges on rocks perhaps caused by flowing water. Why search for water? We know that life needs water to survive, and we think that conditions on Mars may have once been favorable to life, but only if water existed there as well. This is why we are exploring Mars so eagerly. It would be a great triumph to finally verify that water exists there in the form of ice and could, therefore, have been in a liquid form during the early days of the planet.

Observation

Our observations of Mars have revealed a barren world, if one with some interesting topography. From the early observations of Schiaparelli to those of Lowell and others, the quest to resolve the details on the surface have led to the development of new telescopes and more careful imaging. We rely now on remote spacecraft to provide us with finer views of Mars than could ever be obtained from Earth, but the view through a telescope is still something to seek out. In a recent apparition, or period of good viewing of Mars, thousands of people lined up at telescopes to see the red planet. What brought out the crowds? Mars was closer to Earth—a mere 34,648,840 mi—

than it has been or will be for about 50,000 years. The *Hubble Space Telescope* was even pointed at Mars to obtain a close-up view (Fig. 7.10). Much of the detail on the surface was visible, including the striking canyon Valles Marineris, which is almost 2500 mi long and several times deeper than the Grand Canyon. Observing Mars with a telescope will tell us little more than we already know. The age of Martian exploration has arrived.

Properties

Mars has canyons, volcanoes, craters, and polar ice caps. We know that the planet is about half the size of Earth, has a thin atmosphere composed mainly of carbon dioxide, and is fairly cold, rarely getting above freezing, even near the equator at mid-day. Mars has complex weather. The *Sojourner* rover took images of dust devils moving across the surface; orbiting cameras have snapped pictures of dusty regions on the surface etched with the snail-like tracks left by these Martian dust devils. Occasionally, the entire surface of the planet is covered by gigantic dust storms that represent a global weather phenomenon we do not yet understand completely.

We still seek water and life on our nearest neighbor—not just because we want to know if life ever existed on Mars, but perhaps also to determine if we can ever live there. The terrain is not so different from that in the American Southwest, with dune fields, rolling hills, mesas, buttes, and even a crater or two. But the climatic conditions present a great challenge for us. To send astronauts, we must provide them with a power source to survive on the planet's surface—enough power to run lights, provide heat, and process air to make a livable base. Such power requires nuclear energy and technology we have not yet

Photo courtesy of NASA, J. Bell (Cornell U.) and M. Wolff (SSI)

Figure 7.10—Hubble's Closest Approach Image of Mars

developed for flights into space. Such exploration also costs money, money that many think should be spent here on Earth. Whether we get to Mars or not, our probes will continue to provide a close-up view, and our instruments will provide more detailed measurements. We go to Mars because we can, because we want to learn, and because it is our nearest neighbor and the only likely place for us to ever find a second home.

SUMMARY

The terrestrial planets are (in order of distance from the Sun) Mercury, Venus, Earth and Mars.

Mercury is a hot, cratered world, which is locked in a special orbit around the Sun. Three rotations of Mercury on its axis are made for every two revolutions of the planet around the Sun. We have sent a probe to Mercury and plan to send more. We still do not have a complete map of its surface. Using radar techniques, astronomers have found evidence of ice in the polar regions of Mercury, despite it being very close to the Sun.

Venus is veiled in a thick atmosphere that is full of clouds. Its thick atmosphere retains the heat it receives from the Sun, and its surface temperature is in excess of 900°F. Only a few Russian probes have landed on the surface. A U.S. satellite has used radar to map out Venus' surface. It consists of three general features, smooth basins mainly composed of cooled lava, high mountainous areas with extinct volcanoes, and a transition region between these two extremes. Liquid water cannot exist on the surface of Venus.

Earth is the only planet we know of that has liquid water in abundance. It also has polar caps of frozen water. Its sectioned crust is active, with plates moving about through a process known as plate tectonics. New material is made in the ocean basins and is ultimately subducted or taken back downward toward Earth's center, where it is remelted and can surface through volcanoes. Erosion plays a dominate role on our planet, with water and wind modifying land forms and releasing chemical elements from rock. The dynamic interaction of water, air, and rock is known as the hydrologic cycle. Earth has a moon. It appears that it was formed through a gigantic impact with a large object and the early Earth during the early days of the solar system.

Mars is now a target of exploration by humans, and a number of robotic probes have visited the planet. It is perhaps the only other place in our solar system beyond Earth and the Moon where humans will ever walk. There is a chance that life was also formed on Mars, and that is one of the main reasons we are actively exploring it. Two rovers that landed on Mars in 2004 found evidence of liquid water over longer periods of time, so it may be just a matter of time before we find evidence of early life on Mars.

THE JOVIAN PLANETS

KEY TERMS

Jovian planets, outer planets, belts, zones,
Great Red Spot, heliosphere, heliopause, albedo

The four largest planets in the solar system (Jupiter, Saturn, Uranus, and Neptune) are known as the Jovian planets, after the largest planet of all, Jupiter, which is named for the King of the Roman gods. All four are similar in nature. Astronomers have found that they are composed of gases, mainly hydrogen and helium. As far as we know, they have no solid surface like here on Earth. As the solar system formed, they slowly gathered the hydrogen and helium gas in the outer solar system through gravity. As small clouds of gas moved near a central core, they would be drawn in by the force of gravity, building up over time into the large planets we see today. Because they inhabit the outer solar system, they are sometimes called the outer planets, but this term includes all the Jovian planets and also the small, icy planet Pluto, which we discuss in the next chapter.

Although Galileo was able to observe and follow Jupiter and Saturn with his small telescope, the other, outer Jovian planets, Uranus and Neptune, were not discovered until many hundreds of years later. How is it that two giant planets—planets about eight times as large as Earth—escaped detection for so long? Because they are so very far away (about 20 and 30 times as far as Earth) from the Sun, they are very dim. Although the giant planets are large, they do not emit light on their own. They are visible only due to light they reflect from the Sun. This is why they are so faint. Imagine someone with a signal mirror very close by. It is easy to see the sunlight reflected in the mirror, but if you move it hundreds of miles away, the same sunlight would be far dimmer.

The fact that they are faint makes it difficult to study these planets in great detail from Earth. However, by sending spacecraft to them, we can see them much better. Launched in 1989, the spacecraft Galileo has made an extensive study of Jupiter; another probe, Cassini (named for a great Italian astronomer of the seventeenth century), scheduled to launch in July 2004, will study Saturn. In the 1980s, the world watched in wonder as the two Voyager spacecraft made a grand tour of the outer solar system, studying the Jovian planets. Much of what we know today about these planets is due to the pioneering Voyager missions and the ongoing missions sent by NASA to learn more. Humans will never be able to visit the Jovian planets themselves, but perhaps one day we may visit their moons. Until then, our robot explorers will have to help us learn about these distant giant planets. Table 8.1 gives properties of the planets.

Name of Object	Diameter of Object (in miles)	Distance from the Sun (in miles)
Earth	7,926	92,960,000
Jupiter	88,850	483,600,000
Mars	4,222	141,600,000
Mercury	3,032	35,983,605
Neptune	30,780	2,799,000,000
Pluto	1,454	3,674,000,000
Saturn	74,900	888,200,000
Sun	863,710	—
Uranus	31,760	1,784,000,000
Venus	7,521	67,230,000

Table 8.1—The Physical Characteristics of the Planets

JUPITER: KING OF THE SOLAR SYSTEM

Just how big is Jupiter? More than 1000 Earths would be needed to fill up its interior volume. Almost 35 Earths would be needed to surround its equator if placed side by side. But the grand scale of the planet is not its only impressive characteristic. It is truly beautiful. Sweeping bands of color in the upper atmosphere surround the planet parallel to its equator. A large equatorial band runs around Jupiter's middle with alternating dark and light bands that appear above and below the equatorial band. The dark bands are known as belts and the light-colored bands are known as zones. Jupiter's atmosphere shows colors from darkish red or brown through orange and white.

The most prominent characteristic of the surface appearance of Jupiter, a large oval structure, is actually a large atmospheric disturbance that moves through the belts over time and is aptly known as the Great Red Spot (Fig. 8.1). The Great Red Spot is thought to have first been observed by English scientist Robert Hooke (1635–1703) in 1664, almost 400 years ago. Although documented proof of the existence of the spot is difficult to find prior to 1879, it has been around since then and it is still present today. It is a rotating, hurricane-like weather pattern that appears never to fade. However, instead of being a region of low pressure, like hurricanes here on Earth, it is a region of high-pressure and actually pokes up above the surrounding cloud tops.

Photo courtesy of Hubble Heritage Team (STScI/AURA/NASA) and Amy Simon (Cornell U.)

Figure 8.1—The Great Red Spot of Jupiter

Grand Weather, Deep Mysteries

As the largest planet in the solar system, Jupiter also features the greatest gravity; this and its dynamic atmosphere lead to unbelievable conditions that we can only begin to imagine. By carefully photographing the surface of Jupiter with telescopes and tracking the atmospheric patterns like the Great Red Spot, astronomers have determined that each of Jupiter's belts and zones moves at different speeds. This is similar to the wind patterns here on Earth. But on Jupiter, the winds move much faster. Measurements of Jupiter's winds show that, depending on the latitude, the winds can be as high as several hundred miles per hour. The Galileo mission dropped a probe that plunged into Jupiter's atmosphere and measured increasing wind speeds as it got deeper. The final measurements from the probe indicated wind speeds of almost 400 mi/h.

Because of Jupiter's fast rotation speed, about 10 h per full rotation, and its tremendous size, the velocity of the planet's equator relative to an observer at rest is almost 27,000 mi/h. This rapid rotation causes the equator to bulge slightly, like a soccer ball that someone is stepping on. The rotation is also responsible for the striking weather patterns visible on the surface, such as the Great Red Spot.

The atmosphere of Jupiter is unlike Earth's. The highest clouds we can see are made of ammonia ice. Deeper clouds are formed of water vapor, water ice, and other gases, such as methane and even hydrogen and helium. The temperature increases rapidly from about 100° below freezing at the highest layers to about boiling 100 mi down. Eventually, the pressure becomes so great it is difficult to call the regions an atmosphere at all. Deep in the interior of Jupiter is a region of very dense hydrogen that exists in a liquid state, but because of the high pressure it demonstrates characteristics of some metals. This exotic state of hydrogen is called metallic hydrogen. Hydrogen in this state can freely move electrons around. This ability, as in the liquid metal core of the Earth, is what gives rise to Jupiter's very strong magnetic field.

Jupiter's Moons

Galileo was the first to observe Jupiter through a telescope. Not only that, he found that Jupiter had four moons of its own (signaling the death knell of the Earth-centric solar system). Through his telescope they appeared as simple bright dots, but they also changed position over time. Galileo was able to track them and ultimately predict when they would be visible. Since at the time most scholars felt that everything in the heavens had to orbit Earth, this discovery was quite controversial. Some people thought Galileo had rigged his telescope to show these images and that there was no way a planet could have its own moons.

Today we know that not only does Jupiter have its own moons, it has a lot of them. Besides the four largest there are at least 57 other satellites. The four main moons, Callisto, Europa, Ganymde, and Io, are often called the Galilean moons in honor of Galileo, who first discovered them. More moons are discovered on a regular basis as our telescopes and techniques get better. We don't know much about the non-Galilean moons; they are all small and rocky, and some are probably covered with ice. We know more about the four larger moons.

Callisto

Callisto is about 3,000 mi in diameter and is the furthest out of the Galilean moons. Callisto is about the same size as Mercury, but measurements reveal it is much less massive. This likely means it does not have a large core, like the Earth or Mercury. The surface is highly cratered and appears to be very old. By counting the number of craters in a given area of the surface and comparing it to other solar system objects, like our Moon or Mercury, astronomers are quite sure that Callisto's surface has remain more or less unchanged since the very beginning of the solar system. This also means that Callisto has not had any volcanic activity, which would cover the surface over with new material.

Callisto, like Mercury, has had some very large impacts. The Valhalla basin is a large impact scar more than 1500 mi across, similar to the Caloris basin on Mercury (Fig. 8.2). The moon appears to be largely composed of rock and iron—about 60%—and is about 40% ice. This ice makes the impact features on Callisto appear bright to observers. Callisto has a very thin atmosphere of mainly carbon dioxide, but it has much less atmosphere than Mars, the single planet with a thin carbon dioxide atmosphere.

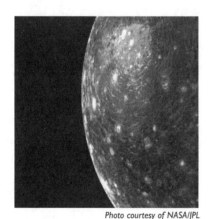

Photo courtesy of NASA/JPL

Figure 8.2—The Valhalla Basin on Jupiter's Moon Callisto

Europa

Europa is slightly smaller than our Moon and is composed mostly of rock, but it has a thin outer layer of ice. It is the second closest Galilean moon to Jupiter. Unlike Mercury or Callisto, the surface of Europa is very smooth, with hardly any cratering. This probably indicates that somehow the surface is repaved when impacts take place. Close-up images taken by Voyager, which was able to map only a fraction of Europa's surface, bear a striking similarity to sea ice here on Earth, complete with icebergs and large cracks that crisscross the surface (Fig. 8.3). Scientists now think that Europa has a water ocean under its icy outer skin and are planning missions to investigate what might be under the thick ice. The ocean could be as much as 30 mi deep, but the ice itself is probably at least 1 or 2 mi thick. It will be a great challenge to burrow through the ice to investigate what lies beneath.

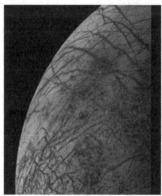

Photo courtesy of NASA/JPL

Figure 8.3—Jupiter's Moon Europa

Europa has a thin oxygen atmosphere, but it is not related to the action of plants, as on Earth. As sunlight hits the icy surface, it can interact with various molecules, sometimes releasing oxygen in the process. Even though we know no life could exist on Europa's icy surface, many astronomers now feel that besides the Earth and maybe Mars, Europa's ocean could harbor life. Because Jupiter's gravity is so strong, it heats the Galilean moons through gravitational pulling and stretching. This heating is what keeps Europa's ocean liquid and could also provide just enough heat for life to form. Europa is one of the more enticing mysteries of the solar system and will be the target of many future NASA missions.

Ganymede

Ganymede is the third Galilean moon of Jupiter, orbiting about 620,000 mi above Jupiter's tumbling clouds. It is the largest of Jupiter's moons and the largest moon in the solar system; it is even larger than the planet Mercury, but it is not as massive. Because the Galileo mission found that Ganymede has a weak magnetic field, it is likely that the core of the moon is made of molten metal, probably iron. The outer surface is icy, and it shows significant cratering as well as grooves and ridges. Between the icy surface and the inner metallic core is probably a region of rocky material.

The origin of Ganymede's grooves and ridges is under active debate, but they probably originate from the strong gravitational interaction with Jupiter, or a process similar to the motion of tectonic plates here on Earth. Only further missions will let us fully understand these interesting natural features on Ganymede (Fig. 8.4).

Photo courtesy of NASA/JPL

Figure 8.4—Ganymede's Grooved Terrain

Io

Io is the most interesting of Jupiter's moons. Orbiting only about 260,000 mi above Jupiter, Io is the closest Galilean moon. It has a dynamic surface, with a range of shades and colors. The Galileo probe has shown that Io probably has an inner iron core, with a thick outer layer of rock, similar to that found on Earth. Io has almost no craters. Scientists had a hard time figuring out why this was so until the Voyager spacecraft actually caught a small volcano erupting on the surface. This eruption and the many others subsequently observed, combined with detailed analysis of changing surface features, indicate that Io replenishes its surface so rapidly that any crater will quickly be filled in with new material (Fig. 8.5).

Photo courtesy of NASA/JPL

Figure 8.5—Jupiter's Moon Io

What causes the heating that produces Io's volcanoes? Because Io is so close to Jupiter, it experiences immense tidal effects, like those produced on Earth by the Moon but much greater in force. These tides push and pull Io, constantly heating its interior and causing volcanic eruptions (Fig. 8.6).

Photo courtesy of NASA/JPL

Figure 8.6— One of Io's Volcanoes

Exploration

NASA has sent seven probes to Jupiter, and most of what we know in detail about the planet and its moons comes from these missions. The first two missions were Pioneer 10 and 11. Pioneer 10 was launched in 1972 and Pioneer 11, in 1973. Both flew by Jupiter taking pictures and making measurements of Jupiter's magnetic field. Pioneer 10 is now the second-furthest manufactured object from the Sun. In 1983 it passed Pluto's orbit, the most distant planet from the Sun, and it is still going. Only the Voyager 1 spacecraft is further away from the Sun than Pioneer 10.

Voyager 1 and Voyager 2 have provided most of the knowledge we have of Jupiter and its moons. Launched in 1977, they reached Jupiter at slightly different times. The Voyagers discovered that Jupiter has a thin ring of material high above its equator similar to Saturn's rings that is much thinner and not as easily visible from Earth. They also took detailed images of Jupiter's moons as well as the planet's atmosphere. They measured the composition of the atmosphere and took measurements of the magnetic field around the planet. As with most scientific probes, they left more questions than answers, and scientists proposed sending another mission, Galileo, to Jupiter as soon as possible. The Galileo mission was designed to insert a spacecraft into orbit around Jupiter, drop a probe into its atmosphere, and visit each of Jupiter's moons in order to provide detailed observations of their surfaces. In 2003, the Galileo mission was completed. The mission initially had difficulty because its antenna did not function properly and it could communicate only slowly with radio telescopes here on Earth. However, all the data ultimately made it back to Earth and we learned quite a bit. Galileo's most important discoveries

SUN'S HELIOPAUSE

The Sun, as we will see in Chapter 10, has a strong magnetic field. This field extends far out into space, protecting all the planets from any magnetic fields in interstellar space and helping to deflect charged particles from entering the solar system. This zone of influence is known as the heliosphere, and encloses a huge region of space, extending well beyond the orbit of the most distant planet, Pluto.

Through sheer good luck, the power source on Pioneer 10 is still functioning, but we can no longer communicate with this distant traveler. Its radio signal can no longer be easily detected. However, the Voyager 1 probe, which has a stronger broadcasting unit, can still be tracked by radio telescopes here on Earth. This plucky little probe is of great interest to scientists. Soon it will pass from the region of space dominated by the Sun into true interstellar space. When it reaches the outer edge of the Sun's heliosphere, the region of space where the Sun's magnetic field has dwindled to nothing, called the heliopause, its detectors will allow us to measure the magnetic field, if any, in true interstellar space. Voyager 1 was more than 8 billion miles from the Sun in the summer of 2003 and increasing its distance by almost 350 million miles per year, nearly four times the average distance between Earth and the Sun.

Scientists knew that these outer solar system explorers would ultimately leave the influence of the Sun and continue traveling through interstellar space. In case some intelligent life form were ever to find the probes, messages were composed and placed on board. The Voyagers carry gold records with images and sounds stored on them. Although it will be millions of years before either probe even gets close to a star, it is possible, if remotely, that something made by humans here on Earth may be found by another denizen of the cosmos.

included that Europa does indeed have an ocean under its icy surface; that Io's volcanoes spew out hot material, sometimes very hot; and that Jupiter's Great Red Spot can bring up material from within the deeper atmosphere, occasionally forming ammonia ice clouds in its wake. On its way to the Jovian system, Galileo found that the asteroid 243 Ida (asteroids are discussed in detail in the next chapter) has a small moon, now named Dactyl (Fig. 8.7).

Photo courtesy of NASA/JPL

Figure 8.7—Asteroid Ida and Moon Dactyl

Observation

Observation of Jupiter from the ground continues today, but as we have seen, the best way to study Jupiter is by sending probes there. Jupiter is unique among all the planets in having a strong magnetic field that interacts with its moon Io to form a unique object in the solar system, a plasma torus, composed of plasma (a hot, ionized gas) and a torus (a doughnut-shaped ring of material). Jupiter's plasma torus is formed through a combination of Jupiter's strong magnetic fields and Io's active volcanoes (Fig. 8.8). The gas originates from Io's volcanoes, which erupt quite often, sending sulfur, sulfur dioxide, and other material high above the planet's surface. The speediest molecules can travel quite high above Io, and some of them even escape its gravitational field. These escaped atoms and molecules become ionized by losing one or more electrons and become electrically charged. Because they are electrically charged once they lose one or more electrons, they are captured by Jupiter's magnetic field. Because Jupiter's magnetic field rotates with the planet, these particles orbit at the same rotational speed as Jupiter, making a complete orbit around the planet once every 10 h.

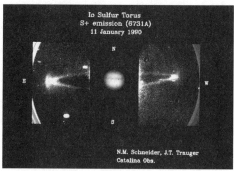

Photo courtesy of G. Orton and NASA

Figure 8.8—Jupiter's Torus from the Catalina Observatory

Observations of Jupiter continue even though we can't see much detail. Astronomers use filters, spectrometers, and other devices to tell them more about the physical properties of the planet. A long-term effort to track Jupiter's weather patterns, led by Reta Beebe of New Mexico State University, has resulted in a long-term record of the Great Red Spot and other atmospheric features. Taking images every clear night, Beebe's team has assembled years of data. Other groups utilize large telescopes to look for faint moons or emission from rare molecules. These observations are hard, but understanding the largest planet in the solar system is worth the ongoing effort.

Properties

The innermost regions of Jupiter are probably solid, but we are not sure of their nature. They could be rocky or even metallic, but if they are made of metal, these regions are not large. Otherwise, Jupiter's density would be much higher than we measure. Even though Jupiter is,

A JUPITER IMPACT

In 1994 astronomers were able to watch as a comet (a small irregular ball of ice, dust, and rock that we will learn more about in the next chapter) smashed into Jupiter. This comet, named Shoemaker-Levy 9 for its discoverers, Eugene and Carolyn Shoemaker and David Levy (and the fact that it was the ninth comet they discovered together), had previously passed close to Jupiter and was partially broken up by Jupiter's immense gravity (Fig. 8.9). After calculating the subsequent orbit, the astronomers determined the pieces were likely to hit Jupiter. A massive observational campaign was set up to observe Jupiter while the impacts took place. Over the period of a week or so, all the pieces of the comet plunged into the atmosphere, making dramatic impact splashes. The comet material heated up and exploded upon impact, and the explosion brought materials from deeper in the atmosphere up to the surface, where they partially absorbed light normally reflected off of the clouds into the atmosphere. Amateur and professional astronomers were glued to their televisions and radios as the impacts took place.

Photo courtesy of NASA/STScI

Figure 8.9—Image of Comet Shoemaker-Levy-9: Black and White Impact Image

On Jupiter, the comet just disintegrated and no permanent markings were left on the gaseous atmosphere, but here on Earth, serious damage could result from such a comet. If a good-sized comet hit the ocean, a bunch of water vapor would be thrown into the atmosphere, causing torrential rains, not to mention a large tidal wave. Coastal areas would be flooded or destroyed and our weather would be affected for years. Thankfully, Earth presents a much smaller target than Jupiter.

on the scale of the solar system, massive and large, it has about five times less material per unit volume than Earth and is only slightly more dense on average than water. Even just 100 mi down in the atmosphere, the pressure is immense and would easily crush humans. The pressure results from the overlying layers of atmosphere and the immense gravity of Jupiter.

SATURN: RING BEARER

When Galileo first looked at Saturn and found that it was not round, he was flabbergasted. No such object had ever been seen before. In a 1610 letter to his patrons, the royal Medici family, he indicated that Saturn comprised three bodies—one large bright one and two fainter ones on either side. We now know these were Saturn's famous rings, but seen through his small, handmade telescope, the rings appeared as separate bodies. He made a sketch of Saturn in his notebook in 1616 that clearly shows the ring structure, even if he couldn't make them out at the time.

Over the ensuing decades, others viewed the planet through their ever-improving telescopes, and the elongation that Galileo saw went away. Explaining why Saturn lost its bulging appearance over time became a major area of research. Finally, in 1655, Christian

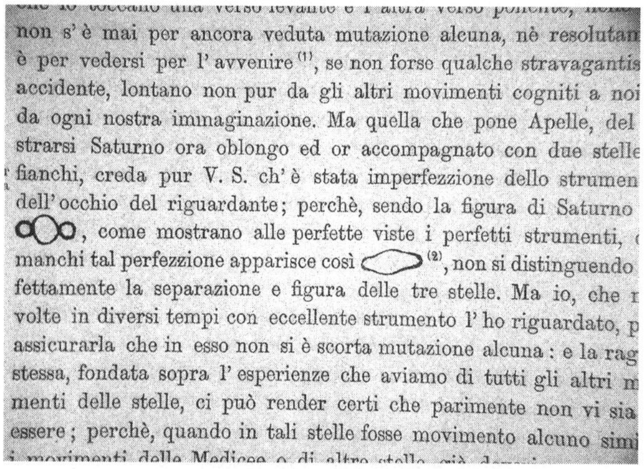

non s'è mai per ancora veduta mutazione alcuna, nè resolutan
è per vedersi per l'avvenire⁽¹⁾, se non forse qualche stravagantis
accidente, lontano non pur da gli altri movimenti cogniti a noi
da ogni nostra immaginazione. Ma quella che pone Apelle, del
strarsi Saturno ora oblongo ed or accompagnato con due stelle
fianchi, creda pur V. S. ch'è stata imperfezzione dello strumen
dell'occhio del riguardante; perchè, sendo la figura di Saturno
∞, come mostrano alle perfette viste i perfetti strumenti,
manchi tal perfezzione apparisce così ⁽²⁾, non si distinguendo
fettamente la separazione e figura delle tre stelle. Ma io, che
volte in diversi tempi con eccellente strumento l'ho riguardato, p
assicurarla che in esso non si è scorta mutazione alcuna : e la rag
stessa, fondata sopra l'esperienze che aviamo di tutti gli altri m
menti delle stelle, ci può render certi che parimente non vi sia
essere ; perchè, quando in tali stelle fosse movimento alcuno simi

Photo courtesy of Biblioteca Nazionale Centrale–Florence

**Figure 8.10—A Picture from Galileo's Notebook
(From the Galileo Project Pages, Rice University)**

Huygens came up with the right answer (rings!), and his well-made diagrams convinced scientists that he was right (Fig. 8.10).

There were some complicating factors. Saturn is tilted, so as it orbits the Sun, its relative tilt as seen from Earth changes over time. From our point of view, the disk of rings around the planet will shift positions as the orbit progresses, moving from an edge-on view (at which we see nothing more than a line) to the maximum angle, back through edge-on and then the maximum angle again, but from the opposite side. This wobbling effect, like a top surrounded by a hula hoop, accurately explains why sometimes the rings stand out so clearly while at other times they are hardly visible.

We know much more about the rings now, and by sending probes to Saturn, we have images of them with far greater detail than Huygens could have ever obtained Somehow, however, their beauty remains intact despite our deep understanding of their structure.

The Wonder and Beauty of the Rings

Photo courtesy of NASA/JPL

Figure 8.11—Saturn's Rings

The rings of Saturn are made up of ice chunks and small, ice-covered rocks (Fig. 8.11). They do not touch the planet's upper surface. The innermost ring visible from Earth is about 44,000 mi above the planet's center and about 6500 mi above the surface, while the outermost ring is more than 87,000 mi above the center. From edge to edge, the rings that are easily visible from Earth are about 43,000 mi in total width, but they are not continuous. The ring system is tipped at an angle of about 26° to the orbital plane of the planet around the Sun, which is why we see the rings differently as Saturn orbits the Sun (see above).

The major rings are labeled alphabetically based on when they were discovered. Some of the larger rings are actually composed of smaller rings, called ringlets. There are gaps between the rings, the largest of which is called the Cassini division, for Italian astronomer and mathematician Giovanni Cassini (1625–1712). These gaps are caused by gravitational interactions with Saturn's many moons, which push and guide the ice chunks and rocks into particular orbits. The moons that have the most influence on the gaps between Saturn's rings are called shepherd moons. The rings are much larger in extent than what we can see from Earth. The probes we have sent to Saturn discovered rings as far as 248,000 mi above the planet's center.

As the Voyager probes passed by Saturn, they discovered that the rings occasionally show dark linear features that run outward across the rings like the spokes of a bicycle wheel (Fig. 8.12). This was a very odd discovery, and scientists are still trying to understand what these spoke-like features are and how they formed.

Photo courtesy of NASA/JPL

Figure 8.12—The Spokes of Saturn's Rings

The rings rotate at different rates based on how far they are from the planet (just like Jupiter's moons or even the planets around the Sun). The innermost rings rotate slightly faster than 44,000 mi/h, and the outermost rings rotate a bit less than 30,000 mi/h. Because the rings appear so solid, you might expect that they have a large mass. They don't. The best estimates indicate that, in total, the rings only have about one-millionth as much mass as our Moon. They are pretty and reflect light well, but they aren't very substantial.

Titan: Saturn's Largest Moon

Titan is Saturn's largest moon. It is about 3200 mi in diameter, but it is not very dense. This means it is probably about half rock and half ice. No surface features have been seen on Titan because it has a smog layer that is orange in color and covers the whole planet. Our best observations indicate that there may be an ocean on the surface of Titan made up of nitrogen, methane, and ethane a bit less than 1 mi deep. The moon has an atmosphere composed mainly of nitrogen with a bit of methane and some more complex molecules composed of hydrogen and carbon, called hydrocarbons. The detection of hydrocarbons originally got scientists excited because hydrocarbon molecules are fundamental to the existence of life, but the temperatures are very low on Titan and there is no liquid water. In the outer solar system, it now looks as if Europa is the only spot where life may possibly exist.

Exploration

We have sent a number of probes to Saturn, including Pioneer 11 and Voyagers 1 and 2. These probes sent back high-resolution images of Saturn, its ring system, and Saturn's moons. The onboard instruments were also able to measure the magnetic field around Saturn and a range of other things, such as the composition of the atmosphere. Voyager 1 performed a key experiment: by directing the probe under the south pole of the planet, its radio signal could be monitored as the probe passed behind the rings. Recording the signal here on Earth, scientists were able to determine the composition of the rings and discover a bit about the sizes of the particles. However, this important knowledge did not come without a price. Because the probe went under the South Pole, it was directed up and out of the orbital plane of the solar system. It would not be able to visit any more outer planets like its sister probe, Voyager 2, which visited Uranus and Neptune. From high above the solar system it took its final picture, a family portrait of the planets, which were so distant they appeared as no more than small bright dots. Lonely Voyager 1 continues on its path away from the solar system and will ultimately enter interstellar space.

The most recent probe to visit Saturn is the Cassini mission, launched in the summer of 2004. When it arrives at Saturn on July 1, 2004, we can expect some fantastic results. One of the more important experiments has Cassini dropping a small probe down into the atmosphere of Saturn's moon Titan. The probe will parachute down, measuring properties of the atmosphere as it goes, and will eventually land on the surface. This will be the first surface landing on an outer solar system object and a tremendous triumph, if all goes well. It also represents a growing partnership between the world's space agencies, an ongoing change in how space exploration is conducted. The probe, named Huygens, was constructed by ESA, the European Space Agency, and NASA built the Cassini orbiter. This continuing cooperation will greatly expand our ability to explore space, expanding our capabilities and keeping the costs to any one country low.

Observation

Saturn is one of the best objects for amateur astronomers to observe from Earth. The striking rings and their constant changes can easily be seen with a small telescope. Professional astronomers also still actively observe Saturn from the ground. Most observations are centered on studying the complex atmosphere of Saturn, which lies hidden under a high altitude haze. One such observation is the study

of stellar occultations. Stellar occultations occur when Saturn (or any other body) passes in front of a much more distant star, and, from our vantage point on Earth, the star is covered up by either the rings or Saturn itself. These observations have enabled scientists to take very accurate measurements of Saturn's atmospheric temperature, although the results depend greatly on how the data are processed.

Another major area of observation is the search for new moons. When the rings present an edge-on appearance to Earth, the amount of reflected light is greatly reduced, allowing observers on Earth a better chance of seeing the reflected light of any small moons. This technique has worked quite well, with 12 new moons being detected during the last edge-on period in 2000. The current count of Saturn's moons is at least 31, but the exact number is not yet certain. Verifying observations have to be made for some of the newly detected ones. This is an area where serious amateur astronomers with special equipment could actually participate, but close collaboration with professional astronomers is necessary. The best way to get involved is to join a local amateur astronomy club, learn good observing techniques, and contact an astronomer working in this area. Reading *Sky & Telescope* or *Astronomy* will let you know which astronomers are performing this kind of research.

Properties

Saturn is the second largest planet in the solar system. Its density is slightly less than that of water. This means that if you could find a large enough glass of water, the planet Saturn would float around on the surface just like a kid in an inner tube. Like Jupiter, Saturn has an active atmosphere, but because it is further from the Sun, the cooler temperature of its atmosphere allows the formation of a high-level haze, which blocks our view of the deeper cloud layers. Jupiter's atmosphere is warmer and no such haze forms. Using infrared observations and special filters, astronomers can peer through Saturn's haze. The winds are slower than on Jupiter, peaking at about 250 mi/h. Again, the greater distance of Saturn from the Sun means that there is less energy to drive complex atmospheric activity.

The inner portion of Saturn is thought to be very similar to Jupiter's, with a metallic hydrogen core deep within the planet. However, because Saturn is three times less massive than Jupiter, the zone of metallic hydrogen is proportionally smaller. The deep inner regions could actually be made of rock, but we don't know for sure. Just like Jupiter, there are immense pressures deep in Saturn's atmosphere, and any probe we could send to the center would be crushed.

Saturn, like Jupiter, has a strong magnetic field. We can tell this from observations of the planet with radio telescopes and also the sensors on the probes we've sent there. It is also why we think it has a metallic hydrogen core, because only through the movement of a liquid metal or metallic-like core can a planet produce a magnetic field.

The atmosphere of Saturn is composed mainly of hydrogen and helium, with methane, ammonia, and other gases playing a lesser part. Most of the differences we observe between Saturn and Jupiter are tied to their temperature differences. Saturn has belts and zones running around the planet parallel to the equator. Its rotational period is also similar to Jupiter's, though slightly longer, about 10 h 14 min. Again, the belts and zones spin at slightly different rates, as on Jupiter, so determining the exact rotation is a challenge.

Saturn has a completely unique weather phenomenon that is seen only every 57 years or so, when it is summer in Saturn's northern hemisphere. A large bubble of warm gas rises to the surface of the planet and is then dispersed by high-speed atmospheric winds. Because it is warmer, it can rise above the hazy regions in the atmosphere and reflects sunlight well, becoming visible as a large white blotch on the planet's surface. Although nobody knows yet why this event takes place, astronomers are actively modeling the planet using computers and think it is related to the heating of the planet during the summertime. In many ways it resembles a gigantic thunderstorm (See Fig. 8.13).

Photo courtesy of NASA/STScI

Figure 8.13—Saturn Storm as Seen with HST

URANUS AND NEPTUNE: JUPITER'S SMALLER COUSINS
Discovery

Uranus and Neptune were both discovered relatively recently. They were not known to ancient peoples because they are too faint to be seen with the naked eye. English astronomer William Herschel discovered Uranus in 1781, using a large telescope with a metallic mirror he made himself. The telescope mirror was 48 in. in diameter, and this large size (for the time) allowed him to detect very faint objects. His main fascination was the observation and cataloging of faint objects in the sky and the detection of comets, but in his searches he came across something that was visibly larger than the rest of the stars, and he suspected it to be a comet. Further observations revealed that its orbit was not that of a comet but very probably a new planet. He named it Uranus after the mythological father of Saturn. It was the first planet discovered with a telescope and the seventh planet known to be in the solar system.

The discovery of Neptune has been shrouded in some mystery and debate. After the discovery of Uranus by Herschel, astronomers carefully followed its orbit and found that it deviated slightly from its predicted path. In 1845, an English mathematician, John Couch Adams (1819–1892), predicted the existence of an unseen planet exerting a gravitational pull to account for the fact that Uranus was being pulled slightly out of position in its orbit. Because all planets closer to the Earth than Uranus were already known, he thought there must be an unknown planet further out. Adams took his calculations to the British Astronomer Royal Sir George Airy (1801–1892), who showed little interest in making the observations to prove the existence of such a planet. The French mathematician Urbain Leverrier (1811–1877) subsequently published a similar prediction, and this made the Astronomer Royal decide to take up the search. However, due to the different methods of calculation used by Airy and Leverrier, the English effort, led by a professor at Cambridge University, James Challis (1803–1882), had to search large regions of the sky, whereas the French method provided more accurate locations. Challis actually sighted the planet several times, but he did not recognize it as a planet; it is hardly noticeable as a planet because it is so far away. The French effort resulted in an identification of the planet on September 23, 1846, during the first weeks of observation using the telescopes of the Berlin Observatory.

With national bragging rights on the line, a battle as to who actually discovered the planet ensued. We now know that Galileo was the first to discover Neptune, but he did not recognize it as a planet at the time. In some sense, the observer at the Berlin Observatory, Johann Galle (1812–1910), is the true discoverer, because he looked for the planet and found it (practically on the first try, so kudos too to Leverrier for excellent calculating ability).

Exploration

Just as with Jupiter and Saturn, we will never land a probe on the surfaces of Neptune or Uranus because they are composed almost entirely of gas. But we can send probes to study them and the Voyager 2 probe did just that, arriving at Uranus in 1986 and Neptune 3 years later. The Voyager probe is our single source of detailed knowledge of these two remote planets. No subsequent probes have been sent, and although some plans have been made to send a probe there in the future, nothing is under construction right now.

Even so, the Voyager probe did a great job capturing pictures and making some important discoveries. Among them was the realization that both Uranus and Neptune have small ring systems just like Saturn's large one and Jupiter's tiny one. Both are hard to see but were detected by the Voyager probe. Both ring systems are challenging to see because the small icy rocks that comprise them are very dark. Astronomers call the reflectivity of an object its albedo. Objects with a large albedo are very reflective (like the Moon or Saturn's rings), whereas objects that absorb most light that hit them have a low albedo. Albedo varies from 100% (a perfect mirror) to 0% (a flat piece of black velvet). The ring systems of Uranus and Neptune have albedos that range from 1% to 4%. These are very dark rings. Saturn's rings, by comparison, have an average albedo of 12% to 40% and are 10 times more reflective.

Observation

Observation of these two distant planets is tremendously challenging, but it is not impossible for amateurs with even modest-sized telescopes. As noted earlier, Galileo, with his homemade telescopes, appears to have been the first to sight Neptune. For a bit of time, it was in the same part of the sky as Jupiter. He made a note of it in his notebooks, but Jupiter moved on past Neptune and he didn't go back to make any subsequent observations. If he had, a good bit of astronomical history would be very different. When professionals study these two planets from the ground, they usually try to characterize the global properties of their atmospheres; study the positions of their moons (to try and find more); or perform occultation experiments to study their rings. Because of their great distance there is little else that can be accomplished without sending a probe.

Properties

Uranus is a little more than 1,780,000,000 mi from the Sun, whereas Neptune is more than 2,790,000,000 mi away. Uranus is pale green,

which is indicative of its mostly methane and hydrogen atmosphere. The ammonia present in the atmospheres of Jupiter and Saturn has frozen out of Uranus's atmosphere, taking with it the oranges, tans, and browns found in Jupiter's skies. The atmosphere of Uranus is completely featureless. Small clouds do appear in the upper atmosphere, although we are unsure how they arise. One notable aspect of Uranus is its rotational axis, which is highly inclined. It is tipped over so much that at certain times of the Uranian year, an entire half of the planet is in darkness while the other is in constant light.

This dramatic inclination would have a much more profound impact if the planet were closer to the Sun. Even so, the temperature of Uranus does appear to be affected by this dramatic tilt. Another consequence of this tilt is that Uranus' moons orbit in such a way that we can look down upon their orbital plane for certain periods of time; every 21 years we see their orbital plane edge-on. However, Uranus takes more than 84 Earth years to go around the Sun one time, so most people only see a portion of one Uranian year. Uranus has five moons visible from the Earth: Miranda (Figure 8.14), Ariel, Umbriel, Titania, and Oberon. The moons are all small and rugged. The largest, Oberon, is about 1000 mi in diameter. Miranda, the smallest of the moons visible from Earth, has impact craters as well as dramatic mountains and valleys. It is only 200 mi in diameter. The moons are composed of rock and ice. Ten additional moons were discovered by Voyager, and even more have been discovered using ground-based telescopes and sensitive detectors. Twenty-seven are now known in all.

Photo courtesy of NASA/JPL

Figure 8.14—Miranda

Neptune is very similar to Uranus, but it is colder because it is further away. The mean temperature in the upper atmosphere is more than -350°F. It is composed mainly of ices, such as water and ammonia, mixed with gases also found on Uranus, such as methane and hydrogen. It takes 165 Earth years for Neptune to orbit the Sun once. Given current life spans, no human will ever see a complete Neptunian year. It is a light green to blue in color, like Neptune, but the images from Voyager show some dramatic atmospheric activity, likely because the obscuring haze found in Uranus has frozen and sunk lower in the atmosphere. Both dark and light regions exist, but there is no banding, as on Jupiter or Saturn. The Voyager 2 probe found a Great Dark Spot similar to Jupiter's Great Red Spot. The Great Dark Spot (Fig. 8.15) is also a region of high pressure, and it is about 18,600 mi across, smaller than Jupiter's spot, but still sizable. Neptune has two moons visible from Earth; the Voyager probe found six more small moons, all small and likely rock-ice conglomerates.

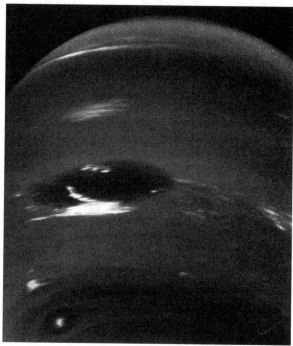

Photo courtesy of NASA/JPL

Figure 8.15—Neptune's Great Dark Spot

THE OUTER SOLAR SYSTEM

The gas giants mark the beginning of the end of the solar system. If we were in a spaceship, traveling away from Earth and the Sun, moving outward into interstellar space, passing by these giant planets would be similar to passing the last few towns in Nebraska before entering Wyoming on a drive from Nebraska to California. Once you hit Wyoming, there just aren't many towns anymore, and the ones that are there are small and far between. Similarly, in the solar system, beyond Neptune not many objects are present. However, there are some objects, and they allow us to understand the very formation of the solar system. Pluto, its moon Charon, the so-called trans-Neptunian objects, and the even more distant comets have all experienced very little change since the time when the solar system formed. In the cold, dark, and distant reaches of the solar system, these small objects are one key to understanding where we came from.

SUMMARY

The Jovian planets are (in order of distance from the Sun) Jupiter, Saturn, Uranus, and Neptune. They are much larger than Earth and composed almost entirely of gasses such as hydrogen, helium, and methane.

Jupiter is the largest of the Jovian planets and was one of the first objects studied in detail with a telescope. It has four large moons, which are easily visible through even a small telescope. They are Io, Ganymede, Callisto, and Europa. Each is very different from the others. Io has active sulfur volcanoes; Europa has an icy surface and probably a water ocean under its icy surface. Ganymede is Jupiter's largest moon and the largest moon in the solar system. Callisto is about the same size as the planet Mercury and is heavily cratered. Jupiter's atmosphere exhibits extreme weather conditions and high-speed winds. The Great Red Spot, an anticyclone, has been in existence since Galileo first observed the planet in the early1600s.

Saturn is the next planet out from the Sun and is similar in composition to Jupiter. It has a system of rings that are composed of small rocks and icy dust. Saturn has its own system of moons, including the moon Titan, which has a relatively thick atmosphere and probably an ocean of methane. Saturn's atmosphere is less active than Jupiter's because it is further from the Sun and less energy is available to power an active atmosphere.

Uranus is tipped nearly on end, with an inclination nearly four times that of Earth. This means that during some parts of the Uranian year, its north pole points directly at the Sun and its south pole points away. Six Uranian months later, the opposite is true. Uranus has a system of rings and also moons. The Voyager 2 probe is the only probe to have visited Uranus and sent back images of the planet. It is shrouded in an all-encompassing cloud layer that hides any details.

Neptune, despite being so far from the Sun, shows a more active atmosphere. Partly this is due to the formation of ices of certain obscuring gas molecules in its atmosphere that are present in Uranus. By forming ice, they fall in the atmosphere and reveal more details. Neptune has a Great Dark Spot, an atmospheric disturbance similar to the Great Red Spot of Jupiter, as well as other atmospheric phenomena such as clouds and high-speed winds.

KEY TERMS

Kuiper Belt Object, comet, coma, tail, meteors, meteorites, Oort cloud

PLUTO: QUESTIONABLE PLANET

In recent years, Pluto has been mired in controversy. When Pluto was first discovered in 1930, we knew of no other objects in the most distant regions of the solar system. It seemed very clearly to be a planet, if a small one. We have now found many objects of all different sizes beyond the orbit of Neptune, in the region of the solar system where Pluto orbits. These objects are sometimes called Kuiper Belt Objects, for Dutch-American astronomer Gerard Kuiper (1905–1973), who predicted the existence of a large number of objects beyond Neptune's orbit. (Now we generally call them trans-Neptunian objects, mainly because a large number of astronomers over the years have predicted their existence, though none as precisely as Kuiper.)

These objects come in a variety of sizes, but due to their extreme distance from the Sun, we do not know much about them. Because Pluto has a significantly different orbit from the rest of the planets and because it shares some characteristics with these trans-Neptunian objects, some astronomers prefer to think of Pluto as the largest trans-Neptunian or Kuiper Belt Object instead of a planet, although the exact definition of a planet is an open topic of debate. However, Pluto is quite a bit larger than the other trans-Neptunian objects and also has a moon of its own, just like Earth. It is unlikely that the controversy over Pluto's status will end anytime soon.

Discovery

Pluto was discovered by American astronomer Clyde Tombaugh (1906–1997). Tombaugh was the only American to discover a planet in our solar system and most likely is the last. No other planets have made themselves known, although some distant and small objects have been found in quite significant numbers, as we see later in this chapter.

After the discoveries of Uranus and Neptune, astronomers actively worked to determine if there was another planet lurking far out beyond Neptune. Different calculations gave different answers. Great debates were held concerning whether another planet existed. Many people worked on predicting the location of Pluto, and searches were carried out in these regions, but the calculations are quite challenging; nobody succeeded in repeating the success of the astronomers who predicted the location of Neptune and then went to the telescope and found it.

One wealthy American amateur astronomer, Percival Lowell, discussed in Chapter 7, became interested in the search for a planet beyond Neptune, and he began a search project using his Flagstaff, Arizona, observatory.

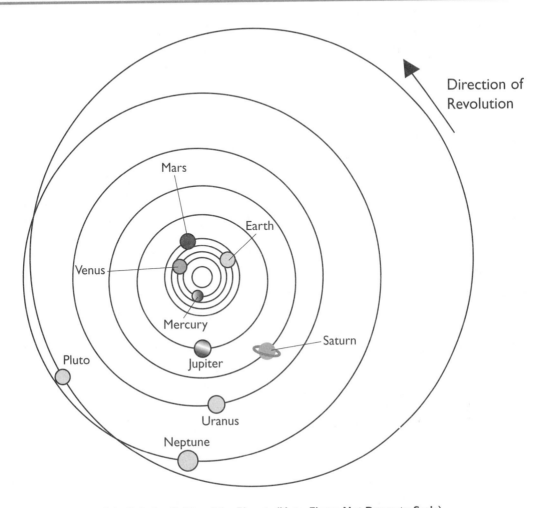

Figure 9.1—Relative Orbits of the Planets (Note: Figure Not Drawn to Scale)

Such searches are long and difficult. Lowell's method involved calculating the predicted position of the planet and then observing the region. The planet was thought to be large and therefore bright. Despite using a 40 in. telescope (large by the standards back then), no planet was detected. Although Lowell died in 1916, the search he began continued after his death and ultimately resulted in the detection of Pluto by Tombaugh in 1930.

Tombaugh used a technique that involved taking photographic plates of the sky at regular intervals and then comparing the plates to see if any objects had changed positions. Because stars are so far away, anything that changes

positions over a short period of time must be relatively close to us, likely in our solar system.

However, it is not the motion of the planet itself, but the motion of Earth that causes the change in location of an object recorded on the photos. From Earth we see objects in the solar system projected against the distant stars. As Earth moves in its orbit, these objects appear to change their positions slightly when compared to the stars. There is a special time when this position change is maximized. Imagine a planet far out in the solar system moving slowly along its orbit. You can see from Figure 9.1 that as Earth (moving much faster in its orbit than the outer planets) catches up to and passes between the planet and the Sun, the projected location of the distant planet changes very quickly. Within the space of one month we see it projected against very different stars. Because the figure is not drawn to scale, the change seems more dramatic than it actually is. In reality, the change in position is not so extreme, but it is detectable.

Tombaugh became interested in astronomy as a child and built his own telescope using parts of a car axle to serve as the telescope mount, grinding and polishing the mirror himself. He then used his telescope to make his own sketches of the planets, which he sent to the director of Lowell Observatory, Vesto Slipher (1875–1969). Slipher was so impressed with the sketches that he hired Tombaugh sight unseen. Clyde took the train from his home in Kansas to Flagstaff to begin his work at the age of 22. He arrived before the new telescope ordered by Slipher had been assembled, and so he spent some of his early time at the observatory doing construction work. He began taking plates with the newly installed 13 in. telescope and used a special device to compare plates taken a few weeks apart. On February 18, 1930, when comparing two plates he noticed a small object that clearly shifted position. After making follow-up observations and having other Lowell Observatory astronomers verify his observations, the announcement of the detection of a new planet was made on March 13, 1930.

Exploration, Observation, and Properties

No probe has yet been sent to Pluto. A research team led by Dr. Alan Stern of the Southwest Research Institute's department of space studies in Boulder, Colorado, is planning a mission to Pluto. They hope to have NASA launch their probe sometime in 2006 so that it reaches Pluto sometime in 2016 and some other Kuiper Belt Objects in 2026. The mission takes so long because Pluto is so tremendously far away. On the average, it is about 40 times further away from the Sun than Earth, but its erratic path brings it closer to the Sun than Neptune for a portion of its orbit. Such a mission faces tremendous challenges, but NASA is developing new technology that takes advantage of radioactive materials' ability to provide electricity and propulsion, which may make the mission easier and also faster.

Despite the great distance to Pluto, we do know some basic facts about it. It has a moon, Charon, which is about one-half its diameter (Fig. 9.2). Pluto is about 1500 mi in diameter,

Figure 9.2—HST Picture of Pluto and Charon   *Photo courtesy of NASA/STScI*

about 600 mi narrower than our Moon. Charon is about 740 mi in diameter. The density of the planet as estimated from the orbit of Charon is about two times the density of water and indicates that the planet is likely composed of a rock-ice mixture.

By monitoring the light of stars that Pluto passes in front of, or occults, we can learn something about its atmosphere. It is very sparse, having at most three-millionths of the surface atmospheric pressure as we have here on Earth. Models of Pluto's atmosphere predict that it will be made mostly of nitrogen, with some methane and carbon monoxide. Because of Pluto's eccentric orbit, some theorists predict that its atmosphere may actually freeze onto the surface when it is furthest from the Sun. This is one reason why those who want to send a mission to Pluto want it to happen sooner, while the planet is closer to the Sun and therefore warmer, rather than later.

The surface of Pluto is quite reflective, probably due to ice, although the surface is red due to organic molecules frozen onto its surface—unlike Mars, which is red in color due to the iron oxide (rust) on its surface. Pluto's surface has been mapped with the Hubble Space Telescope, and although the images show bright and dark regions, the details are a great mystery (Fig. 9.3). Pluto is so distant that the smallest thing we could possible see on its surface—even with the power of the Hubble—are at least a few hundred miles across. Are there mountains and valleys, or is the surface smooth like a billiard ball? We just don't know. One thing the images do show is that the planet has polar caps that are more reflective than the equatorial region.

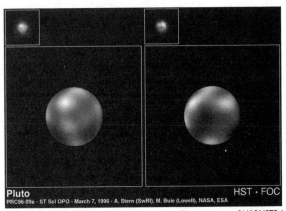

Photo courtesy of NASA/STScI

Figure 9.3—Pluto's Surface from HST

Just how cold is Pluto? Estimates of the surface temperature vary and depend upon the local reflectivity of the surface, but are likely no warmer than –350°F. This is much colder than the coldest temperature recorded at Earth's poles, about –132°F.

We know only the basics about Pluto and Charon. Only significantly improved observational techniques or a probe's arrival at the system will allow us to solve the mystery of this distant pair of ice-covered worlds.

Our solar system is, even now, not completely known. Astronomers announced the discovery of the most distant object in our solar system yet detected in March 2004. The object, which has a diameter between 730 and 1,470 mi, is similar in size to Pluto. The object, tentatively named Sedna, probably has its own moon. It is about 3.6 billion miles from the Sun on average and has a dark red color, again due to the large amount of organic material that is likely on its surface. The surface is even colder than Pluto with a temperature of about –400°F. Further observations are necessary to understand this object more completely, and it is almost certain that more such objects will be found as telescopes get better.

COMETS

Comets are the dancers of the solar system. Halley's comet, last visible from Earth in 1986, is probably the most famous, and many readers may remember seeing comet Hyakutake in 1996 as it filled up almost as much of the sky as the Big Dipper (Fig. 9.4). Spending most of their time in the outer portions of the solar system and dipping closer to the Sun only occasionally, comets, like some asteroids (discussed in the next section), visit both the inner and outer portions of the solar system, making them unique members of our planetary system.

In ancient times, comets were often thought to bring bad luck or calamity, which they certainly would if they actually hit Earth's surface. Luckily, this has happened only rarely and is not likely to happen in the near future. Try to imagine just how dramatic the appearance of a comet in the sky must have been. There was no television, radio, or other media. There were no satellites. There was no understanding of what the objects in the sky were; even the Moon was a great mystery. The starry sky dominated the nighttime lives of everyone in creation, and the regular constellations and slow parade of the planets was a known and accepted part of everyday life. Suddenly, the sky changes—cut into by a bright object with a huge tail that rapidly moves across the sky. It is clear why these hairy wanderers (the name comet comes from a Latin phrase meaning long-haired stars, a reference to their dramatic tails) had such a dramatic impact on people.

Comets have a bright nucleus, the inner portion of the comet, sometimes called the core. The part we see is a gaseous region very close to the comet but not the comet nucleus itself.

Photo courtesy of M. Newberry, W. Brown, J. McGaha, and J. Dolby

Figure 9.4—Comet Hyakutake

A comet's nucleus is rarely more than a few miles in diameter, although the region we see can be much larger. This extended visible region of a comet is known as the coma.

A comet has a broad sweeping tail that lights up due to reflected sunlight as it orbits closer to the Sun, appearing bigger if the comet comes close to the Earth. The tails are made of both gas and dust and can give us some insight into the composition of the comets themselves. Because of their orbits, some appear to move quite quickly through our night sky, whereas others appear to move more slowly. This is a trick of their relative distance from Earth. The fastest have speeds of nearly 200,000 mi/h, whereas in the outer part of their orbits, they slow down to a crawl, moving only a few hundred miles per hour. However, it is the rather fast speed of the Earth combined with the distance from us to the planet that dictates how fast or slow a planet will appear to move in the sky from day to day.

The Structure of Comets

Comets appear to be loose agglomerations of ice, rock, and dust. They do not appear to be held together very well and have been known to break up from gravitational interactions with larger solar system objects. The comet Shoemaker-Levy 9, discussed in the previous chapter, came close to Jupiter; through this interaction it broke into pieces, which later plowed into Jupiter, vaporizing as they entered Jupiter's atmosphere.

Close observations have revealed that comets actually have two tails. One of the tails is mainly gas and the other is made of dust. The gas tail always points directly away from the Sun, even when the comet is moving away from the Sun. As the comet moves away from the Sun, it is preceded by its tail. The Sun directs the comet's tail away from the Sun; we learn how it does this in the next chapter. The basic reason is that the Sun gives off a wind of particles that push against the gas released from the comet's surface, streaming it away from the Sun. The comet's dust tail tends to follow the comet's orbital path, like a boat's wake. However, unlike a boat's wake, the dust comes from the comet itself; it's not passing through any dust.

Both the gas and dust tails are generated by sunlight falling on the comet. Sunlight heats the ice-dust mixture that makes up a comet and, through sublimation (the conversion of an ice directly to a gas without converting to a liquid first), the ice is converted into a gas, which forms the gas tail, and the dust that was mixed in with the ice is also released and left behind the comet as it continues its orbit. Liquid states of gasses cannot exist in low-pressure environments like open space or the surface of a comet. The tails change from night to night and even hour to hour. The comet itself spins, presenting different surfaces to the sun. The sunlight heats different portions of the surface differently, based on terrain and dust composition, so different amounts of gas and dust leave the surface,

sometimes explosively, causing changes in the tail and even the brightness of the coma.

Occasionally, Earth passes through the orbits of comets, which are littered with dust and small bits of rock. These "comet remains" enter our atmosphere, making dramatic streaks of light in the sky. We call these streaks meteors, or, informally, shooting stars. Because the orbits of the comets that create meteors are fixed in space, there are regular periods of time when many meteors are visible. These are called meteor showers. They usually happen on a single night or two, as Earth passes through the region of the comet orbit with the most dust, but the period of time when more meteors are visible than on average can last several weeks. Slightly larger pieces of rock that hit the surface of Earth, including any miscellaneous piece of space rock that hits Earth's surface, whether it originally came from a comet or not, is called a meteorite. The Earth runs into a surprising amount of space junk; luckily, these days most of it is relatively small, simply making a beautiful display in the sky as it burns up in the atmosphere. This is also why the best time to observe meteor showers is in the very early morning hours before dawn. This portion of the sky is directly overhead, oriented almost exactly in line with Earth's direction. Any debris orbiting through space that is in Earth's way at this point is overtaken by Earth, and the speed at which the debris enters the atmosphere is maximized. At other times, like sunset, Earth is rotationally pulling away from space debris, and the impact speed is reduced. This decreases the brightness of any meteors as they streak through our atmosphere. So if you want to be a successful meteor observer, get a good alarm clock and go to sleep early so you can wake up at 3:00 or 4:00 in the morning to get the best views. Most meteor showers are widely

METEOR SHOWERS

No special equipment is required to observe meteor showers. However, you have to do a bit of planning (they occur only at certain times of year). Also, you will be able to see more meteor showers if you get away from city lights. The darker the sky is, the more faint meteors you will be able to see. Because meteor showers go on for several hours, even a whole night, you will need to be comfortable outside. If it is cold, bring proper clothing. Also, it is a good idea to have lawn chairs or a blanket and a pillow to relax in as you watch the night sky for these spectacular sky streaks. The best time to view is from midnight to dawn, so get plenty of sleep the day before so you can stay up late.

Name	Morning to View	Typical Count per Hour	Constellation
Quadrantids	Jan. 3/4	40	Bootes
Lyrids	Apr. 22/23	15	Lyra
Eta Equarids	May 4/5	20	Aquarius
Delta Aquarids	Jul. 30/31	20	Aquarius
Perseids	Aug. 12/13	50	Perseus
Orionids	Oct. 21/22	20	Orion
Taurids	Nov. 4/5	15	Taurus
Leonids	Nov. 16/17	15	Leo
Geminids	Dec. 13/14	50	Gemini
Ursids	Dec. 22/23	15	Ursa Major

announced on television, and you can always read about them in specialty magazines or on the many Internet resources now available.

The Origin of Comets

Comets come in two basic groups, those that orbit the Sun on relatively short periods, which we see again and again, and those that have very long period orbits, which we see only once (if at all). Some simply whip in and out of the solar system, never to return. Just where do all these comets come from?

The Dutch astronomer Jan van Oort (1900–1992) theorized in the 1950s that comets originated in the very furthest reaches of the solar system. This area, now called the Oort cloud, is made up of clumps of material left over from the formation of our solar system. This residual material is mainly composed of ices; frozen water is one such ice, but many of the gasses we commonly find on Earth are also frozen at the very low temperatures found in the outer solar system. These frozen gasses include carbon dioxide, methane, oxygen, nitrogen, and many others. Oort theorized that the occasional gravitational pushes and tugs on these comets from Uranus and Neptune or from stars that occasionally pass near our Sun (though not too near and not too often) could nudge these pieces of primordial space junk into slightly different orbits, causing them to fall into the solar system on highly elliptical orbits, creating comets. Some simply come in, zip around the Sun, and are never seen again. Some interact with the planets and have their orbits reduced considerably. We see these comets, known as periodic comets, again and again. They can be quite famous, like comet Halley, which returns every 76 years and last visited the inner solar system in 1986. It will return in 2062.

HALLEY'S COMET

Comet Halley was first predicted to be a periodic, or returning, comet by Edmund Halley. Halley used Newton's theory of gravitation to determine its orbit. Although he did not live to see his prediction proved true, the comet duly returned in 1758, just as he had calculated. Since then, people have searched historic records to see how far back this comet has been seen by humans. The first recorded observation was by the Chinese astronomers in 241 B.C.E. Kepler observed the comet in 1607, and the first photos of it were taken in 1910. In 2024, it will reach the furthest point in its orbit, which is almost as distant from the Sun as Pluto. Its orbit does take it out of the plane of the solar system though, which has greatly reduced the chances it will ever actually impact a planet. We see the debris of this comet as the Eta Aquarid meteor shower, which takes place in early May each year. So, although the full comet will not likely impact Earth, pieces of it have come as meteorites.

Space Probes to Comets

Although observing comets with telescopes can be useful for some studies, particularly those concerning the gas that comets emit when they approach the Sun, the only way to actually see the nucleus itself is to travel to a comet. Because of their small size, rapid speeds, and odd orbits, comets are challenging targets for space missions. Even so, several probes have made it to a variety of comets.

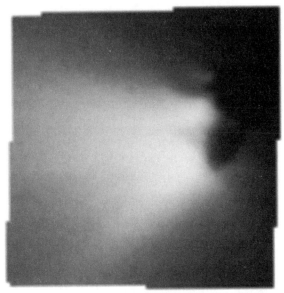

Photo courtesy of ESA/Giotto

Figure 9.5—Comet Halley's Nucleus

The first real effort to send a probe to a comet took place with the last visit of comet Halley in 1986. Japan, Russia, and the European Space Agency (ESA) sent probes to comet Halley. The ESA probe, Giotto, took a picture of the nucleus itself (Fig. 9.5).

The Halley nucleus was measured at 7 mi across and was found to be oblong in shape. Instead of the surface being mainly ice, it was very dark and covered with dust. Giotto continued on after being hit by dust from comet Halley (traveling almost as fast as bullets) and also had a flyby of comet Grigg-Skjellerup in 1992. The ESA is now the undisputed champion of comet fly-by missions and is launching another one, Rosetta, in 2004. Rosetta will be the first attempt to land a probe on the surface of a comet. Rosetta will fly a circuitous route to rendezvous with comet Churyumov-Gerasimenko in 2014. Releasing a small probe onto the icy nucleus, Rosetta will spend the next two years orbiting the comet as it heads toward the Sun. On the way to the comet, Rosetta will receive gravity assists from Earth and Mars and fly past some asteroids.

ASTEROIDS

Asteroids are large chunks of rock and metal. Most asteroids are located between the orbits of Mars and Jupiter, and some people have theorized that they are the fragments of either a never-formed planet or a planet that broke apart for some reason. However, when we add up the total mass of the asteroids, there is not enough stuff to make up even a medium-sized planet. This small total mass makes it quite likely that these objects didn't have enough gravity to coalesce into a planet.

The largest asteroids are so large their gravity pulls them into a spherical shape. Ceres, about 570 mi in diameter, was discovered by Italian astronomer Giuseppe Piazzi (1746–1826) in 1801. Since then, many thousands have been discovered. There are a little more than 10,000 asteroids known, and more get discovered with some regularity. Amateur astronomers with advanced equipment can discover a new asteroid. Whoever discovers an asteroid, or minor planet, as they are also known, gets to name it. Each one receives a catalog name and then a proper name. Some discoverers have named them for themselves (4151 Alanhale); some are named for other people as an honor (12373 Lancearmstrong). There is even one named after a Louisiana city (11739 Batonrouge).

We know a bit about the composition of asteroids because pieces of them have entered our atmosphere as meteors, eventually hitting the surface of our planet as meteorites. Meteorites allow us to hold a piece of another world (if a small one).

Meteorites come in a variety of types. Some are metallic, known as irons. They aren't made entirely of iron, but an alloy of nickel and iron, which is crystalline in nature; sometimes smaller amounts of other metals are present, too. Most are made of chrondrites. Chondrites are rocky materials that contain small, spherical mineral formations named chondrules, which are formed through melting processes; these formations are held together with other minerals that did not melt. Achondrites are similar to chondrites, but they lack any chondrules. About 80% of meteorites are chondrites. Achondrites make up 10% of the meteorites found. Less than 1.5% of all meteorites are the stony iron type, a mixture of iron-nickel and mineral matter. Meteorites are found in regions where there are not many rocks on the ground (so you can tell them apart from Earth rocks) and where there is not much rain, which erodes them away if they are the rocky types or rusts away the metallic types. Deserts are particularly good places to look for meteorites. Another recently discovered treasure trove includes areas in Antarctica where ice motion has slowly accumulated meteorites near rocky outcroppings and then the ice has been slowly worn away by wind erosion. These Antarctic meteorites have proved particularly exciting; including some discovered pieces that are thought to come from Mars, not asteroids.

We have sent some probes to asteroids. The probe NEAR (short for Near Earth Asteroid Rendezvous) landed on the asteroid 433 Eros on February 12, 2001. It was not designed to land on the asteroid initially, but mission planners opted to gently crash it into the surface after it had performed its mission mapping the asteroid's surface. The mission also visited 253 Mathilde (Figs. 9.6 and 9.7). The surface features of these asteroids were quite similar, with craters covering the surface. They also had many large boulders.

Photo courtesy of NASA/JHU

Figure 9.6—Asteroid 253 Mathilde

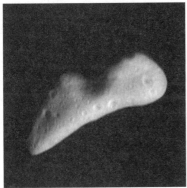

Photo courtesy of NASA/JHU

Figure 9.7—Asteroid 433 Eros

On its way to Jupiter, the Galileo probe snapped a photo of the asteroid Ida and found a surprise: Ida has a small moon, now named Dactyl (Fig. 9.8). Ida is only about 30 mi long and 15 mi wide, about the size of the Hawaiian island of Oahu, and Dactyl is just a mile or so in diameter. You could walk all the way around Dactyl completely in about 15 min. Although other asteroids were known from indirect observations made from the ground to have companions, this was the first time such a pair had been imaged. Other missions are planned, including sample-return missions, when a probe lands on the surface of an asteroid and sends back a piece for study using a smaller craft carried to the asteroid on the main probe. We expect such a sample to be similar to the meteorites we find here on Earth. One such mission, being planned joint-

ly by the Japanese space agency ISAS and NASA, is named MUSES-C and will land a probe on the asteroid 25143 Itokawa in 2005, returning a sample in 2007.

Photo courtesy of NASA/JPL

Figure 9.8—Asteroid Ida with Moon Dactyl

One asteroid class is a bit worrying. Near Earth Objects (NEOs) are asteroids with orbits that take them near Earth, which potentially pose a direct threat to life on Earth; the risk is quite low but present nonetheless. We know that large impacts have taken place on Earth in the past, and we expect that at sometime in the future other impacts are possible, but these impacts are quite rare. Several groups are actively trying to identify all NEOs and track them over time. Exactly what we would do if we discovered an asteroid on a collision course with Earth is unknown. We wouldn't necessarily blow it up, because we risk getting hit with many smaller asteroids; the combined damage could be just as devastating. A better tactic is to try to redirect the asteroid, nudging it just slightly so that its orbit misses Earth. The current development of nuclear-powered propulsion devices (not planned for launching rockets from Earth's orbit, for use only in deep space) gives us some hope of being able to perform such a difficult maneuver. The power-ful thrust capability provided by a nuclear-powered electrical propulsion system is tremendous. Were we to face a life-or-death situation, we could try to land many such propulsion units on the asteroid and guide it away from Earth. However, this technology is in its infancy, and so we must put our trust and faith in the low probability of such a collision actually taking place.

THE FURTHEST REACHES OF THE SOLAR SYSTEM

Just where does the solar system end? We are only now beginning to be able to answer this question. Beyond Pluto, objects get smaller and further apart. Temperatures drop as we move further from the warming light of the Sun. Beyond Neptune is a range of small objects, probably made of rock and ice, the biggest example of which could be Pluto. Beyond Pluto, a range of small bodies exists, out to probably 50 to 60 times the distance of Earth to the Sun. Beyond the orbit of Pluto, Oort cloud objects begin to appear, comets slowly orbiting the Sun in the near blackness of space far away from the Sun. At about three times the distance from the Sun as Pluto, even the Oort cloud objects begin to get sparse. We think this happens about 2 light-years from the Sun, or nearly 12 trillion miles from its surface. The nearest star to our Sun, Alpha Centauri, is a little more than 4 light-years away. If it has an Oort cloud as does our Sun and if its Oort cloud ends about 2 light-years from its surface, then the two clouds at some level can interact—even exchange —proto-comets. In a sense, then, there is no edge to our solar system; it simply blends into the system nearest our Sun, and that system blends into the next, and so on. Another way to define the edge is based on the Sun's waning influence. The region where the Sun finally stops influencing the surrounding region is known as the heliopause. This region, discussed in greater detail in the next chapter,

marks the boundary where the Sun fades into the cosmic background, appearing as just another star. The Voyager spacecraft are nearing this zone, and their magnetic field–sensing instruments will soon let us know just where the extreme edge of our solar system lies.

SUMMARY

The outermost regions of the solar system are cold due to the remoteness of the Sun. Pluto, the furthest planet from the Sun, is a frozen ball of ice and rock. It has a companion moon named Charon, which is about half of its size. No probe has yet visited Pluto-Charon, but one may soon. Pluto is the only planet discovered by an American, Clyde Tomabugh.

Comets are thought to originate in the distant regions of the solar system. They are composed mainly of ice and dust with some rock. Through gravitational interactions with each other and the major planets, they occasionally fall into orbits that bring them very close to the Sun. During these close passages, they heat up, releasing gas and dust from their surfaces and forming gigantic tails that light up through reflected sunlight. The most famous comet is Halley, which has a periodic orbit of about 76 years. Meteors that we see as shooting stars here on Earth originate with comets. As Earth passes through their orbital paths, particles left behind from previous cometary passages enter Earth's atmosphere, burning up as they enter our atmosphere at high velocity.

Objects more distant than Pluto that aren't comets are known as Kuiper Belt Objects. They are similar in nature to Pluto, though generally smaller. More are discovered each year, and a full inventory is yet to be made.

Asteroids are found generally in orbits between Mars and Jupiter. Though numerous, their total mass is not even a fraction of one of the terrestrial planets. Through collisions and gravitational interactions with each other and the planets (especially Jupiter), they occasionally move into orbits that bring them to Earth. When pieces of asteroids fall to Earth, they are known as meteorites. There are three general classes of meteorite: irons, chondrites, and achondrites. These rocks have provided information about the early stages of the solar system and are a valuable scientific resource.

CHAPTER 10

OUR SUN

KEY TERMS

galaxy, photosphere, chromosphere, corona, core, sunspots, convection, nuclear fusion, thermodynamic equilibrium, quiet Sun

Each day, the Sun rises into view above our horizon, slowly moves across the sky, and sets in the evening. The light it provides makes plants grow, enables us to see, lights up the Moon, and tans our bodies when we are at the beach. After Earth, the Sun is easily the most important astronomical object in our lives. But the Sun is not a quiet place. It is a seething soup of extremely hot gas. Eruptions on its surface can cause magnetic storms here on Earth that hinder airplane navigation and disrupt communications. In this chapter we learn about out nearest star, the Sun, and the many ways it affects our lives.

PHYSICAL PROPERTIES

By Earth standards, the Sun is very large. Its diameter is 864,400 mi. This is more than 109 times the diameter of Earth (7926 mi), just less than 10 times the diameter of Jupiter. The Sun is about 93 million miles away from us. Because this distance is used so often when speaking about the solar system, it has a special name, the astronomical unit. If the Sun were much closer, liquid water could not exist on Earth: the heat would vaporize it, and it would all be in gas form. If the Sun were much further away, the loss of heat energy would likely turn all the water on Earth to frozen ice. We are in the sweet spot of the solar system, where the overall average temperature on Earth, thanks in part to the warming effect of our atmosphere, is just above freezing. This important fact is what has enabled life to take hold here on Earth, because liquid water is a fundamental necessity for life as we know it.

Even though the Sun appears huge to us, it is actually a rather average star. Many stars are larger and many are much smaller. Some stars are as many as ten times more massive. The Sun's mass is about 4.5×10^{30} pounds (lb), Technically, pounds are a unit that measures weight, which is the force an object of a given mass exerts when close to the Earth. The metric unit for mass is the kilogram and the Sun has a mass of 1.98×10^{30} kilograms, which is again somewhat average for stars. We know now that the Sun is just one of many billions of stars in our galaxy, or grouping of stars and their orbiting planets, gas, and dust. We learn more about galaxies in Chapter 14. For now, you need only to know that every star you see in the sky is similar to the Sun and every star you see exists within our galaxy. Other galaxies exist, but they are tremendously far away.

The photosphere is the part of the Sun that we see each day, where the gases that comprise the Sun finally become transparent and the light from the very hot gas can escape into space. The region where the bubbling surface begins to interact with free space is known as the chromosphere. The chromosphere is relatively thin, about 1000 mi thick, but the gas in this region absorbs light from the photosphere and results in the formation of spectral absorption lines, which we can study from Earth using telescopes and spectrographs. The tremendously hot region beyond the chromosphere is called the corona. The gas in this region has temperatures in the millions of degrees. The corona is also quite large and extends far above the Sun, tapering off about a million miles above the photosphere. When we see solar eclipses, we can often see the corona, which varies in shape over time and can be dramatically different from one eclipse to the next. It looks like a bright circular curtain that surrounds the Sun and can appear extremely regular and symmetric or very ragged and asymmetric.

The Sun rotates. This was one of the first properties of the Sun determined by telescopic observations. Sunspots were the key. These darker regions appear as dark blotches on the surface. Since these spots exist on the surface for quite a while, astronomers can track their motion by observing the Sun with properly filtered telescopes. By observing the Sun each day and tracking the sunspots as they move across the surface, the Sun's rotation has been determined to be about 26 days at the equator and a bit longer at the poles. If you were able to pick up a sunspot and move it away from the Sun, it would appear quite bright, nearly as bright as the photosphere itself. But because it is slightly cooler than the photosphere, it appears as a dark spot. We learn more about sunspots in the section on the active Sun later in this chapter. (See Figure 10.1.)

SUN SAFETY

Although the Sun provides the light we desperately need for life on Earth, it can be dangerous. We should never look directly at the Sun; especially through any magnifying device such as telescopes or binoculars. Our eyes have evolved over time to be able to handle the intense light from the noonday Sun, but gathering far more light than we gather with our eyes can be dangerous. Telescopes and binoculars are designed to gather light and concentrate it to make faint things bright. But this ability, when used to look at an object as bright as the Sun, can be devastating. Even small telescopes and binoculars can concentrate enough light to set paper placed in front of their eyepieces on fire. Imagine what such concentrated light could do to our eyes. For safety's sake, we should never look at the Sun with an optical device without proper shielding. We can use special filters on our telescope to safely look at the Sun without damaging our eyes (or the telescope optics, which can also be damaged by the extreme heat).

Even though our atmosphere blocks most of the harmful ultraviolet (UV) rays from the Sun, some make it through to the surface of Earth. This short-wavelength light interacts with molecules in our skin to darken it, giving us a tan, but excessive exposure causes damage (a burn). If we go outside for any length of time in bright sunlight, it is a good idea to use protective lotions to save our skin from damage. Some doctors say that receiving too many dark tans can be cumulatively harmful to our skin. A doctor should be consulted about skin safety for further advice on how to be protected. The Sun is necessary for life, but we have to protect ourselves from the damage that it inevitably causes unprotected skin.

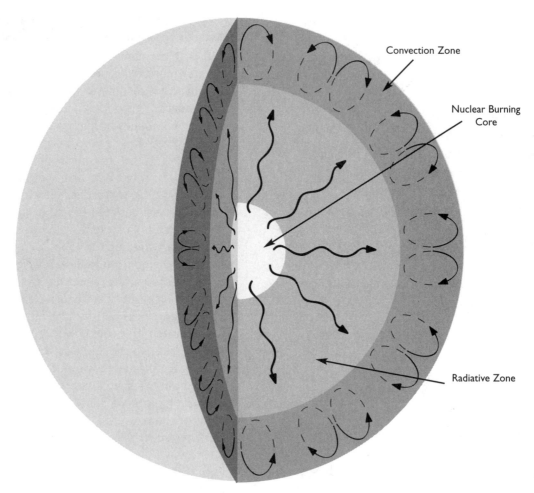

Figure 10.1—Internal Structure of the Sun

Deeper into the Sun, the density increases and light cannot easily escape; it slowly makes its way to the surface through multiple scattering processes. This radiative region, or region of the Sun where energy is transported by the motion of photons, ranges from the center of the Sun to within about 90,000 mi below the surface. Because the Sun is about 432,000 mi in radius, almost the whole Sun is radiative. Beyond the radiative zone, convection dominates. Convection in the Sun is similar to the process you see when water boils. Parcels of water bubble up to the surface, release their energy, and then fall back to the bottom of the pot of water. The same process takes place on the Sun. Hot parcels of gas take up energy at the top of the radiative zone, rise due to their energy uptake (their density actually drops, so they rise like corks in water), and, when they reach the top of the photosphere, release their energy; the gas then falls back down to repeat the cycle. Careful observations of the photosphere show this bubbling motion in the form of granulation. Granulation is the pattern of the hot gas rising and the cool gas falling on the Sun, similar to water boiling. The Sun boils relatively slowly, with granules appearing on the surface over a period of 10 min or so and then falling back down over the same timescale (Fig. 10.2). Any given granule is huge. The average granule is roughly 800 mi across, about the size of Texas.

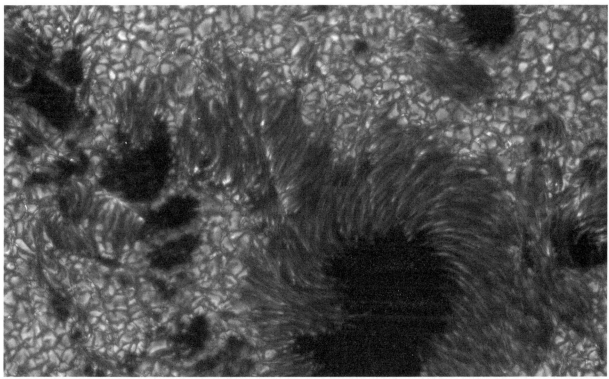

Figure 10.2—Granulation

Photo courtesy of Royal Swedish Academy of Sciences

HELIOSEISMOLOGY

Like a vat of bubbling, boiling water, the motions of gas within the Sun are accompanied by noises. We cannot hear the sounds here on Earth, because sound cannot travel through the emptiness of space. But were we to stand on its surface, the Sun would be a loud place. The sound waves that the Sun produces can be observed from Earth, even though they can't be heard. Because the rising and falling clumps of gas come in all different sizes, they make a continuum of sounds, just like a ringing bell. This ringing makes itself apparent through the overall velocity of the gas we see at the photosphere. A low-frequency ringing would imply that a few, very large pieces of gas are moving up or down. High-frequency ringing is represented by many small packets of gas moving up or down. By measuring the detailed velocity structures of the photosphere, scientists can calculate the ringing frequencies. Why is this important? The interior structure of the Sun moderates the ringing (imagine putting a sock inside a bell), and we can learn about the interior by studying the ringing frequencies. The real difficulty is that some of the very lowest frequency motions also propagate very slowly, and to study them a worldwide system of telescopes had to be established. Just such a network, coordinated at the National Solar Observatory in Tucson, Arizona, is operating right now. Nicknamed GONG, for Global Oscillation Network Group, this connected system of telescopes is located in mainly clear and dry regions, works around the clock to measure the motions of the gas in the photosphere, and studies the deep interior of the Sun simply by listening to the Sun's "ring." They also have an extensive Web site, which was used as the basis for this sidebar.

All this energy comes from the core. The core of the Sun is, thankfully, a region unlike any you can experience here on Earth. The density is immense. The solar core is where all the Sun's energy comes from. Due to the huge amount of material and the mutual gravitational attraction of the accumulated gas, the pressure at the Sun's core is several trillion times the atmospheric pressure on Earth's surface. Such a phenomenal pressure crushes atoms at the core close together. Due to the high temperatures, the atoms are also moving very fast. With a temperature of about 15 million degrees Fahrenheit and a density 10 times that of lead, the conditions are not something easily visualized or even imagined. The Sun is not "on fire." We might expect that during the collapse of a star-forming cloud that a great deal of friction would heat up the gas, and this might be why the Sun is hot. Although such heating does take place, it is not enough, nor does it last long enough to explain the Sun's brightness we see today. The process from which the Sun's energy comes is called nuclear fusion. Due to the intense temperature and density at the core, hydrogen atoms can fuse together and become helium atoms, releasing energy. When the hydrogen atoms come together, they ultimately form a helium atom. Four hydrogen atoms are needed to make one helium atom, but hydrogen atoms have only protons, while a helium atom has two protons and two neutrons. Two of the hydrogen protons convert to neutrons, which are less massive than protons. This small change in mass results in the release of energy and this is where the Sun gets its energy. The energy comes from the conversion of matter into energy, predicted by Einstein's famous equation $E = mc^2$. This transition results in the production of only a small amount of energy, but so many reactions are taking place that, in total, a great deal of energy is produced in the

form of gamma rays or X-rays. These high-energy photons propagate outward, heating the material in the Sun and ending up in the convection zone. Each day, the Sun converts about 3×10^{17} pounds of hydrogen into helium. This immense amount is about the same as half a million SUVs. You might think that the Sun would use up all its hydrogen quickly, but due to its immense size and huge amount of contained mass, the Sun has used only a small fraction of its total mass and can easily carry on producing energy for the next 4.5 billion years or so, and it has been fusing hydrogen into helium for about the same amount of time.

Gravity and Heat: A Delicate Balance

With the intense nuclear reactions going on at the core of the Sun, one might expect the Sun to explode just like the hydrogen bombs developed by the United States and the former Soviet Union (and tested in the South Pacific in the 1950s and 1960s). But the Sun doesn't explode, because the very large amount of material that composes the Sun is held together by gravity. This special balance between the heat and energy produced by nuclear reactions at the core and the force of gravity pulling together the material that makes up the Sun is called thermodynamic equilibrium. The thermal energy is balanced by the dynamic force of gravity holding the Sun together. If the nuclear reactions were to speed up, the Sun would expand a bit. More energy with the same amount of gravity means a bigger star. Slower nuclear reactions would result in the Sun collapsing a bit, because less energy would be available to offset the gravitational attraction.

All stars, not just the Sun, are in thermodynamic equilibrium most of the time.

Sometimes there are slight changes, which lead to dramatic changes in the star. For example, when a star uses up most of its core hydrogen and begins to fuse helium into other elements, the amount of energy produced changes and the star changes shape. We talk more about this in the next chapter. Thermodynamic equilibrium is one of nature's great wonders. We see thousands of these delicate balancing acts when the stars come out at night. They are not just twinkling lights, they are seething nuclear fusion explosions balanced by the force of gravity into a state of stability, allowing us to watch their fiery shows.

SUN CYCLES

The Quiet Sun

After centuries of observation, astronomers have determined that the Sun has cycles, with relatively active times followed by relatively quiet times. The cycle is roughly 11 years long, sometimes longer, sometimes shorter. The quiet Sun is when the Sun shows little surface activity; during this period the surface shows granulation (or the boiling of the photospheric gases discussed earlier) but no dramatic sunspots or large eruptions. Some dramatic features do appear, such as spicules. Spicules are jets of gas that originate in the photosphere of the Sun and transport energy into the chromosphere. In just a few minutes these jets of gas can climb 6500 mi or more into the chromosphere, depositing their energy there, and heating it.

The Active Sun

The active Sun, on the other hand, is a violent place. In the active Sun, regions of activity appear on the Sun's surface, sometimes covering a large fraction of it. These active areas exhibit sunspots, flares, bright eruptions of energy, and prominences. Prominences are large plumes of a material that originate near the photosphere of the Sun and expand away from it in spikelike projections. This activity is linked to the Sun's magnetic field and the complex rotation of the Sun. The poles move more slowly than the equatorial region, resulting in a magnetic field that is tangled and twisted. This odd rotation property is possible with an object that is not a solid, like Earth. Solid bodies rotate differently than fluid or gaseous objects. When the magnetic field adjusts to eliminate these twists and tangles, active regions result.

Sunspots

Sunspots are dark regions on the photosphere that normally form in groups. Each has a dark central core known as the umbra and a fainter outer region known as the penumbra. Surprisingly, if you picked up a sunspot and moved it away from the Sun, it would appear bright, not dark. Although darker than the normal photosphere, sunspots are quite bright on their own. You could easily see them from Earth if they were by themselves in open space.

Sunspots are intimately linked with the Sun's magnetic field. In fact, sunspots are regions where the convective motion of the photosphere has concentrated the magnetic field and is moving it downward into the photosphere. Like magnets on Earth, a magnetic field is usually tied to a material. In a magnet, it is tied to the metal of the magnet itself. In the Sun, the magnetic field is tied to the gas that composes the Sun, and therefore it can move around as the gas is moved around. The increased concentration of the magnetic field in these downward moving photospheric regions modifies the photosphere, depressing it slightly and causing the sunspot region to cool relative to the surrounding area. Because a cool material gives off much less light than a hot one (the amount given off is proportional to T^4), the sunspots appear dark. Sunspots change shape slowly over time, and observations over a period of days can easily show this shape change.

Sunspots can be used to measure the rotation rate of the Sun. As the activity cycle progresses, sunspots appear closer and closer to the equator. Few sunspots ever appear near the poles. This is probably because the magnetic field of the Sun is relatively ordered at these locations. Only in the other, more chaotic regions of the Sun's surface do we see sunspots.

Flares

Flares are dramatic and rapid releases of energy in the form of light of many wavelengths, including X-rays, that occur when magnetic fields break apart and reconnect. Through careful observation, astronomers have found that flares occur most often near the active regions of sunspots. The release of energy undoes the twisting and kinking caused by the fact that the Sun's poles move more slowly than the equatorial regions. The magnetic fields are connected with the gas in both locations, and the different rotational motions cause the winding up of the magnetic fields. The flare begins out in the corona (where the magnetic fields can most easily wobble due to the low density) and then actually grows downward into the chromosphere. This odd situation is caused by the fact that the energy release begins at the weakest point in the magnetic fields, which arc upward from the photosphere into the chromosphere.

In movies available on solar observatory Web sites (listed in the appendix), one can see how dramatic the flares are, with regions much larger than Earth erupting with bright light and material seemingly dropping along the reconnected magnetic fields toward the Sun's surface. The exact reasons for the flares are still unknown, so we cannot accurately model them, although we do understand in general how they work. Because these flares are the main source of the dangerous particles in the solar wind that can injure astronauts, it is important we continue to study the Sun so that we can one day predict when such potentially damaging flares will take place.

Prominences

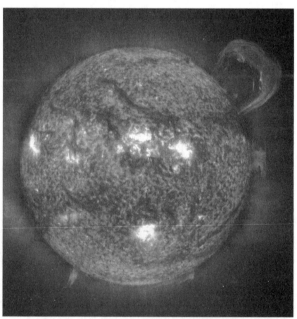

Photo courtesy of SOHO–EIT Consortium, ESA, NASA

Figure 10.3—Image of a Prominence

Prominences are the grandest spectacle visible in our solar system (Fig. 10.3). Found above sunspot groups, prominences appear to be eruptions of hot gas, usually occurring in loops (revealing a relationship to magnetic fields) that erupt upward into the Sun's corona. They

SPACE SOLAR OBSERVATION

NASA has sent a large number of satellites into orbit to study the Sun. Because it is nearby and very bright, large, expensive telescopes are not necessary, making small orbiting satellites the best way to observe the Sun. Above Earth's atmosphere, wavelengths of light not normally visible from the ground can be captured, and more information can be gathered from the light from the Sun. One recent satellite, called the Solar and Heliospheric Observatory, or SOHO, has provided some dramatic images of the Sun in a whole range of wavelengths. The satellite studies the corona with a number of instruments, as well as performing helioseismology observations and observations of the particles in the solar wind (explained later). To study the corona effectively, the Sun's bright photosphere must be blocked out, and this is accomplished with a small blocking device in the telescope. SOHO has captured images of eruptions of material into the corona, and, most interestingly, comets actually falling into the Sun itself (Fig. 10.4). Movies are available on the SOHO Web site (http://sohowww.nascom.nasa.gov/).

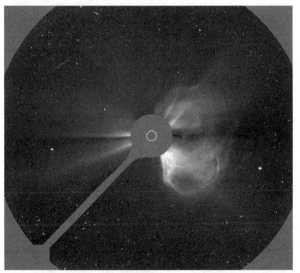

Photo courtesy of SOHO/LASCO C3 (ESA & NASA)

Figure 10.4— Large Coronal Mass Ejection (CME) of April 20, 1998

can be longer than the Sun's diameter and are visible for many hours to perhaps a day or two. Careful observation shows that a prominence may fade away, only to reappear more or less in the same physical shape a few days later. This strongly suggests that the prominence is related to the magnetic field emanating from the active region. Sunspots are regions where the magnetic field is concentrated, and perhaps the prominences light up when larger clumps of magnetic field come into the sunspot region. Active observation of the Sun to more completely understand prominences is ongoing from the ground and from space. The missions include the Solar-Terrestrial Relations Observatory, which will study how the Sun influences Earth through its steady wind of particles and the release of energy through solar flares, and the Solar Dynamics Observatory, which will study a number of solar issues, including the role of magnetic fields on the Sun.

The Impact of the Sun on Earth

Another feature of the cyclical Sun is a slow and steady loss of mass from the Sun in the form of a wind of charged particles, mainly protons and electrons. This solar wind originates in the hot region of the corona. Because the temperatures are so high, particles in this region can escape the Sun's gravitational field because molecules or atoms that are hot have high velocities. This wind of particles moves quickly, with a variable speed between 670,000 and 1,800,000 mi/h. Just like winds here on Earth, the solar wind has gusts, periods when it is faster. It also is faster over active regions on the Sun and slower overall in the quiet Sun times. The solar wind also carries magnetic fields. The wind takes about 4 to 5 days to reach Earth. Predicting when strong gusts will hit Earth is an important part of

THE SPACE ENVIRONMENT CENTER

Each day, the National Weather Service, through its national and local offices, produces weather forecasts for cities and towns across the United States as well as global forecasting. They also predict space weather through a small facility in Colorado known as the Space Environment Center (http://www.sec.noaa.gov/). A small group of solar astronomers and physicists work to predict the space weather near Earth each day. Such weather is caused by the Sun and its solar wind. This predictive service helps our country in a number of ways. Most obviously, scientists can prepare satellites for disruptive solar wind gusts and modify the way they operate, sometimes moving the satellites to minimize any service disruptions. Air travel across the poles, such as flights from Chicago or London to Japan or China, can have their navigational equipment malfunction in certain solar wind events. With notice that a solar wind event is coming, they can make arrangements to use different equipment or fly slightly different routes. Finally, strong solar storms can also affect our electrical distribution systems, which act something like large antennas, picking up the intense radio waves given off by the solar storms and disrupting the flow of electricity and also the control systems that govern how it flows along the power lines. Beyond predicting solar weather's impact here on Earth, the researchers study how solar eruptions occur to improve their predictive capability. Although we generally have a few days in which to prepare, it is useful to know even earlier. As we increase our human presence in space, it will be very important to be able to predict space weather to maintain astronaut safety. Large solar storms can significantly damage astronauts through increased exposure to charged particles and intense electromagnetic radiation. Perhaps in the future so many people will be in orbit that our TV news will carry regular space weather reports; when they do, they will get their information from the Space Environment Center, just as those who need to know do today.

solar research, and NASA, the Air Force, and the National Oceanic and Atmospheric Administration support an active group of scientists that warn satellite operators and astronauts of impending solar wind gusts. Because satellites and astronauts can be damaged from these bursts, such research is vital.

When particularly strong gusts hit the Earth, the wind and particles interact with the Earth's magnetic field. This creates stronger aurora. Aurora are impact zones, the spots where the solar wind is captured by Earth's magnetic field and guided along its field lines to just above the North and South poles of Earth. In these regions, the high-speed particles interact with the atmosphere and cause air molecules to give off light. No harm comes to us here on the surface; we just get to enjoy a dramatic light show. Unfortunately, only people living near the Polar Regions get to see the aurora on a regular basis, and there they are best seen at night, when it is extraordinarily cold. Fans of the aurora say the lights warm them up inside, but watching the aurora remains a cold nighttime activity.

THE SUN'S PLACE IN THE GALAXY

The Sun is but one of billions and billions of stars in our galaxy, the Milky Way. The stars close to us appear as bright points of light, whereas those far away fade together into an arc of faint light that extends across the whole sky. Our galaxy has a central region, known as the bulge, composed mainly of older stars and a large disk of younger stars. The Sun orbits about two-thirds of the way out from the center in the disk. The Sun is only about 4.5 billion years old, a relatively young star. Its age has been determined from measurements of radioactive material in Earth. Radioactive materials decay at a steady rate; by measuring how much radioactive material remains, an accurate age for any given rock sample can be determined. Because the Sun and Earth formed at the same time, we can infer the age of the Sun by measuring the age of Earth.

All stars in the galaxy rotate around the galactic center, but not all have the same period, which is the amount of time it takes to go around the center one time, just as not all the planets have the same period. Stars close to the center have shorter periods than stars further out in the disk. Because the Sun is located in the outer part of the galaxy, it orbits pretty fast, about 500,000 mi/h. Despite this fast speed, it still takes a long time to orbit the galaxy because the galaxy is so big. The Milky Way is about 100,000 light-years, or 5.9×10^{17} mi, across. The Sun is located about 30,000 light-years, or 1.8×10^{17} mi, from the galaxy's center. Assuming a circular orbit, the Sun has to travel about 189,000 light-years, or 1.1×10^{18} mi, to go around the Milky Way once. Given this great distance and the fast speed of the Sun, you might think it wouldn't take too long to orbit the galaxy, but it does—roughly 225 million years. This means that in the 4.5 billion years the Sun has been in existence, it has made 20 orbits. We are in our twentieth galactic year, with about 20 to go. We'll learn more about the Sun's ultimate fate in Chapter 13.

SUMMARY

The Sun is the source of energy for life on Earth. It is 109 times the diameter of Earth and located about 93 million miles from Earth. The visible part of the Sun is the photosphere. The surrounding regions are known as the chromosphere and corona. It has a dense core, in which nuclear reactions take place that provide its energy. The Sun is in thermodynamic equilibrium, a state where the energy from the nuclear reactions at its core balance the pull of gravity trying to pull the material in the Sun together.

The Sun goes through active periods when sunspots, solar flares, and prominences can occur. Sunspots are caused by magnetic fields and appear as darker areas on the Sun's surface. Solar flares are explosions on the surface caused by the reconnection or untwisting of magnetic field lines. Prominences are immense pillars of hot gas that extend from the surface of the photosphere into the corona.

The Sun can seriously impact Earth through solar storms, or eruptions of high energy particles. These bursts can interrupt satellite communications and cause other problems. The Sun should never be looked at directly without proper filters, especially with telescopes or binoculars. The intense light can cause serious eye damage.

STARS

KEY TERMS

blackbodies, luminosity, main sequence

From Earth, stars appear as small, glowing points, twinkling as the light streaming from them is distorted by our atmosphere. But these remote specks of light are suns in their own right. Some are larger than our Sun and some are smaller. All share the common characteristic of thermodynamic equilibrium discussed in the last chapter. A star in thermodynamic equilibrium undergoes regulated thermonuclear explosions and is held together by the immense gravity generated by its huge mass. They use these reactions to produce light, which ultimately allows us to see them.

Scientists have learned much about stars, although there is much more to learn. One of the great triumphs for astronomers in this century is the determination of how stars produce light and how they change over time. This chapter explores the fundamental properties of stars, from where they are to how big or bright they can be.

WHERE ARE THEY?

Stars are tremendously far away from us. We know this just by noticing that, day by day, they appear in the same relative positions; whether it is spring, summer, winter, or fall, the fundamental constellations remain unchanged. This means that the motion of Earth around the Sun, a total trip of about 584,000,000 mi, does not cause them to appear to change position. But why does this imply great distance?

When you hold your finger out in front of your face at arm's length and alternately open and close each eye, you will see that your finger appears to change position relative to the background of whatever you are looking at (such as wallpaper or some distant trees). The effect of apparent change of position that occurs when a distant object is viewed from different points of view is called *parallax*, and this apparent change in position of Earth can be used to determine the distance of remote celestial objects. Careful measurements with telescopes indicate that some stars show parallax effects; that is, they appear to change position as the Sun orbits Earth. This allows us to calculate the distance to such a star: knowing the orbit of Earth precisely and using basic trigonometric equations, we can find out, for example, that the nearest star (the one that shows the largest parallax effect) is about 2.4×10^{13} mi away. Even if you were in a rocket ship going 6 trillion miles per year (which is roughly how far light travels in 1 year), it would take you more than 4 years to reach this star, named Alpha Centauri. And this is the *nearest* star; most are much further away.

The distances to the stars are so great that astronomers don't use miles or meters to measure them; they use units that represent much larger distances. The easiest to understand is the light-year, which you'll remember is the distance light travels in 1 year. As just stated, it is equal to about 6 trillion miles. Another unit is the parsec, which is about three times as great as a light-year. A star 1 parsec away would display a parallax effect of exactly 1 arcsec. (Recall that an arcsecond is a very tiny angle, 1/3600 of a degree) In absolute terms, a parsec is 3.26 light-years, or almost 20 trillion miles.

When we look out at the night sky, every star we can see is located in our galaxy. The stars are not uniformly distributed on the sky but are concentrated into a flattened band that arcs across the sky and is known as the Milky Way. This faint band of light is actually the light of very distant stars, blended together due to their great distance. The fact that we can see so many stars means that most of space must be pretty much empty. If there were any dust particles or other material out there, the light from the distant stars would not be able to reach us but would be absorbed or scattered. We do notice that there is some dust, but there is not much, and it tends to simply redden the light (by scattering the blue light more than the red) and dim light from distant stars slightly. (There are regions of dense dust in our galaxy that are forming stars; we discuss these regions in the next chapter.)

The Milky Way has about 200 billion stars, of which the Sun is but one. They are aligned in a flat disk, with a central bulge, kind of like a compact disk with a table tennis ball stuck in the middle. Surrounding the galaxy are self-gravitating clumps of stars (stellar groups that are held together by gravity), called globular clusters, composed of tens of thousands to a hundred thousand stars (Fig. 11.1). These globular clusters are orbiting the galaxy, but they do so very slowly. We cannot detect any

Photo courtesy of NASA/STScI

Figure 11.1—A Globular Cluster

motion directly, although we can detect their Doppler shifts and, from that, their motion toward or away from us. Even with 200 billion stars moving around, there are almost never any collisions; there is too much empty space. Direct collisions probably only occur once or twice during the lifetime of the Galaxy.

HOW MASSIVE?

Our Sun has a mass of 1.98×10^{30} kg. Although this sounds like a lot of material, especially compared with Earth's mass of 5.97×10^{24} kg, the Sun is just a mid-mass star. As with distance, astronomers have defined a particular unit to use when speaking of the mass of stars or galaxies: the *solar mass*. One solar mass is simply the mass of our Sun. The smallest stars known have masses of about 0.1 solar mass, and the most massive stars have masses exceeding 10,000 solar masses.

However, by number, most of the stars are smaller in mass than the Sun. Big, heavyweight stars are exceedingly rare.

How can astronomers determine the mass of a star? When astronomers first began observing stars carefully, they found that some changed brightness in a regular way. For a few days or more, a star would be of a certain brightness; then, over the course of a few hours, it would dramatically decrease in brightness and then increase again to its original level. Through careful study and thought, astronomers determined that such stars were actually pairs of stars slowly orbiting one another and that the dimming of the light happened when one star crossed in front of another, obscuring the light from the brighter of the two stars.

Stars that appeared to be close to each other in the sky had been seen as soon as the first telescopes were built, and through careful observation, some of these visual binary stars were shown to be orbiting each other. It was just a quick leap of intuition to predict that some of the stars that periodically dimmed would be similar systems. Stars that periodically appear to be dimmed but are aligned so that we would see one star pass in front of the other are called *eclipsing binary stars*.

Using eclipsing binary stars, astronomers are able to use Newton's laws of gravitation to determine the mass of each of the stars in the system. This is because the special alignment of such systems removes our uncertainty of their alignment in the sky. If one star blocks another out, we know that we must be looking directly along the orbital plane of the system.

Although eclipsing systems provide the best measurement of the masses of stars, other

binaries can be used to determine the ratio of the mass of one star to its partner (even though we don't know the tilt of the system's orbit relative to Earth as we do for the eclipsing binary systems). Visual binaries, simple pairings of stars that can be seen with a telescope or by eye, that show rotation about a common center of mass can be used in this way. Kepler's laws state that the sum of the masses of two stars locked in orbit around one another is related to the size of the orbits and the period of rotation. If we can measure the orbital sizes and the period of rotation, then we can determine the sum of the masses. This method for determining stellar masses requires a lot of work over a long time and some way of measuring the distance to the stellar system so that the size of the orbits can be determined (usually measured using parallax, discussed earlier).

Spectroscopic binaries are stars that are located so close together that, even with the largest telescopes, we can see them as only one star. They can also be used to measure the mass of binary companions. However, because they are rotating about each other and they each emit light separately, we can sometimes detect a Doppler shift effect from the light emitted by each star. In Figure 11.2, you can see that when one of the stars is moving toward us, the other is moving away. The star moving toward us emits light at a certain wavelength, but due to its motion, the wavelength is blueshifted, while the light given off by the star moving away from us is redshifted. By making spectroscopic observations of these systems over time, the period and the velocity of the stars in their orbit can be calculated. This velocity is used to measure the size of the orbit (a star moving at a certain speed, say 1000 mi/h, completes one full orbit in 10 h, so it has traveled 10,000 mi). Once the size of the orbit

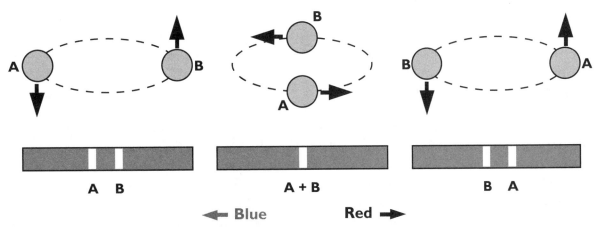

B

A ○····················↑**B**

↓

B○←
○**A**→

B○····················○**A**↑

↓

A   B

A + B

B   A

← **Blue**   **Red** →

Figure 11.2—Diagram of Spectroscopic Binary Stars

and the period are known, Kepler's laws can again be used to determine the sum of the masses of the two stars. However, once again, we do not know the tilt of the orbit of the stars (unless it is an eclipsing system), and therefore the mass measurement for each star is uncertain. Only eclipsing binary stars give us the true masses of the stars, and this is why they are so important to study.

HOW BIG?

As we saw in the last chapter, the Sun is huge, about 864,000 mi in diameter. Although many stars are smaller, some are much, much larger. To speak easily about the diameters of the stars, astronomers use a special unit, scaled to the size of the Sun: the *solar radius*. Predictably, 1 solar radius is equal to the radius of our Sun, or about 432,000 mi. The smallest normal star (see the section at the end of this chapter for the size of some special stars) has a radius of about 0.1 solar radius, whereas the largest normal star has a radius of about 300 times the solar radius. Again, some special stars can be bigger, but not by much.

If all stars look like points of light in even the largest telescopes, how can astronomers

determine their size? One way is with eclipsing binaries, as we have learned. This is a very accurate method for determining stellar size, but it is limited to those stars that show eclipsing phenomena.

Another very accurate method for measuring the diameter of stars uses the interference properties of light (discussed in Chapter 3). By combining light gathered in different spots here on Earth in a special way, astronomers can simulate a telescope with a much larger diameter. Because the resolving power of a telescope is related to its diameter, bigger telescopes (even simulated ones) should be able to measure the sizes of stars. Such devices, known as interferometers, are now becoming commonplace, but the first experiments in optical interferometry were undertaken by American astronomer A. A. Michelson (first discussed in Chapter 4). He arranged two small openings in front of a 12-in. telescope and observed the moons of Jupiter. He knew he should be able to resolve these moons using the interferometric technique because they are visible as small disks in even a modest-sized telescope. By adjusting the slits so that the light from one of the moons appeared dimmest, the size of the moon could be calculated. He completed his first observations in 1890. Various attempts since then have led to more refined techniques, and now dedicated groups of optical telescopes perform the same kind of observation (see the appendix for a list of these telescopes). These interferometric methods have allowed astronomers to accurately measure the sizes of stars. Most importantly, they have measured the diameters of stars not found in binary systems. We have no guarantee that binary stars and normal stars are exactly the same. Measuring the diameters of individual stars is a very important goal, because it allows us to make sure that binary stars and isolated stars share the same properties.

Another method of measuring stellar size involves observing the light from a star as the moon moves in front of it, occulting the star so that we cannot see it. A special kind of interference pattern can be observed as the edge of the moon blocks the starlight; it is called *Fresnel diffraction*, for the French scientist Augustin-Jean Fresnel (1788–1827), who was made famous for designing lenses for lighthouses that are still used today in overhead projectors). The pattern observed is related to the diameter of the star. This method is useful, but it works well only on bright stars that are relatively nearby, and it is not as accurate as other methods.

HOW HOT?

The temperatures of stars are determined by their color. Hot stars are blue; cold stars are red. This runs opposite to our everyday color associations for hot and cold. Normally we think of blue, the color of water, as cold and red, the color of a hot stove burner or candle flame, as hot. But this is only our perception;

it is not how nature actually works. Light given off by hot objects produces a particular distribution of colors and intensities, first calculated by German physicist Max Planck (1858–1947). He determined that as the temperature of an object increases, the amount of light at all wavelengths increases, and the dominant color of the light from the object shifts toward the blue end of the spectrum. Cool objects are dim and reddish in color (very cool things are so red, they give off most of their light in the infrared portion of the spectrum, which we cannot see with our eyes). Very hot objects are very bright and give off most of their light in the blue portion of the spectrum.

Planck used basic physics and some clever mathematics to calculate the distribution of light as a function of wavelength for perfect emitters and absorbers of light that he called *blackbodies*. Although such perfect objects do not exist in nature, stars come fairly close to following the exact relationships calculated by Planck. The light given off by blackbodies is known as *blackbody radiation*.

The results of his calculations are normally displayed in a plot like those shown in Figure 11.3, where the vertical axis represents the intensity of the light given off, and the horizontal axis represents the color or wavelength of the light emitted. This so-called Planck function depends only on the temperature of the object emitting the light. If you can measure how much light the object gives off of a particular color, then you can determine its temperature. Astronomers use this powerful tool to measure the temperature of stars.

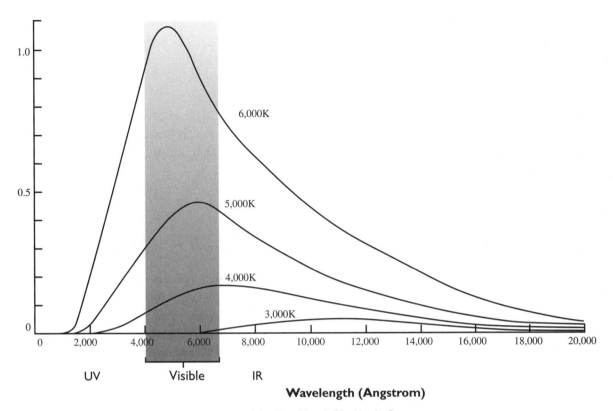

Figure 11.3—The Planck Blackbody Curve

CLASSIFICATION OF STARS

Spectral Type

Stars were a puzzle to astronomers in the late 1800s and early 1900s. The observational techniques available, combined with the large telescopes, had allowed increasingly detailed observations of stars to be made. Spectroscopic observations using photographic plates had been made for thousands of stars and although some patterns did appear, it was not certain what they meant. American astronomer Edward Charles Pickering (1846–1919) realized that some insight into how stars worked must be hidden in the stellar spectra. Spectra, as discussed in Chapter 4, are images of the amount of light of each color coming from an object. Spectra are made by dispersing— or spreading out—the light from an object and measuring the wavelengths, or color, as well as

the intensity. In 1896 Pickering, the Director of Harvard College Observatory, hired American Annie Jump Cannon (1863–1941) to classify the spectra obtained from telescopes in the southern hemisphere and to classify variable stars detected on photographic plates at Harvard's many observatories. She excelled at both tasks and eventually became a full-fledged astronomer. Her classification system of stellar spectra, based on the appearance of certain spectral lines, led to the stellar classification system we still use today. Although her system has had to expand slightly to allow the addition of two other classes of stars and has received some fine-tuning, it is still substantially her creation. She began classifying the stellar spectra in the Harvard plate archives in 1911 and completed the task in 1915. During the peak of her classification days, she would look at and classify three stellar spectra per minute.

Annie Jump Cannon's monumental effort—classifying more than 253,000 stellar spectra and then assembling them into a coherent pattern—stands as one of the triumphs of modern astronomy. It took her several years to prepare her work for publication, and it finally appeared in 1924 as the Henry Draper Catalog, named for American astronomer *Henry Draper* (1837–1882), whose wife presented Harvard College Observatory with a substantial gift to memorialize her husband. Henry Draper was the first American astronomer to actively pursue astronomical photography and was the first astronomer ever to obtain a photograph of a nebula.

Annie Jump Cannon found that stars could be grouped into seven basic types and gave each type a letter designation. The letters for the types are O, B, A, F, G, K, and M. Sometimes astronomy students use a mnemonic device, or phrase of words, whose first letters match

WOMEN IN ASTRONOMY

The sciences have not always allowed women to participate in scientific research. In earlier times, it was felt that women did not possess the skills or intellect necessary to carry out research. Nothing could be further from the truth. In astronomy, many of the most brilliant insights have come from women researchers, sometimes while struggling against the status quo and experiencing direct discrimination on a number of different levels. It is a truly a waste that for so many years potentially half of our most brilliant astronomers were not even allowed to participate.

To be sure, observatories made use of their skills, sometimes even their research insights, but only rarely were they given proper credit. Edward Pickering, at the Harvard College Observatory, was but one of many observatory directors who hired hard-working women astronomy enthusiasts to undertake the sometimes monotonous or mundane tasks necessary to classify, catalog, and index the data that telescopes were producing.

Here are just a few of the great women astronomers and what they accomplished: Henrietta Leavitt (American; 1868–1921) determined that the absolute magnitude of a class of variable stars known as Cepheids was related to their period of brightness fluctuation, allowing distances to galaxies to be estimated more accurately than ever before; Maria Mitchell (American; 1818–1889) discovered a comet using a telescope and was an important teacher of other women astronomers at Vassar College; Caroline Herschel (British; 1750–1848) helped her brother, William Herschel, perform observations on the way to discovering Uranus; Mary Agnes Clerk (British; 1842–1907) documented the early days of astrophysical astronomy in books for the general public; Beatrice Tinsley (British-American; 1941–1981) performed fundamental research in cosmology, especially in the area of galaxy mergers and collisions and their role in the evolution of galaxies over time. All are worthy of further investigation.

Today, the American Astronomical Society is working to increase the number of women participating in astronomy and has reached a membership total of 35% women for members under the age of 35. For the youngest members, aged 18 to 23, more than 64% are women. This is the best distribution of women physical scientists for any physical science society. We hope this trend will continue and an equal partnership between the sexes in the discovery and exploration of the universe will lead to new knowledge and insight more quickly than with just one gender leading the way.

Spectral Type	Temperature Range	Example
	(K)*	
O	> 25,000	Lambda Cepheid
B	11,000 to 25,000	Rigel
A	7,500 to 11,000	Sirius
F	6,000 to 7,500	Polaris
G	5,000 to 6,000	Sun
K	3,500 to 5,000	Arcturus
M	< 3,500	Betelgeuse

*The unit of temperature known as Kelvin (and abbreviated K) is an alternative measurement system to Fahrenheit and is used most commonly by physicists and astronomers. 32°F is equal to 273.15 K and 212°F is equal to 373.15 K.

Table 11.1—Spectral Types and Temperatures

the system. (My personal favorite, submitted to me for extra credit by one of my students, is "Oh be a fine grader, Kevin Marvel.") Many such phrases exist, but they have no special significance. They exist only to help us remember the order of the spectral classification system. Because a finer subdivision in the spectral types is needed for detailed study, numerical classifications can be added to a letter to indicate slightly different spectral characteristics. For example, the Sun is a G2 star.

The spectral classification system is linked closely to a star's photosphere temperature. The Sun is yellow, and its spectral type is G2. Red stars like Betelgeuse, the star marking the shoulder of Orion, are cool and have spectral types K and M. Blue stars like Sirius are very hot and have spectral types of A, B, or O. Table 11.1 shows the connection between spectral type and temperature with some example stars of each type

Luminosity

Astronomers measure the brightness of stars using a unit called the magnitude. It is derived from an ancient system developed by early Greek astronomers in which the brightest stars were named stars of the first magnitude and dimmer stars were stars of the second, third, and so on, magnitudes. This system, although the opposite of how we typically measure quantities (larger numbers usually measure bigger things), continues to be used today. The apparent magnitude of a star is how bright a star appears from Earth. It is the combination of a star's inherent brightness and its distance from Earth. Given two stars of equal brightness, one placed nearby and one distant from us, the more distant one is fainter. In fact, the brightness of an object decreases as the square of its distance from us. A star 2 times as far away would be 4 times fainter. A star 4 times as far away would be 16 times dimmer. Apparent magnitudes are not especially useful in understanding the inherent properties of a star because they are so linked to the star's distance from the viewer. Astronomers therefore use a related system of measurement, called absolute magnitude, which removes the effect of distance. By definition, the absolute magnitude is the apparent magnitude of a star that is 10 parsecs, or a little more than 30 light-years, away from Earth. However, to calculate the absolute magnitude, we must know either the distance to the star or its inherent brightness. The Sun has an apparent magnitude of more than −26 but an absolute magnitude of +4.8. Its apparent magnitude is large (a big negative number is a very bright object) because it is so close. Compared to all other stars, it is not so absolutely bright after all.

Luminosity is the measure of how much total energy a star is giving off, per unit time, in all directions. It is directly related to the absolute magnitude of a star. The luminosity can be used to classify stars, just like the temperature or spectral type. It simply is a measure

of how much light the star is giving off at all wavelengths. Because the luminosity and the spectral type are complementary measures of stellar characteristics, they can be used together to try to understand stars.

Two astronomers in the early 1900s, American astronomer Henry Norris Russell (1877–1957) and Danish astronomer Ejnar Hertzprung (1873–1967), independently developed a graphical classification system based on the spectral type and luminosity of stars. The relationship between a star's spectral type and its luminosity need not be clear-cut. The amazing thing about Russell and Hertzprung's work is that stars, when graphed using their system, follow very clear patterns. These so-called Hertzprung-Russell (or HR) diagrams, enabled astronomers to understand how stars produce energy and how they change over time (Fig. 11.4).

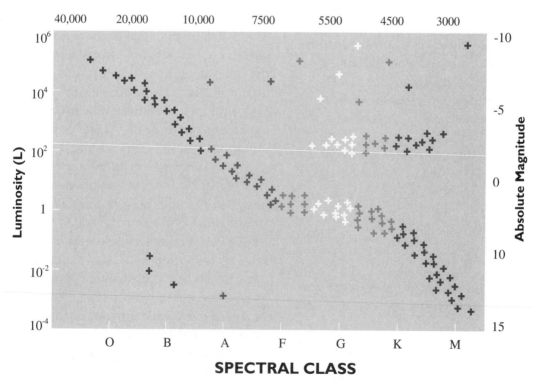

SPECTRAL CLASS

Figure 11.4—A Classic HR Diagram

The *main sequence* is a zone that cuts across the center of an HR diagram, in which most stars fall when their luminosity and spectral type are plotted. Stars on the main sequence follow a rather simple pattern: the higher the temperature (like O, B, or A stars), the greater the luminosity; the lower the temperature, the lesser the luminosity. How is it that most stars follow such a simple track across the HR diagram? Something must be similar among all of them. The similarity is that stars on the main sequence are fusing hydrogen into helium.

So why does the luminosity increase as the temperature increases? Remember that stars are in thermodynamic equilibrium. If more energy is produced, the star expands a bit. The luminosity depends on the size and temperature of the star (a bigger, hotter star produces more total energy in all directions because its surface size is larger and its temperature is greater). So O and B stars on the main sequence must be very large (their luminosities are large and their temperatures are high) and M stars on the main sequence must be small (their luminosities are small and their temperatures are low). Using the size-determining observations discussed earlier in this chapter, astronomers have verified that this is the case.

Stars on the main sequence are sometimes called *dwarfs* because they are the smallest stars at any given temperature (except for some special cases) located on the main sequence of an HR diagram. The Sun is often called a G-dwarf, which tells us it is a G-type star on the main sequence, fusing hydrogen into helium.

Another zone of stars begins in the middle of the HR diagram and arcs upward toward cooler temperatures and higher luminosities.

These stars must be different than the hydrogen-fusing main sequence. This so-called giant branch is composed of cool stars with large luminosities. For a cool star to have a large luminosity, it must be truly grand in size; in fact, these stars are very large indeed. If we were to place the largest of the giant branch stars where the Sun was, its photosphere would extend beyond the orbit of Mars.

STELLAR EVOLUTION

Over time, stars change. Stellar evolution is a process by which the temperature, luminosity, and other fundamental characteristics of stars are altered over time. In the next chapter we learn more about how stars form. Here we consider stars when they first arrive on the main sequence. They begin their time on the main sequence hotter and brighter than when they leave, slowly cooling and contracting as the hydrogen in their cores is converted to helium. When the star begins fusing helium to make hydrogen, it expands dramatically and also cools, but it gets brighter, moving onto the giant branch. After most of the helium is fused into other atoms, such as carbon, nitrogen, and oxygen, the star becomes unstable and ultimately ends its life in one of many ways. In Chapter 13, we discuss these outcomes in more detail.

Some astronomers in the 1980s believed that stellar astronomy was a done deal, that no new insight into stars would ever be made because everything had been figured out. Nevertheless, improved instrumentation and long nights at the telescope have resulted in some significant new discoveries, including some new classes of stars.

RECENT ADVANCES IN STELLAR ASTRONOMY

Sensitive studies of very faint stars have revealed two new spectral classifications now considered part of the system developed by Annie Jump Cannon: L and T dwarfs. With the development of new detectors sensitive to the infrared portion of the spectrum, astronomers began a search for stars fainter and redder than the M-dwarf stars. Such stars would not be visible very far from the Sun because they are not very luminous and most of their dim light would be emitted in the infrared.

In 1998, J. Davy Kirkpatrick and colleagues announced the discovery of a new class of stars, the L-dwarf spectral type. Initially based on only 20 objects found in a sensitive infrared survey of the sky, the class has grown to include more objects as deeper observations have been made. The L-dwarfs do not contribute much matter to the Galaxy. Individually they have only one-twentieth the mass of the sun. By number, however, they probably outnumber *all* other stars. Of all the stars we see with our eyes at night, none are L-dwarfs. However, as a class, they impressively outnumber all other stars, perhaps by as much as 2 to 1.

Using the same deep survey, astronomer Adam Burgasser and his collaborators discovered yet another new class of stars, named the T-dwarfs, although the first clear member of this class was found in 1995 by the Japanese astronomer Tadashi Nakajima and his collaborators. Due to the excitement caused by the discovery of this new class of stars, several teams of researchers have been actively pursuing research projects to understand them better, and their understanding is changing rapidly; indeed, a friendly competition has started up to find stars with lower and lower temperatures. The T-dwarf stars are even cooler in temperature than the L-dwarfs; they are so cool that methane can form in their photospheres. Methane is a common constituent in the atmospheres of Jupiter and Saturn and it is not too far from the truth to say that Jupiter could have been a T-dwarf were it only a bit more massive. These stars are cooler and smaller than the L-dwarfs and are on the main sequence, fusing hydrogen into helium just like other larger and hotter stars.

Understanding where stars come from, some of their properties, and that they change over time allows us to ask the next obvious question: what happens to them as they age? Do they just fizzle out like a used sparkler on the Fourth of July? Do they turn black like a lump of burnt-up coal or make cosmic ashes of some sort? Stars end their lives in a variety of ways that depends almost entirely on their initial mass. The next chapter describes just what these end states are and how the stars get there.

SUMMARY

The stars we see in the night sky are similar to our Sun, but they are at a great distance from the Earth. They have a range of masses and sizes from smaller than our Sun to much larger. The stars we see in the sky are all contained within our galaxy, the Milky Way. We can see other galaxies that are also composed of stars and are at immense distances from the Milky Way.

Stars are classified based on their spectra, or the different colors of light that they give off. Annie Jump Cannon, an American astronomer, developed the system we use today. Letters indicate the general class of the star; O, B, A, F, G, K, M, and a numerical designation provides a finer division within each class. Two new classes have been added, L and T, which are both cooler and smaller than the M stars.

The apparent magnitude of a star is how bright it appears to us here on Earth. The absolute magnitude is how bright it would be if it were a given distance from Earth. The total energy a star gives off in all directions is the luminosity. The luminosity is related to the size of the star and its temperature.

The Hertzprung-Russell diagram plots stellar luminosities versus spectral type. Stars do not fall randomly on this graph; instead they appear in certain regions based on their mass and what stage of their life they are in. Stars spend most of their time on the main sequence, a region that slopes from high luminosity and spectral type O to low luminosity and spectral types M, L, and T. Stars on the main sequence are fusing hydrogen into helium. As stars use up their core hydrogen, they change location on the HR diagram. This change in position is known as stellar evolution.

ORIGIN OF THE STARS

Stars are the building blocks of our universe. Galaxies are made up of billions of stars, sometimes hundreds of billions. But where do they come from? Although stars form very slowly, it seems sensible to expect that we can observe some stars forming somewhere in our galaxy, and in fact we can. Astronomers have found stars that are forming right now, hidden away in areas of dense dust. They have found stars that have just begun their lives on the main sequence as well as stars that have not yet begun to fuse hydrogen into helium in their cores, and they have even found loose clouds of dust and gas that seem to have formed just the barest beginnings of a star. In the process, they have learned much about the birth cycle of stars, even though we will never be able to watch a star form directly, in real time.

BETWEEN THE STARS

Clearly, stars have formed from something. The search for "star seeds" occupied astronomers for a long time. The first true hint came soon after telescopes were first used to take photographs of the sky, in the form of nebulae. *Nebulae* are bright regions of gas and dust that appear cloudlike in space. These clouds indicated that there was matter between the stars. The space between the stars is known as *interstellar space*.

The material we find between the stars is known as *interstellar matter*. Interstellar space and interstellar matter taken together are often referred to as the *interstellar medium*. Although astronomers long expected that material was there (due to the presence of the nebulae), determining what and how much interstellar matter was present took a long time and necessitated the creation of new observing methods and even new kinds of telescopes.

Looking at our galaxy, the Milky Way, we can see regions where there appear to be fewer stars. Peering more closely with sensitive telescopes, it becomes clear that the reason we see fewer stars is not because there actually are fewer stars, but because certain regions of our galaxy have dense dust clouds that obscure the light from background stars. Only stars on the near side of the gas clouds are easily seen with normal telescopes. Early on in the study of the galaxy, a great debate took place over whether these dark regions were caused by dust absorption or by "rifts" in the stellar distribution, allowing us to see beyond our galaxy. It was not settled until the observational evidence for the presence of interstellar matter was overwhelming, in the mid-1930s. Light from distant stars that did make it through the dust clouds was reddened and dimmed, the exact signature of dust.

Dust is not the only material between the stars. Using radio telescopes and sensitive spectrometers, astronomers have found that various types of gas are present as well. The most common gas is hydrogen. This is not too surprising, because we know that the stars are composed mostly of hydrogen. If stars form from the interstellar medium and they are made mainly of hydrogen, then we expect the interstellar medium to be mainly hydrogen.

We see hydrogen in two basic forms in the interstellar medium. With radio telescopes we can see very cold hydrogen gas that emits radio light with wavelengths of 21 centimeters (cm), or about 8.3 in. This gas is seen just about everywhere we look in the galaxy. About half the hydrogen we know about is thought to be in this cold state. Another form we can see with telescopes is ionized hydrogen. This gas is normally seen near hot, young stars of classes O and B. These stars, with their high luminosity and high temperatures, can produce large quantities of short-wavelength light that effectively strips an electron from the cold hydrogen, ionizing it. Once ionized, the hydrogen can grab free electrons; this process generates a particular wavelength of light in the red

portion of the electromagnetic spectrum (sometimes called H-alpha). These ionized gas clouds make great photographs (Fig. 12.1) and are a regular target for amateur astrophotographers (and professionals too). Other regions we can see are blue. These *reflection nebulae* are regions in the interstellar medium that are formed when light from stars scatters off the dust particles in interstellar space and directs some of the blue light toward us. A similar process makes our own sky appear blue.

Spectroscopic observations reveal a remarkable variety of molecules in the interstellar medium. From simple atomic gasses such as carbon, nitrogen, and oxygen to complicated molecules such as ammonia (NH_3), methane (CH_4), and even acetic acid, the interstellar medium is a complicated place. However, astronomers find these very complicated molecules only within the dark dust clouds, where temperatures are cool and the dust absorbs any ultraviolet light from hot stars. Complex molecules are sensitive. If they are exposed to extreme conditions—hot temperatures or intense ultraviolet light—they break apart. This is why they are found in the cool comfort of dark dust clouds.

Because these dark dust clouds in the interstellar medium contain large amounts of gas and a remarkable variety of molecules, they are often called *giant molecular clouds*. These clouds are typically a few tens of light-years in diameter, are composed mainly of hydrogen, and have very high densities compared to the rest of interstellar space. (In absolute terms, the density of a giant molecular cloud is actually a better vacuum than we can create here on Earth in a laboratory.) They have a range of different masses, from 10,000 solar masses to 1 million solar masses or, rarely, even more.

Photo courtesy of NASA/STScI

Figure 12.1—Interstellar Gas Cloud

THE RACE TO DISCOVER MOLECULES

In the late 1960s and early 1970s, a great race took place within the astronomical community. Technological developments allowed astronomers to measure incoming short-wavelength radio light. Wavelengths from just a centimeter to a fraction of a millimeter became visible to the right kind of telescopes with the right kind of receiver. When the curtains on this observational window were drawn open, astronomers rushed to try to detect various molecules in space. By collaborating with their colleagues in chemistry, they were able to determine the exact wavelengths for particular molecules (chemists had done numerical calculations and laboratory work to measure them here on Earth); they then needed only to hunt for the most likely places such molecules could exist, hoping to find a match for the molecules' signature wavelengths. Given the few specially equipped telescopes, competition was sure to surface, and it did. Astronomers were very secretive about just what frequencies or molecules they were hunting for. Successful detections were kept secret until papers could be published and bragging rights secured. These were heady days. Some astronomers used every resource available to be the first to detect certain molecules, including digging through trash bins to see if the previous observers had left any hints as to the right wavelength to observe for a particular molecule. In retrospect, this competition was rather silly. Eventually, the number of molecules detected became so large that finding another one was no big deal (we now know of more than 150 different kind of molecules in interstellar space). However, the competition did serve a useful purpose. More molecules were found more quickly, and the receivers used were under constant improvement. Competition is good for science as long as nobody gets hurt.

With the advent of radio telescopes capable of observing the light given off by molecules, astronomers have performed many detailed studies of these regions, mapping them all across our Milky Way, since the dust does not absorb light at radio wavelengths. Only optical light and shorter wavelengths are absorbed dramatically.

So, in between the stars is a bunch of gas and dust. Do stars just puff into existence from this material? Are there particular conditions needed to make stars? Just where does all this dust and gas come from anyway? As we will see in the next chapter, stars and the interstellar medium work very much like a forest. Seeds grow into trees, which then spread more seeds. When trees die, the material that makes them up is reprocessed into the soil and is ultimately used by new trees. Stars work in a similar way, both coming from the interstellar medium and contributing material back to interstellar space. Stellar ashes eventually spark new light.

FROM ASHES TO LIGHT

The constellation Orion is easily visible in early March. The three bright stars that form the belt of the heroic hunter Orion from Greek myth make this constellation easy to recognize. Just below and east of his belt is Orion's sword. This small set of three stars hides a beautiful, brightly colored gas cloud known as the Orion nebula. It is one of the nearest regions of active star formation to the Earth.

Looking at the nebula with a normal telescope, you can see a bright region filled with many young, bright stars and filaments of dust crossing the bright light, emitting gas.

It is a favorite object for amateur astronomers and can even be seen with binoculars. Although astronomers suspected that this region was a stellar nursery, a place where new stars are formed, it took the development of infrared telescopes to reveal the remarkable scale of this nearest star formation region. Observing in the infrared allows astronomers to peer within star-forming regions, which are always very dusty; they don't pass visible light well. The infrared observations reveal that the Orion star-forming region covers nearly the same area in the sky as the constellation itself, and literally thousands of stars are either formed or being formed within its sheltering darkness.

Star-Formation Theory

The laws of physics govern the material in interstellar space. Even the smallest dust grains feel the tug of gravity. Deep in giant molecular clouds, gas and dust are much more closely packed than in the rest of interstellar space. Within these regions, the gas slowly cools down because there are no stars to heat it up. This means that it moves much more slowly than outside of the clouds. Isaac Newton believed the laws of physics were universal and first put forward the theory of the gravitational collapse of large clouds of gas. He felt that in *gravitational collapse*, if a cloud were cold enough, the force of gravity would be able to pull the material together into an ever-denser clump of matter, thus forming stars. This is still the central idea in our ideas of star formation; only the details are different.

This gravitational collapse process inevitably heats up the gas, so there is a chance that some collapses may not form stars in the end. If there is not enough mass, the heat of the gas may be enough to stop or prevent the collapse

at some point. If there is enough mass, the collapse proceeds until the temperature balances the pull of gravity, and, if the temperatures are hot enough, nuclear fusion begins and a star is born. An object that is in the process of formation but has not yet begun nuclear reactions is known as a *protostar*. The Orion nebula is full of protostars. Other nearby regions containing protostars can be found in the constellations Taurus and Ophiuchus.

As you might expect, just as there are different stars, there are different protostars, each forming in a slightly different way. Massive protostars, the precursors of massive stars, form quickly (more gravity pulls things together more quickly); the temperatures at the core of a massive protostar are so hot that nuclear reactions can begin before the star is fully formed. Once these massive stars "turn on," or begin to fuse hydrogen into helium, the light ionizes the surrounding interstellar medium, forming *emission nebulae*, nebulae that emit their own light (as opposed to simply reflecting the light of nearby stars). A strong wind from the star then blows away the material still surrounding the star. Stars of about the mass of the Sun form more slowly, do not ionize their surrounding hydrogen gas, and often form jets of material from the poles of the star that can eat away at the surrounding cloud. These jets are an active area of research today.

The formation process doesn't proceed quite as simply as the previous paragraph describes. The clouds of material can be spinning, which modifies the process slightly and makes using equations to model the process much more difficult. There are magnetic fields in interstellar space, which can act to prevent the collapse in certain directions. Also, the exact composition of the interstellar medium can have an effect as well. Having a higher fraction of heavy atoms (called metals by astronomers, but really just atoms that are not hydrogen or helium) allows radiation to escape more easily, cooling the gas and speeding up the collapse. Astronomers are actively working on figuring out how the process works. But overall, the picture of gravity pulling together clumps of gas to form protostars that ultimately begin nuclear fusion is accepted by astronomers as the most likely way that stars form.

Observations of Star Formation

Infrared and radio telescopes are the only tools that allow astronomers to peer into the dark stellar nurseries where stars form. Despite the limited set of tools available, a great deal can be seen. Stars appear to form in groups or clusters. We have not found cases where stars are forming in isolation. This implies that the conditions for star formation occur over a large fraction of a giant molecular cloud more or less at once. Astronomers think that star formation is triggered, or initiated, when giant molecular clouds bump together or pass near one another. The influence of gravity on the gas then sets off small collapse regions where the density of the molecular cloud is slightly higher than in surrounding regions. If we had a movie camera and enough film for a few million years or so, we would be able to watch the process. Unfortunately, such cinematography is impossible, but by observing many different star forming regions in different stages of star formation, we can get an overall idea of the process.

Imagine two of these grand clouds moving gently through interstellar space, and colliding, with the rapid collapse of stars taking place in an almost random pattern through both of the clouds. Once the collapsing has begun, the small protostars rapidly get warmer until fusion can begin, altering the material out of which they formed. Star formation shuts itself off when there is no more material for more stars to form. Astronomers call this effect self-quenching; the process of star formation disrupts the surrounding interstellar material so that no more stars can form.

Observations with radio telescopes have confirmed the gravitational collapse model. Infalling gas can be detected by measuring the Doppler shifts of gas near protostars. Because we see jets of material leaving protostars along their polar axes (both in infrared light as well as in the radio wavelength range), we should expect to see some outflow signatures—and we do. Once again the Doppler shift allows us to see gas and gauge its velocity. Additionally, signs of rotation of the overall gas cloud from which the protostar is condensing are visible, along with clear evidence of magnetic fields. The observations confirm, overall, the gravitational collapse model.

RECENT ADVANCES ON STELLAR BIRTH

The *Hubble Space Telescope* (HST), in conjunction with observations made by sensitive radio interferometers, has really opened up the study of star formation. *Hubble* allows us to see newly formed stars with unprecedented resolution, especially once the residual dust and gas have been cleared out by stellar winds. We see disks of material around protostars. These disks are spinning. It is thought that these disks can ultimately form solar systems much like our own. Because they are cold and composed mainly of dust, we see them as dark donuts against the bright background of emission nebulae. Although some ground-based telescopes can make similar observations with special adaptive optical systems, the *HST* can provide excellent images of these kinds of sources anywhere in the sky. Future space telescopes should be able show us these protosolar systems in greater detail. The *HST* has limited resolving power and cannot show us the baby planetary disks in any greater detail.

One recent result made with an array of telescopes located on the Mauna Kea volcano in Hawaii (extinct and so safe for an observatory) seems to indicate the presence of forming planets. The Submillimeter Array, or SMA, was used in 2003 by Dr. David Wilner to image a protostar named epsilon Eridani. He found a ring of material with hints of some small clumps of material that were emitting blackbody radiation and detectable with the SMA. They could be *protoplanets*, or small clumps of matter formed through the gravitational action of a planet. Future observations are needed to understand this interesting source, but for now we can only guess as to the true nature of this matter.

Sensitive interferometers, especially those that observe very short-wavelength radio light, such as the Owens Valley Radio Observatory in California or the Plateau de Burre interferometer in France, are capable of observing many different molecules near protostars. Some we see associated only with the outflow. Others we see in disks of material around the protostars, whereas others can be seen falling in toward the protostar, remnants of the gravitational collapse process. A new telescope, the Atacama Large Millimeter Array, which should near completion around 2010, will be far more sensitive to a wider range of wavelengths than the current telescope interferometers. We expect to see star formation in greater detail.

We should be able to make detailed maps of the rotating disks, the infalling material, and the outflowing jets. Combined with images now being made with the infrared-sensitive Spitzer Space Telescope, which primarily captures material in the jets emerging from the protostars, a more complete understanding of the detailed process of star formation will be possible. We are entering a golden age for the study of stellar birth. Understanding how stars form will help us understand where planets come from and, ultimately, where we came from. As we see in the next chapter, we already know a great deal about how stars end their lives.

SUMMARY

Stars are formed from the gas found in interstellar space. This interstellar medium is formed from the processed gas from older stars and the material found in the galaxy.

Stars form in the densest and coldest gas clouds, known as giant molecular clouds. Because of the cold temperatures and very dense conditions, fairly complicated molecules can form there, such as ammonia and methane.

Stars basically form through the action of gravity that pulls together the gas in the giant molecular clouds into protostars. Once the core temperature of a protostar is hot enough, nuclear fusion can begin and a star is born.

Star formation can be observed directly only with infrared and radio telescopes. Once stars are formed and move the obscuring dust from their stellar nurseries, they can become visible to optical telescopes.

THE LIFE AND DEATH OF STARS

This chapter discusses that portion of a star's life when it has finished fusing hydrogen to helium (the main characteristic of the main sequence). Certain stars never leave the main sequence. These small stars hardly have enough mass to sustain nuclear fusion in their cores and can, therefore, spend a huge amount of time on the main sequence. Some stars out there, small, very dim, very red, have been around since the very beginning of the universe, glowing embers sprinkled through the cosmos.

The really exciting stars quickly fuse hydrogen into helium and end their lives in spectacular explosions. Stars like the Sun take the middle road, transitioning from fusing hydrogen into helium to fusing helium into other atoms. Perhaps the most amazing aspect of this whole process is that we have figured it out at all. It is one of the great triumphs of stellar astronomy. Let's see how stars change over time and how astronomers uncovered the mystery of stellar life and death.

THE IMPORTANCE OF MASS

Mass drives stellar evolution. When a star forms, its mass is based on the peculiarities of where it formed, how much matter was available in the interstellar medium, whether any other stars formed nearby, and so on. Just as humans are born with slightly varying sizes and weights, stars, too, are formed within a range of parameters.

Astronomers still can't predict exactly how many stars of some particular mass might form out of a generic interstellar molecular cloud. We do understand the general trend, and active research is ongoing to figure out the inner workings of the process. By observing a large number of stellar clusters, astronomers have determined in a general sense the fractions of stars that are formed given a range of parameters. The *initial mass function* is a function that tells us just how many of each kind of star we might expect to see formed from a giant molecular cloud. A great deal of research has been done on this function. Initially, astronomers felt that it must be a uniform property of the universe. The same rough fraction of each kind of stars must be the same everywhere. What we typically find is that the situation is more complex. The number and type of stars that form from a giant molecular cloud appear to vary based on the properties of the giant molecular cloud and the gas and dust it contains. It also seems to vary from galaxy to galaxy. Just as the fraction of people of a given size varies from country to country, the number of each kind of star changes depending on where we are looking.

More massive stars fuse hydrogen into helium faster than less massive stars. This is due mainly to the increased density and temperatures found in the cores of the massive stars. More mass means more fusion, and more fusion means that the core hydrogen will be used up more quickly. It is kind of like the gas tank of a sports car versus the gas tank of an economy car. Economy cars can go further on a tank of gas (if the tanks are the same size) because they use gas less quickly. Smaller stars fuse hydrogen into helium less rapidly and can, therefore, last longer on the main sequence.

Astronomers also know almost exactly how a newly formed star transitions from an object with no nuclear fusion to a star on the main sequence fusing hydrogen into helium. This was an active area of research in the 1950s and 1960s, and the advent of computers helped greatly increase our understanding. Although some details remain to be worked out, much of the early formation process is understood. Given just the mass and chemical makeup of a star (e.g., just how much of each element is in the star), computer programs can predict the physical characteristics of the star as it approaches and "lives" on the main sequence and even much of its later stages of life.

STELLAR CLUSTERS

No theory is worthwhile unless it can stand up to observational tests. Astronomers use observations of *stellar clusters*, groups of related stars, as tests for the computer models used to predict how stars form and move onto the main sequence.

There are two basic types of stellar clusters: open clusters and globular clusters. Open clusters have from a few hundred to several thousand stars. They are found in the disk region of the Milky Way (and the disks of other galaxies) and have a range of stellar types and ages. Some clusters have many young stars, whereas other clusters have mainly older stars. Open clusters have no defined shape. Some are roughly spherical, and some are like squashed pancakes. Because they sometimes have so few members, characterizing their shape can be a challenge.

Globular clusters are the jewels of the night sky. Comprising 10,000 to 1 million stars or more, they are spherical in shape, with many stars located toward their centers and fewer toward the outer regions. They are in orbit around the Milky Way (and other galaxies, even elliptical galaxies, have globular clusters too). We see many of them far out from the center of our Galaxy and a few closer in, some even in the plane of the Milky Way itself. This can be understood using Kepler's laws. Just like comets, globular clusters move fastest in their orbits when they are closest to the galactic center and move slowest when they are at the furthest reaches of their orbits. This is why we see so few in the galactic plane. On galactic time scales, they zip through the plane quite quickly, although we cannot detect their motion within the frame of a human lifetime.

Presumably, stellar clusters represent stars that all formed at the same time, from more or less the same material. We see them grouped together in the sky, so they haven't moved away from each other; perhaps gravity might be holding them together strongly, or perhaps they are a young cluster that hasn't had time to split up due to the random motions of the stars themselves. Additionally, the stars in a stellar cluster are at more or less the same distance from us here on Earth. There are slight differences in distance, but compared to the huge distance from us to them, they are

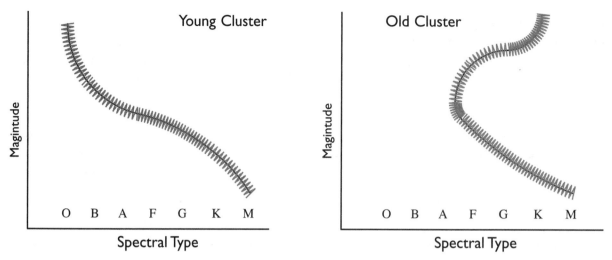

Figure 13.1—Young stars, which are hot and bright, are not present in the old cluster HR Diagram

essentially equally distant. This fact greatly helps the analysis of the clusters because the relative brightness of the stars indicates not a difference in distance, but a true difference between the brightness of the stars themselves.

Astronomers use the fact that the stars in a cluster are all at the same distance to measure their relative luminosity. By additionally measuring their colors (in other words, their temperature), a Hertzprung-Russell diagram for a particular cluster can be created. By observing many different clusters, a rough idea of how stars age can be created (Fig. 13.1).

From this research we have learned that hot O and B stars are very young stars. Only some clusters, which still have observable gas and dust nearby and appear to be gravitationally bound, have these bright stars. When we look at older stellar clusters, they typically have none of these stars. It is through the comparison of HR diagrams for clusters that we have determined that O and B stars form first, quickly fuse their hydrogen into helium and leave the main sequence. As clusters age, the main sequence slowly disappears from the top left of the diagram to the bottom right,

and stars show up in the top right of the HR diagram. Our computer models predict just such a change over time.

It makes a certain kind of sense. We know that the mass of stars decreases from the upper left of the HR diagram to reach a minimum, at the bottom right. Because nuclear fusion proceeds fastest for stars with the most mass, we should not expect them always to be present in clusters. They burn hot and bright, but they do so for only a short length of time. The insight gained by studying clusters of stars and understanding how clusters change over time compared to computer models has allowed us to learn about how stars themselves age. We even know how most stars will end their lives. We understand, in essence, the stellar lifecycle.

STELLAR LIFECYCLES

The study of clusters of stars combined with computer modeling has allowed us, more or less, to determine how stars will change over time. This section reviews a few of the typical lifecycles.

HOW DO WE KNOW THE AGE OF STELLAR CLUSTERS?

Human ages are pretty easy to figure out using visual cues. Wrinkles and potbellies begin to appear in the late thirties, extreme wrinkles and infirmity generally settle in during our late sixties. Clusters of stars have a similar set of characteristics that we can follow by studying HR diagrams and knowing a bit about how stars create energy (Fig. 13.1). Once we understood that stars fuse hydrogen into helium for a good portion of their lives, it was possible to calculate how long they would spend on the main sequence. Imagine doing such a calculation for a normal cluster. When the cluster is first formed, it has some massive stars, a larger fraction of midmass stars, and a whole bunch of low-mass stars. This is the initial mass function. Because higher-mass stars fuse hydrogen into helium faster than their lower-mass brothers and sisters, they don't spend much time on the HR diagram. In fact, a medium-age cluster should show no hot O and B stars in the main sequence portion of its HR diagram. Very old clusters should have few, if any, midmass stars, because they, too, will have burned up their nuclear fuel and left the HR diagram. Only dim, low-mass stars should remain. By making good guesses as to what the initial mass function for a cluster may have been, the cluster's age can be determined just by making an HR diagram and comparing it to the numerical models for clusters of different ages. The point on the HR diagram where the main sequence stars are just leaving the main sequence is known as the main sequence turnoff, and it is the location of this point that is the fundamental unit for determining the cluster age.

As stars of any mass condense from the interstellar gas, they heat up and contract until nuclear fusion begins. During the contraction phase, their brightness increases as their temperature goes up. This process takes a relatively short time on the cosmic time scale; for a star like the Sun it takes about 50 million years. More massive stars take less time to reach the main sequence, and lower mass stars take longer.

Once fusion begins, the surrounding dust and gas, which is still continuing to coalesce onto the star, begins to be blown away by the newly initiated stellar wind or, in the case of very massive stars, ionized by the stellar light. Not surprisingly, massive stars have stronger stellar winds than less massive stars. We often see young, low-mass stars that still have material around them while young O and B stars have clear bubbles blown out around them, indicating the power of their winds and the short-wavelength ionizing light they emit.

Once the star is on the main sequence, it proceeds to fuse hydrogen into helium. Again, this process depends on the mass of the star, with more massive stars fusing faster and lower mass stars fusing more slowly. Eventually, the star fuses almost all the hydrogen in its core into helium. Once enough helium is around, it can begin to fuse the helium into carbon. Because this nuclear process produces less energy than hydrogen fusion, the star's state of hydrostatic equilibrium is affected. The core of the star collapses, becoming smaller and denser, its temperature goes up, and further nuclear fusion reactions can take place. Fusion doesn't stop with carbon. Various processes can make nearly every naturally occurring element up to iron. Fusion reactions involving iron actually take energy, instead of producing energy. Only very massive stars are able to sustain these ongoing fusion reactions. Stars like the Sun make it only to carbon, and less-massive stars may not even reach the point where helium reactions can take place.

THE END OF STARS

Brown Dwarfs

Brown dwarfs are the normal end state for stars with much less mass than the Sun. The star spends a very long time on the main sequence fusing hydrogen into helium. Some of these low-mass stars, formed soon after the beginning of the universe, are still on the main sequence. However, eventually they use up the hydrogen in their cores and shrink, heating up in the process. Although they heat up, the temperature and density in these cores are insufficient to support further fusion of helium into carbon. They slowly cool over time, from a few thousand degrees to ever-cooler temperatures. As they cool, their color changes from dark orange-red to very dark red to colors that can be seen only in the infrared. Brown dwarfs, by number, are an immense population. We are not sure how many there are, but there are easily thousands within just 30 light-years of Earth. However, they are so dim in the visible portion of the spectrum that we must use special telescopes to search in the infrared. Even so, they emit so little light (their luminosities are low because they are so small) that it is nearly impossible to detect them. Only recently have astronomers found objects they truly believe to be brown dwarfs. The search will continue, because we can learn much about the life cycle of low-mass stars by observing what remains when their main sequence life ends.

White Dwarfs

White dwarfs are the normal end state for stars with masses close to that of the Sun. After these stars leave the main sequence (stop fusing hydrogen in their cores), their core shrinks, because the helium-to-carbon fusion reactions produce less energy, and gravity therefore makes them contract to compensate. A shell of hydrogen around the core continues to be fused into helium. When the core contracts, this hydrogen shell increases in temperature and produces more energy, which puffs up the outer portion of the star, increasing its luminosity but decreasing the overall temperature; these stars are called *red giants*. The amount of expansion varies, depending on the initial mass of the star, but it can be on the order of a factor of a hundred or so.

Red giants are stars fusing helium into carbon. Compared to the amount of time the stars spend on the main sequence, the time they spend as red giants is relatively short, something like one-tenth of the time they spend on the main sequence. Eventually, even the helium they formed in their core is used up. They contract and heat up, leaving the portion of the HR diagram known as the giant branch. Depending on their mass, they can spend some time in a region of the HR diagram known as the instability strip, pulsating slowly over time. When the helium fusion reactions in their cores stop, they shrink more. The helium fusing reactions still take place in a shell around the core. Because the helium reactions are very sensitive to temperature changes, the small fluctuations in the shell cause the star to begin to pulsate. As the rate of the helium shell reactions changes, energy production is in turn changed, causing the outer portions of the star to expand and contract. Such unstable stars begin to blow off their outer atmospheres, ultimately forming an object known as a planetary nebula. A *planetary nebula* (which in fact has nothing to do with planets) is a region of gas illuminated by an old star (known as a white dwarf) that has a carbon core and a shell of helium fusion reactions. The star becomes very hot and very small because no fusion reactions

THE CEPHEID VARIABLES: KEY TO THE DISTANCE SCALE

Cepheid variable stars, named because they vary in brightness and because the first detected example of this kind of star was delta Cepheid, are very important for determining distances in the universe. These stars, with masses just a bit greater than the Sun, are moving from the red giant portion of the HR diagram to the white dwarf portion of the HR diagram. They are pulsing regularly due to the fluctuations in the nuclear fusion rates of the helium shell around their carbon cores. Henrietta Leavitt (1868–1921), an astronomer at the Harvard College Observatory, is responsible for discovering how they can be used to determine distances. She found out that the star's period of fluctuation, how long it took to go from a bright state to a dim state, was directly related to its true brightness. More luminous Cepheids varied more quickly; less luminous ones varied more slowly. By simply measuring the fluctuations of the Cepheids, their distance could be measured.

Cepheids are very luminous stars, sitting above the main sequence in a diagonal strip from about the location of the Sun to the very uppermost regions of stellar luminosity. Because they are so bright, they can be seen individually in the nearest galaxies with telescopes on the ground and in more distant galaxies with telescopes from space. The *Hubble Space* Telescope had as one of its original goals the measurement of Cepheid periods in a range of galaxies, which it succeeded in capturing. These observations have helped to calibrate the true distances to the galaxies, something known as the cosmological distance scale. There is still some uncertainty in this scale, as some alternative distance-measuring methods don't agree with the Cepheid data, but the Cepheids remain important because they connect the distance scale we can measure here in the Milky Way with the distance scale of the whole cosmos (which we learn more about in Chapter 15).

are taking place in the core to offset gravitational contraction.

White dwarfs are located below the main sequence, in the bottom left-hand portion of the HR diagram. They have low luminosities because they are small, but they are very blue due to their hot temperatures. Because they have insufficient mass to fuse carbon, they slowly cool down, shifting toward the bottom right of the HR diagram. They are like the dim coals left over after a bright campfire, slowly dimming over time until they are practically invisible at any great distance from Earth.

Novae, Supernovae, and Black Holes

In 1572, Tycho Brahe witnessed a unique and previously unrecorded event. A new and very bright star appeared in the sky, where no star had been before. Calling the event "nova stellae," or new star, Tycho made observations with his instruments and noted its appearance in his notebooks. Astronomers have subsequently seen hundreds of these kind of events and call them novae. Novae are stellar explosions that result in the sudden brightening of stars by factors of tens of millions. They do not, however, blow apart their host star.

Novae take place in binary star systems. In such a system, two stars, which do not have to have the same mass, evolve along the main sequence at different rates. One of them leaves the main sequence before the other, ultimately becoming a white dwarf. The other, less massive star evolves more slowly and becomes a red giant only after the more massive star has already become a white dwarf. Remember that red giant stars are constantly losing mass through stellar winds, and in such a binary system some of this material finds its way onto the surface of the white dwarf. Once enough mass has accumulated, hydrogen fusion reactions can begin. When they do, they begin suddenly and quickly spread across the whole surface of the star. All the hydrogen contributed to the white dwarf by the red giant ignites in a sudden explosive event, increasing the brightness of the system tremendously; material is ejected in the process as well. High-resolution observations of such systems after such a nova has taken place reveal the material released during the explosion being ejected from the system. Some novae repeat. Matter continues to accumulate on the surface of the white dwarf until the red giant itself becomes a white dwarf, finishing the nova phase of the system.

In contrast, supernovae can never repeat, because they disrupt the host star. Although there are a variety of supernovae, the basic mechanism is the same in all cases. A star several times more massive than the Sun is able to pass beyond the normal helium fusion reactions and progressively fuse heavier atoms into ever-heavier atoms until a core of iron is produced. Shells of fusion reactions surround the iron core. The inner temperatures are high enough to begin to fuse iron, but such a reaction actually takes energy instead of producing it. The hydrostatic equilibrium of the star is seriously disturbed. Imagine a stream of water coming out of a hose. Now imagine suddenly switching on a reverse pump located along the hose. The water would not only cut off, it would reverse itself. This is what takes place when a star begins to try to fuse iron into heavier atoms. A sudden collapse takes place.

The surrounding shells of fusion reactions rapidly collapse. The densities and temperatures at the core become immense. A rebound reaction takes place in which the collapsing layers encounter this immensely dense core and bounce off it, rapidly expanding outward and blowing the star apart.

In the process, a dense core is formed that is composed entirely of neutrons, a so-called neutron star. Its formation is fairly complex, but a *neutron star* is formed basically through nuclear reactions that change protons into neutrons, which are then drawn together into a very small object due to immense gravity. If you could put a small amount of neutron star material into a matchbox, it would have more mass than the whole Earth! This is because neutrons, not having electric charge, can be pressed very close together. This is the densest configuration of matter that we know of. Neutron stars do not collapse because they are as densely packed as can be. There is no empty space between the particles. They are called degenerate in this state, as they do not have properties of normal matter but act in slightly different ways. Because they are degenerate, they hold up neutron stars from further collapse, just as the nuclear reactions held up the star through the production of energy.

Depending on the exact conditions, such neutron stars can be observed as pulsars. *Pulsars* are rapidly rotating neutron stars with strong magnetic fields. Electrons moving in the magnetic fields of the neutron star emit radio wavelength light, and because the star is rotating, the beam of the radio waves produced sweeps across our line of sight with regularity, in a kind of lighthouse effect. The discovery of these objects was made in 1967 by English astronomer Jocelyn Bell Burnell (1943–), who now teaches at the Open University in England. Because nature does not usually produce such regular signals, their initial discovery was discarded as being interference, and some thought they might represent communications from alien life. Although such communication would be amazing (see Chapter 16), it is equally amazing that such signals come from an immensely dense, fast-rotating remnant of a supernova explosion.

Very massive stars go one step beyond the neutron star stage. When the mass of the core remnant after a supernova is massive enough, the support from the tightly compressed neutrons cannot keep the star from further collapse, and a runaway collapse takes place. The gravitational field is so strong around such objects that light cannot escape from them. A *black hole* is created, the most massive object we know of, in which the gravitational field is so strong that light cannot escape from it. Although light cannot escape from a black hole's surface, the matter surrounding it is swirled around in small orbits at great speeds, creating tremendous heat and light. Astronomers feel they have detected clear signs of black holes in the centers of galaxies and also nearby in certain stellar systems that give off tremendous amounts of X-rays. Active research into these objects is testing the limits of our understanding of physics. The general and special theories of relativity are necessary to understand these objects with their immense gravity, which can warp space and time. What would happen to Earth if the Sun were replaced with a black hole with the same mass as the Sun? Nothing. As long as the mass was the same, the Earth would continue to orbit it, although it would get awfully cold.

GAMMA RAY BURSTS, A NEW UNDERSTANDING

In the 1960s, the American government launched a series of satellites to monitor the nuclear testing activities of the Soviet Union. A nuclear explosion gives off large quantities of the shortest wavelength light known, gamma rays. By measuring from space when large amounts of gamma rays appeared on Earth's surface, our military hoped to be able to monitor when nuclear testing took place. However, the satellites they launched indicated that about once a day a nuclear bomb was going off—or, more precisely, a large amount of gamma rays were detected. For a while nobody could figure out what was going on, but ultimately astronomers realized that these gamma ray bursts were coming from celestial objects. They were actively studied throughout the 1970s and 1980s. In 1991, a special telescope, the *Compton Gamma Ray Observatory*, was launched into space to provide continuous observation of these enigmatic releases of energy. They appeared uniformly around the sky, which either means they are close by or at tremendous distance. Their distribution in brightness favored the more distant option. By developing a network of ground-based telescopes to respond quickly when the satellite indicated a burst had gone off, follow-up observations could be made. The distance was determined: they were tremendously far away. Astronomers now think that these gamma ray bursts are uniquely strong supernova explosions that produce large quantities of gamma rays in addition to the tremendous light that is emitted. The mystery was solved, but the details are still under active study. Why do only some supernovae produce these bursts? Is it simply a function of mass? Is it because the explosions occur along a preferential axis, and only when the axis is pointed toward us do we see the gamma rays? Stay tuned as this mystery is unraveled.

However, if a much more massive black hole were placed where the Sun is now, Earth would follow a more-or-less straight-line orbit right down into the black hole itself. Although the immense gravitational forces would tear Earth apart, this scenario is not something we have to worry about, fortunately. The Sun will end its life as a red giant (not that this is good news) and has insufficient mass to become a black hole.

Many odd effects take place around a black hole, including the slowing down of time itself. Were you to be able to get close to a black hole, you could look back out at the universe and watch it as if in fast-forward. Stars would form and explode; galaxies would collide as if you were watching a sped-up movie. This odd effect is a direct result of Einstein's theory of relativity, which tells us how nature acts in the extreme cases of large gravity or very fast speeds.

SUMMARY

As stars fuse hydrogen to make helium, they slowly use up their core hydrogen. Depending on the mass of the star, different changes are possible once the core hydrogen is depleted.

If the star is not very massive, it simply cools over time very slowly, using up the available hydrogen. If it is a bit more massive, about the same mass as the Sun, it can fuse helium into carbon and becomes a giant star, swelling up to many times its normal size. When the helium is used up, it collapses to become a hot white dwarf, which slowly cools over time. If it is much more massive than the Sun, at least five times more massive, it can ultimately become a supernova, a star that explodes putting material back into the interstellar medium. Additionally, massive stars can form remnant stars composed entirely of neutrons, so-called neutron stars, which are very dense and, if rotating, can become pulsars, strong and regular emitters of radio waves. If the star is massive enough, when the core fusion process stops, the star collapses into a black hole, an object so massive and dense that light cannot escape from its surface.

Stars typically form in clusters. The number of stars of each type of star formed in a given cluster is known as the initial mass function. By understanding how stars change with time, we can learn the rough ages of clusters and better understand the star formation history of our Milky Way.

CHAPTER 14

BEYOND OUR GALAXY

KEY TERMS

spiral galaxies, elliptical galaxies, irregulars, quasars, local group

EARLY UNDERSTANDING OF GALAXIES

When astronomers first began gazing at the sky through telescopes, they quickly found, in addition to innumerable stars, fuzzy patches of light in the sky. These patches were all called nebulae, although they did not all look alike. Some, as we saw in the previous chapter, were related to stars in our galaxy—either the remnants of a supernova explosion or the ejected outer atmosphere of a red giant. Other regions were simply glowing gas illuminated by bright young O and B stars or regions that were collapsing to form new stars. However, some of the nebulae had spiral shapes. They looked like little pinwheels in the sky. Closer examination revealed a whole range of shapes, including some spirals with barlike structures onto which the spirals seemed to attach (Fig. 14.1).

Photo courtesy of NASA/ESA/STScI/AURA

Figure 14.1—A Face-on Spiral Nebula (Galaxy)

These spiral nebulae were an active topic for debate in the astronomical community from the late 1800s to the early 1900s. Just what were they? Another major question concerned their whereabouts. If they were in the Milky Way, then we might expect to be able to detect their motion in the sky or their own internal motions, just as we can detect the motion of some of the closer stars. Some astronomers thought they could (and even claimed that they did) measure the motion of the bright clumps of gas in the spiral nebulae. They had no idea what they were looking at.

In 1917, American astronomer Harlow Shapley (1885–1972) made the assumption that the spiral nebulae were extremely distant stellar systems and not objects within our galaxy. Guessing that the brightest stars in a remote galaxy would be similar in brightness to the brightest stars in our own galaxy, he determined that the minimum distance to the Andromeda galaxy would be 1 million light-years. The actual value as measured today is 2.2 million light-years. Given the prevailing wisdom of the day, he wasn't far off.

A debate was arranged by the National Academy of Science in 1920 between a champion of the so-called island universe theory (i.e., that the spiral nebulae represented other galaxies) and an individual who held that they either existed within our own galaxy between the stars or, at worst, in an extended halo around the Milky Way. Representing the island universe theory was the young Harlow Shapley, and representing the alternative was Heber Curtis (1872–1942). Curtis, the older astronomer, had the upper hand through much of the debate, but because no distance to the spiral nebulae was available, no conclusions could be drawn from the event. However, the pressing need for a distance measurement was made very clear.

The debate concerning the actual nature of the spiral nebulae continued until American astronomer Edwin Hubble (1889–1953) published a paper in 1929 in which he reported on his use of the 100 in. Mt. Palomar telescope to resolve individual stars in the outer regions of the largest visible spiral nebulae, known as M51 (now known as the Andromeda galaxy). Additionally, he discovered Cepheid variables in the galaxy and used the work of Henrietta Leavitt on Cepheids in our own galaxy to derive a distance to Andromeda of about nine times the distance to the Magellanic Clouds. The Magellanic Clouds are visible from locations in the southern hemisphere. They are, in fact, the nearest galactic companions of the Milky Way. This distance clearly placed them beyond the disk of the Milky Way and the island universe theory was confirmed.

The faint spiral fuzzy patches of light seen with telescopes were not nearby gas clouds, but whole systems of stars, millions and billions of light-years way—distances so great that the light leaving a young star could travel toward Earth and not reach us until the star had exploded as a supernova. Imagine a string of light from such a star leaving the star when it reaches the main sequence and its fusion reactions begin, traveling through space toward us for millions of years, and then the star exploding as a supernova. The supernova flash serves as a final end note to the light from the star, traveling swiftly through space and just waiting for an eager amateur or professional astronomer here on Earth to look its way.

We now call the spiral nebulae galaxies, and they are an active area of research for many astronomers. We want to understand how they form, interact, and change over time, what makes them have particular shapes, and how those shapes influence the rates of star formation within the galaxies. The first step in any scientific study is basic classification and the study of galaxies is no exception. Let's take a look at what kind of galaxies there are and their basic properties.

TYPES OF GALAXIES

Astronomers have actively characterized galaxies ever since they could take reliable photographs of them. Surprisingly, there are only a few types of galaxies. *Spiral galaxies* are large disks of stars and dust with large central bulges. They have the general appearance of a compact disk with a lime stuck in the center. *Elliptical galaxies* are football-like distributions of stars, with little dust or star formation. All the rest of the galaxies fall into either a transition class that has characteristics of both elliptical and spiral galaxies or into a generic class known as *irregulars*, which do not look like elliptical or spiral galaxies. Although this basic classification covers all galaxies, much remains to be discovered through the study of galaxies, the irregular galaxies in particular. Some irregular galaxies are apparently formed through gravitational interactions with other galaxies or even outright galaxy collisions. Origins of others are unclear, but spirals dominate.

Many different classification schemes have been developed, but the most enduring is the one first proposed by Hubble. During the early part of the 1900s he worked as an observational astronomer at the Mt. Wilson Observatory. Through careful study of a large number of galaxies (originally 600, but the number expanded over time), he developed a classification scheme where the general type of galaxy is denoted by a letter, either *E* for elliptical or *S* for spiral, followed by a number or letter indicating a sub-type within the over-

all class. For example, a nearly spherical elliptical galaxy would be an E0, whereas a very elongated elliptical would be an E7. The number after the E represents the ratio of the largest axis to the smallest. Similarly, spiral galaxies were classed on their degree of "spirality" and dominance of their central bulge. A very tightly wound spiral would receive an *a* subtype classification, whereas less tightly wound spirals would receive a *c* subtype. Just three letters, *a*, *b*, and *c*, are enough to classify the spiral galaxies effectively. Additionally, because some spiral galaxies have obvious barlike structures, Hubble also defined a barred spiral type with the letters *SB*. Irregular galaxies were given the label *I*. Hubble aligned his classification in a tuning fork diagram, with the ellipticals on the left, proceeding from spherical to more elliptical galaxies and ultimately to the S0 galaxies at which point a split occurs in the barred and normal spiral galaxies. The irregulars were off by themselves. Hubble felt galaxies started out as E0 galaxies and over time changed into the other types. We know now that this is not the case. Just how galaxies form and have particular shapes is still an active area of research nearly 100 years after they were first identified as distant stellar systems.

When Hubble initially proposed his scheme of galaxy classification, astronomers investigated the sky using visible light. Hubble's whole scheme was based on how the galaxies appeared in photographs that captured only visual light. Since then, astronomers have used many different wavelengths of light, from X-rays to radio waves to study galaxies, and many different classification schemes have been developed to try to understand galaxies more completely. Pictures of some galaxies in infrared light show little discernible difference between some of Hubble's classifications.

Although no classification scheme has helped codify the galaxies more effectively than the Hubble scheme, new methods of observation have required new classification schemes. Nevertheless, it is still very useful to understand how the basic types were initially classified by Hubble, because it provides some insight into the natural forces that guide the formation of their shapes.

Spirals

By number, spiral galaxies make up about 77% of all the galaxies in the universe. They vary in size from about 10,000 light-years to about 800,000 light-years in diameter. The Milky Way is an average spiral galaxy with a diameter of about 100,000 light-years. Spiral galaxies are composed of a disk and a bulge. They also have an extended halo.

The stellar disk is very flat, usually only a few thousand light-years thick but as large as several hundred thousand light-years across. Within the disk is an even thinner distribution of gas and dust, often known as the dust disk. This is the home of the giant molecular clouds. This disk within a disk is even thinner than the overall stellar disk, usually only a few hundred light-years thick. Gravity pulls this disk into its flat distribution. The stellar disk is larger due to gravitational interactions between stars and between stellar clusters. Such gravitational interactions can speed up the stars and allow them to have orbits around the center of the galaxy that carry them above the thin dust disk. New stars are constantly being formed in the dust disk.

The disks of spiral galaxies are rotating in different ways. *Solid-body rotation* is a special kind of rotation seen in the innermost regions of disks of spiral galaxies in which the angular velocity remains constant with distance from the center of rotation. This is the kind of rotation you would see if you twirled a baton or broomstick around its center. The outer portions of the baton rotate at the same angular speed as the inner portions. This means that the outer regions have to move much faster in a real sense than the inner regions. The velocity increases with distance from the center. At some point, the solid-body rotation stops and differential rotation takes over. *Differential rotation* is rotation where objects further away from the center of rotation move at a slower angular velocity, like the planets circling the Sun or stars orbiting the outer regions of a spiral galaxy. In the galactic disk, the actual speed stays more or less constant with distance from the galactic center. At great enough distances, we expect the actual speed to begin to decrease, but it does not. This means that more matter is there than we can see. Since we can't see it, it must be dark. Astronomers call this matter Dark Matter. It ends up it is one of the major constituents of the universe and we know nothing about it beyond that it has mass. This is how the solar system works. Most of the mass is in the Sun, so the speed of the planets actually decreases as a function of distance from the Sun. The speeds of the stars in their galactic orbits are quite fast. The Sun is moving at almost 500,000 mi/h in its orbit around the center of the galaxy. Stars further out move a bit slower; those closer in to the center of the galaxy move a bit faster. At this speed, the Sun can make about 50 orbits around the galactic center before it uses up its core hydrogen and becomes a red giant.

The disk makes up the spiral pattern we see. The pattern appears to be caused by spiral density waves. A *spiral density wave* is similar to a sound wave in air, wherein some disturbance in the galactic disk causes material to pile up in a particular pattern. Although we don't know how spiral density waves get started, their origins must in some sense be related to the differential rotation. If the outer material in the disk is moving slow and the inner material is moving quickly, then you naturally get a kind of spiral pattern. However, astronomers can tell that the density wave moves faster than the stellar orbits, so this is not a complete answer. If you were to filter out the hot, young stars, you would not see a spiral pattern in most spiral galaxies. The disk of older stars, like the Sun, is fairly uniform in its distribution. Only the movement of the spiral density waves, piling up gas and dust and forming new hot stars, makes the spiral arm visible to our telescopes.

The bulge is a central distribution of stars that has a shape like a slightly squashed orange. It is composed mainly of old stars and has very little dust. Bulges vary in size according to type of spiral and range from about one-tenth up to one-half the diameter of the galaxy. Sa galaxies have the largest bulges; Sc galaxies have the smallest ones. Some Sa galaxies appear to have no bulge whatsoever. The formation of the bulge, how it changes over time, and why some galaxies have large bulges whereas others have only small ones is an active area of research.

The halo, a region that surrounds the center of spiral galaxies, is a bit of a mystery. First, it is hard to study because not much is there. We see stars at very great distances from the galactic center that are not associated with the disk. These stars tend to be quite old and, therefore, quite faint—as well as red. The bright O and B stars, formed in the disk, just don't have time to get very far above the galactic plane before they die.

Halos also have a gaseous component, which can be detected with radio telescopes. This gas can range from cold to very hot. It is thought that the hot stars in the stellar disk heat up the gas and that it arrives in the halo due to the ejection of material by supernovae in the disk. Such supernovae can eject material up and out of the disk easier than through, or along, the disk (because the gas and dust are relatively thick in the disk). This forces the material from supernova explosions upward into so-called chimneys that pump hot gases from explosions outward to the halo. We also know from the orbital speed of the disk material that there is some *dark material* in the halo, material we cannot see but that has influence on the overall gravitational field of the galaxy. This dark matter must exist because of the observed orbital speed of gas and stars in the outer disks of galaxies, but we do not know what it is exactly.

Ellipticals

By number, ellipticals represent about 20% of all galaxies, and they vary in size. The largest have diameters of almost 1 million light-years; the smallest can be less than 1000 light-years across. They have a wide range of masses, from as small as 10 million solar masses or so up to 1 trillion solar masses or more. The very smallest ellipticals are called dwarf ellipticals in recognition of their very small size and mass. These little galaxies are only slightly larger than globular clusters, and the two objects may have formed in similar ways. We call them galaxies because globular clusters are always associated with larger galaxies, whereas dwarf ellipticals can be found in isolation or in orbit around larger galaxies. The largest elliptical galaxies are known as giant ellipticals.

To put their immense size in some perspective, if the largest known giant elliptical were placed with one tip at the Milky Way, the opposite side would reach to the Andromeda galaxy, our nearest large spiral companion galaxy, nearly 2.2 million light-years away. The overall range in size for ellipticals is much larger than that of the spiral galaxies. Ellipticals overall have very little gas or dust and don't show much evidence of star formation. Not surprisingly, given these observed facts, the stars that comprise them appear to be mostly older stars that all formed more or less at the same time, perhaps in parallel with the formation of the elliptical galaxy itself.

Research on ellipticals is ongoing and recent results show that some definitely formed through the accumulation of other galaxies. The giant ellipticals in particular, which often sit at the centers of large groups of galaxies called clusters, appear to have been built up over time through the accumulation of galaxies whose orbits brought them into the gravitational influence of the giant elliptical. In some sense, they gobbled up their cluster companions, making themselves larger in the process.

Irregulars

Irregular galaxies represent about 3% of all the galaxies we see. They are very rare. They have masses from 100 million up to about 10 billion solar masses. They have odd shapes and are often subdivided into two categories, peculiar and normal. Normal irregulars are symmetrical but do not fall into either the spiral or elliptical groups, whereas peculiar irregulars look odd in some way. Most peculiar irregulars appear to have had some kind of gravitational interaction with other galaxies, which has caused their shapes to become

highly distorted. Some even have what looks like the remains of a spiral galaxy stuck through an elliptical galaxy or even odder combinations. Irregulars tend to have a good amount of gas and dust and often are experiencing active star formation. They are irregular just because their physical appearance lacks symmetry. Because they are so odd in their appearance and so rare, many people are interested in trying to understand them, and they remain an active area of research today.

Interacting Galaxies

Interacting galaxies are galaxies that are exerting gravitational influence on each other (Fig. 14.2). They can be easily identified because the symmetrical appearance of the interacting galaxies is disrupted. A spiral arm of one may be closer to another galaxy than it appears it should be. In extreme cases, immense tails of material can be thrown out into space while two galaxies merge together. As these interactions take place, stars often form in regions where the enhanced gravitational field has pulled gas and dust into more compact distributions. Astronomers have even found a few cases in which an elliptical

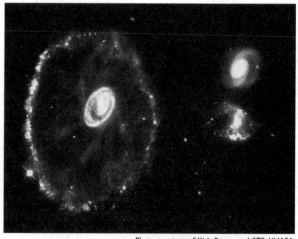

Photo courtesy of Kirk Borne and STScI/NASA

Figure 14.2—An Interacting Pair of Galaxies

galaxy has plummeted directly through the center of a spiral galaxy, forming an expanding ring of star formation propagating outward from the impact point, just like waves move away from a rock thrown into a pond. These dramatic interactions make spectacular photographs and also allow astronomers to study how star formation can be triggered through gravitational influence.

Active Galaxies

Some galaxies that appear otherwise normal are giving off large amounts of light, X-rays or radio waves for no apparent reason. Careful study of these objects has revealed that most have large black holes deep within their centers and that much of the activity we see is linked to these extreme objects. Although the gravitational field of a black hole prevents light from leaving its surface, the extreme force of the field swirls gas and dust (and even whole stars!) around at tremendous speeds. This motion causes intense heating of the gas and leads to the strong X-rays and bright optical light we see from active galaxies. One notable type includes the quasars. Quasars were initially detected by radio astronomers, who called them quasi-stellar radio sources. They were small, almost point-like, and emitting tremendous amounts of radio waves, just as stars give off large amounts of visible light. Study of quasars revealed that they were at great distances from Earth; very recent observations using the *Hubble Space Telescope* have confirmed that quasars are always associated with galaxies. *Quasars* are simply galaxies with so much activity (like emission of X-rays, ultraviolet and visible light and sometimes radio waves)that they are visible clear across the universe.

THE LOCAL GROUP

As we look out from our home here in the Milky Way, we see a number of galaxies that either appear quite large or quite bright. The largest nearby spiral galaxy is the Andromeda galaxy, about 2.2 million light-years away. It has two elliptical companions, a spiral companion and a dwarf elliptical with many globular clusters. We, too, have some companions, the large and small Magellanic clouds, which are the largest and a number of dwarf galaxies known by the constellation we see them in: Ursa Minor, Draco, Carina, Sextans, Sculptor, Fornax, Leo (I and II). Along with a few other isolated and small galaxies, this hodge-podge of galaxies is known as the local group. The *local group* is our immediate cosmic neighborhood, dominated by the Milky Way and Andromeda galaxies, plus a few other isolated and small galaxies.

The Milky Way and Andromeda galaxies are similar in size (Andromeda is a bit larger), and the other galaxies orbit one of the two of us or are so distant they effectively orbit both galaxies. The overall width of the local group is about 5 million light-years. There are about 30 galaxies in all and, except for the possibility of some very faint galaxies hiding behind the Milky Way or Andromeda, we know who all our neighbors are. The center of the local group is about halfway between Andromeda and us, the two dominant galaxies in the association.

CLUSTERS OF GALAXIES

In the grand scheme of things, the local group is kind of a backwater. It is not especially big and doesn't have many members. Galaxies tend to form in groups, and some tremendous clusters exist, some not too far away. One of

DARK MATTER RESEARCH

So how do you study something you can't see? Because dark matter has gravitational influence on normal matter, astronomers can learn about it by studying its gravitational effect on normal stars or galaxies. One of the best places to study its influence is in very large clusters of galaxies. In these clusters, a lot of dark matter and a lot of galaxies exist. In these clusters, the galaxies are moving faster than they should be if the only matter in the cluster were in the luminous matter we can see in the galaxies. They are moving faster because of the presence of dark matter. More matter means more gravity and more gravity means faster moving galaxies. The other way to study dark matter is to carefully observe how the bright matter in galaxies moves. By comparing the actual orbits of material in the galaxy to their predicted orbits based on the amount of bright matter, we can see that everything is moving faster than it should. This is the evidence for the existence of dark matter, and careful study lets astronomers determine how the dark matter is distributed. It appears that dark matter is in a more or less spherical distribution with a density distribution that more or less matches the distribution of the bright matter, but without the presence of a disk. Further study is needed to confirm the shape of the dark matter distribution and to understand just what the material is.

the largest nearby is the Virgo Cluster, about 60 million light-years away, with more than 2000 members. Our local group appears to be moving toward the Virgo Cluster, which is not surprising given its tremendous mass. The Virgo Cluster (and the local group, too) appears to be moving toward what must be an even larger cluster, or a cluster of clusters, known as the great attractor (and, more generally, as a supercluster). Clusters of galaxies appear to form along large linear structures, with very large clumps of clusters forming where these lines come together. The Virgo Cluster is at the center of the local supercluster (cluster of clusters). Other superclusters are even bigger than ours.

The speed of galaxies in orbits in clusters and from clusters in superclusters provides further evidence for the existence of dark matter. The speeds are greater than we would expect by adding up the masses of everything we can see. Because gravity is the only force making galaxies and clusters move about, there must be some matter present that we can't see given current techniques. Just what this dark matter is remains a significant mystery.

GALACTIC COLLISIONS

Galaxies are closer together, relative to their size, than stars. This means that galaxies tend to interact with and crash into each other much more often than stars. For example, the Milky Way and Andromeda galaxies are both about 100,000 light-years in diameter but are only 2.2 million light-years apart. Their separation is about 22 times larger than their diameter. For stars, this scale is much, much larger. The Sun is about 860,000 mi in diameter, about the same as one of our nearby neighbor stars, Alpha Centauri. However, Alpha Centauri is about 7,854,437,234,000 mi away. The ratio of its distance to the Sun's diameter is 9 million to 1. The stars are much further apart than their typical diameters. This means that stars essentially *never* run into each other (although we cannot rule out an occasional stellar collision), whereas galaxies bump into each other all the time. The collision of two galaxies is like a collision between ghosts: no damage is done. The stars in each galaxy don't run into each other, but the gas clouds and dust clouds do interact and form new stars. Also, the galaxies can influence each other to the point where they become distorted and, possibly, merge together.

THE PROBLEM OF DISTANCE

When you want to measure something in your house, such as the ideal height for a picture frame or the size of a window for a new set of drapes, you use a yardstick or tape measure. These devices provide a linear scale that you can hold up to measure the size of something or the distance between two things, such as the edges of a window frame. We can measure the distance to the nearest stars using parallax, which is based on how they change position as we orbit the Sun. However, beyond this range (about 100 light-years with current techniques) it becomes hard to measure distance. We must compare the true brightness of objects we think we know well and with how bright they appear to be. Cepheid variable stars give us another handle on distances. Their fluctuations in brightness are correlated with their true brightness. By measuring their period of fluctuation, we can estimate their distance. This method works for measuring the distances to the nearest galaxies and was one of the major accomplishments of the *Hubble Space Telescope*. Beyond the distance where we can see individual Cepheid variables, astronomers use a range of objects, from globular clusters to whole galaxies, to try and estimate distances. Supernovae, visible clear across the universe due to their extreme brightness, provide a one-time measure on distances. Like a measuring tape that disappears after one use, they're interesting and valuable but not much good if you want to double-check your measurements. Only the techniques close to home are very accurate. We introduce uncertainty into our distance measurements with each step further away from Earth.

Hubble's Law and the Birth of Modern Cosmology

When Edwin Hubble began studying galaxies in earnest, he found that the light coming from them was Doppler shifted. The galaxies in the local group had a range of shifts, some red, some blue, indicating that some were moving toward us and some away. But more distant galaxies were all red-shifted. In fact, the further the galaxy was from us, the greater was its shift. Hubble proposed a rule, now known as *Hubble's law*, that related a galaxy's distance to its Doppler shift or more properly, its velocity. A constant, now know as the Hubble constant, governed this relationship: velocity = $H \times$ distance, where H is the Hubble constant. He first published this relationship in 1929.

Hubble's law presents us with an interesting fact of the universe. With the exception of those nearby, galaxies are all moving away from us, and many of them are moving very fast, as much as 20 million miles per hour or even faster. (Moreover, the farther away they are, the faster they're going.) How can this be? How is it that all galaxies are rushing away from us? The simplest explanation is that the universe is expanding. Einstein's initial theories of relativity had predicted an expanding universe, but he added in a constant term to keep the universe from expanding. He did this because prevailing wisdom at the time predicted a static universe, one that did not expand. When Hubble discovered the expansion, Einstein called the inclusion of this constant his greatest mistake.

Cosmology, the study of the whole universe, its origin and its ultimate fate, and how it changes over time, was born with this discovery. In the 1980s, astronomers thought they

GRAVITATIONAL LENSING

Einstein's theory of relativity states that the gravitational warping of space by massive objects should deflect the light from more remote objects. Astronomers proved this initially back in 1919 by observing the location of stars near the Sun during a total solar eclipse. Subsequent observations have only solidified the somewhat rough initial measurements. However, certain rare objects prove an even more bizarre prediction of Einstein's theory: the existence of gravitational lenses. When a very massive object, such as a galaxy cluster, lies on the line of sight between Earth and a more distant object, the gravitational warping of space by the massive object not only can modify the direction of the light from the background object, but also can distort and magnify the light from the object. A number of these objects have been found, both in the radio portion of the spectrum and in the optical. Usually, the distorted images of the background object are just multiple images, each with particular brightnesses determined by the exact distribution of mass in the lensing object. However, in rare cases, when a line from the background object passes through the lens and reaches us here on Earth, an Einstein ring can be formed. An Einstein ring is a perfect circle of light that encircles the lensing object. Exceedingly rare, a few of these beautiful objects have been found. They are an elegant and beautiful confirmation of Einstein's theory of relativity. Also, since the bending we see is more than that expected from the gravitational field of the visible matter, they also prove the existence of this mysterious material. See Figure 14.3.

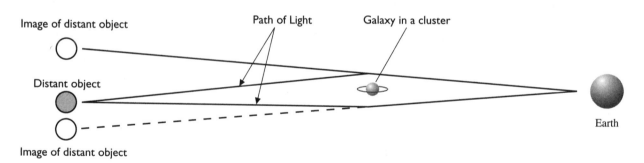

Figure 14.3—Diagram of Gravitational Lens System

had cosmology pretty much licked. This belief was premature. New observations showed that not only did they not have cosmology completely solved, but also that Einstein's greatest blunder was not such a mistake after all; we know about less than 95% of the mass and energy content of the universe. All the objects we can see—the stars, galaxies and clusters of galaxies—represent only 5% or less of the total mass and energy of our universe. The next chapter deals in detail with this exciting area of active research.

SUMMARY

Beyond our galaxy we can see other galaxies. Initially, it was not clear if they were local clumps of gas in our own Milky Way or simply distant groupings of stars just like our galaxy. We know now that they are distant versions of our very own home. The distance to galaxies was determined by the measurement of the period of brightness fluctuation of a type of star known as Cepheid variables. This type of star shows a relationship between its absolute brightness and its period, so it can be used to estimate the distance to remote objects because it is also very bright (and therefore visible very far away).

There are three basic types of galaxies, spirals, which are pinwheel shaped and have disk-like distributions of stars; elliptical galaxies, which are large, almost football-shaped distributions of stars; and irregular galaxies, which have no normal shape and come in a variety of forms.

Spiral galaxies have a bulgelike distribution of stars at their center, with a disk of stars distributed in a flat plane around the bulge. They exhibit active star formation and have dense dusty regions in the center of the plane.

Elliptical galaxies have little gas or dust and limited star formation. They can range in size from dwarf ellipticals that are much smaller than the Milky Way to extremely large galaxies, so that if one edge were placed where the Milky Way is now, the other end would reach our nearest large spiral galaxy neighbor, the Andromeda galaxy, 2.2 million light-years away.

The irregular galaxies come in a variety of forms and are thought to form in very different ways. Some are obviously the result of galaxy collisions, whereas others just appear to be very odd in shape or composition.

Some galaxies show much activity, including strong X-ray emission, radio emission, and large amounts of star formation. We find that all active galaxies have large black holes at their very center, which cause much of the observed activity through heating of the gas that spirals into them in the dense core region of the galaxy.

Our Milky Way is part of a larger group of galaxies known as the Local Group, which is but a small cluster of galaxies compared to other larger clusters we can see in deep space. Measuring distance to these remote galaxies is challenging, but Edwin Hubble, an American astronomer, found that the more distant a galaxy is, the faster it appears to be moving away from us. This Hubble law shows us that we live in an expanding universe, not a static and unchanging one, and it is one of the fundamental observations in the study of cosmology, the understanding of the origin and fate of the universe as a whole.

Cosmology is the study of the entire universe, how it was formed, how it has changed over time, and how it will ultimately end. It is the large-scale, all-encompassing study of everything we can know about the universe. Cosmology is based on a few assumptions and many observations. The assumptions are things that we believe to be true about the universe but cannot prove directly. The observations give us basic information about the universe. By combining the assumptions with the observations, theories about the universe can be developed and then tested against new observations.

THE ASSUMPTIONS

The assumptions are very likely to be true, although they may not be directly provable. The first assumption is that basic physical laws are the same everywhere in the universe. This means that gravity works the same everywhere, the laws of electromagnetism work the same everywhere, and the interactions between light and atoms and between sub-atomic particles are the same everywhere. If this assumption were not true, it would be difficult to develop cosmological theories at all.

The second assumption is that the universe is *isotropic*, which is the belief that space is the same no matter where we look, that there is no favored direction and no place is special, and that there is no center to the universe.

The third assumption is that the universe is *homogeneous*: the universe is smooth on the largest scales. We know that there is some clumping at the smallest scales, represented by planets and stars and galaxies, but on the very largest scales, the distribution of material is smooth. Smooth is a hard word to think about when applied to the universe, but imagine it as a large bowl of cake dough.

THE OBSERVATIONS

Any good cosmological theory must be able to explain adequately a few basic observations. First, all galaxies appear to be moving away from us. As observed by Edwin Hubble and discussed in the previous chapter, when we look at galaxies, they all have a Doppler shift toward the red, indicating movement away from us. How is it that they are all moving away; is this property universal? The most likely explanation and the one accepted by almost all astronomers is that the universe is expanding. But it seems as though the expansion is centered on us, upsetting the isotropic assumption. However, if space itself were expanding, then any observer on any planet in any galaxy would see all the other galaxies moving away from him or her, too.

One way to think of the situation is to imagine a cake baking in an oven. The cake has chocolate chips in it and you, an observer, are located on one chocolate chip. As the cake expands (assume the cake expands uniformly), all chips get further apart from each other at a uniform rate. Because the cake itself is causing the expansion, chips further away appear to be moving faster.

The universe works in a similar way. This cake model explains the observed fact that the galaxies are all receding from us and that more distant galaxies are receding faster than those nearby.

Another key observation was made by American physicists Arno Penzias (1933–) and Robert Wilson (1936–) when they both worked for AT&T Bell Labs in 1965. While using a newly developed radio telescope to

search for sources of radio emission in the Milky Way, they kept detecting a background noise that they did not anticipate. It seemed always present, no matter where they pointed their telescope. After ruling out errors in their equipment and effects on the antenna, such as water and even pigeon droppings, they determined that it was coming from deep space, but they were not quite sure where or from what. With collaborative help from some Princeton physicists, led by Robert H. Dicke (1916–1997), they determined that this weak radio emission was the residual signal from the initial phases of the Universe, just after the expansion had begun. These initial phases of the universe, just after the expansion had begun, are commonly known as the *Big Bang*. If the whole universe is expanding, it makes sense that at some point in the past, if we reverse the process, the universe was in a more compact, denser, and hotter state. The cosmic

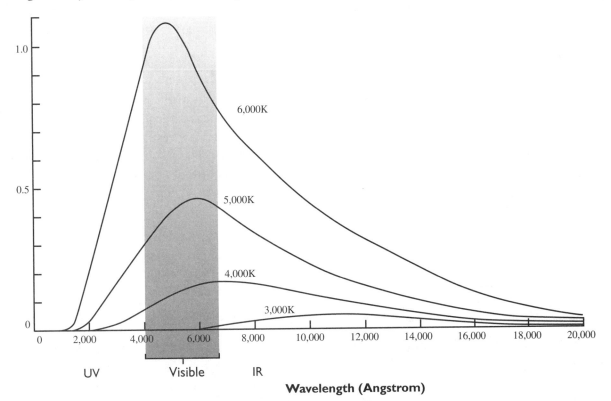

Figure 15.1—Planck Blackbody Curve

background radiation discovered by Penzias and Wilson is an observable fact and must be explained by any cosmological theory.

Additional observations of the cosmic background radiation made with satellites have revealed some important facts. First, the radiation follows the Planck blackbody distribution that was covered in Chapter 11 (Fig. 15.1, previous page). Blackbody radiation comes from objects that are hot and that are perfect emitters of electromagnetic radiation. The distribution of the wavelengths and the relative intensity of each wavelength are dictated only by the temperature of the blackbody. By making observations of the cosmic background radiation at a variety of wavelengths, we now know that the radiation represents a perfect blackbody at a temperature of 2.7 K, or –454.8°F.

If the early universe was extremely hot, why is the radiation we see coming from a blackbody at such a low temperature? The overall expansion of the universe has Doppler-shifted the blackbody radiation and changed its apparent temperature. Assuming a constant Hubble expansion, the initial temperature was almost unimaginably hot, on the order of 1,000,000,000,000°F. It is unknown how matter acts under such extreme temperatures. Even the normal laws of physics may not act in the predictable ways we understand today.

MODELS OF THE UNIVERSE

Cosmology advances by the construction of mathematical models that explain the observable facts about the universe and make other predictions that can be tested in some way. The rules of science dictate that the simplest model that explains all of the observable facts

should be accepted as correct. The Big Bang model, in which the whole universe grew from a small, hot, and dense state to the expanding universe we see today, is now accepted as the most likely model for the birth of the universe.

Alternative theories cannot predict all the observable facts we see. One such competing model is the *steady-state model*, an alternative model in which the universe is not expanding; it cannot predict all the observable facts we see without extreme complications. In this model, which Einstein initially supported, the Doppler shift is caused by other, more complex mechanisms than expansion. Although this model still has a few proponents, the vast majority of astronomers, easily 99%, accept the Big Bang as the most likely cosmological model. The details are constantly argued over, but the overall idea of an expansion from a hot, dense state is the basic unifying theory for all cosmological work.

Before 1998

Since 1998, our understanding of the universe has changed dramatically. Before we get to these exciting new results, it is important to understand what was accepted as the standard cosmological model before this pivotal year.

How We Got Here

The basic observations of an expanding universe and the cosmological background radiation lead us to conclude that the universe began in a hot, dense state; hot because the background radiation has been redshifted to its current appearance through the cosmological expansion and dense because all the material we see around us would have originally been in a very small region. So at the very beginning of the universe, the temperature of the universe would have been infinite. None of our theories or understanding of physical laws allows us to characterize this period of the universe in great detail. All we know is that the universe was small, dense, and very hot. It was so hot that normal matter could not exist. Only electromagnetic radiation existed. The universe was pure energy.

Our understanding of how the universe got from this hot, dense state to what we see now—with stars and galaxies formed, the overall temperature much reduced, and the density so low that light can travel clear across the universe—was built up from basic physics and our observations of the cosmic background radiation and the overall expansion. The easiest way to understand what we know is to turn the history of the universe into a narrative, describing the likely physical conditions and the dominant characteristics of the universe.

Let's begin at the very beginning. Some 13 billion years ago, for reasons we still do not understand, the universe began to expand. The temperature and density are completely unknown to us. No observational information about this period or the initial beginning of the universe is available to us (and will never be available), so the very initial moment of the universe will forever remain closed to scientific inquiry. We do know that the universe began to expand from this hot, dense state, because it is still expanding today. After a very short period of time, roughly 10^{-44} s, the density dropped enough to allow protons and neutrons to be created from the high-energy photons. How can matter be created from energy? Remember Einstein's famous equation, $E = mc^2$. If you have enough energy, mass—matter—can be created. However, this process creates both normal particles and a

type of particle called an antiparticle, which is identical to the normal particle in every way, except for the fact that if it comes in contact with the normal particle, both are annihilated and a photon is created. During this phase, particles are formed and then destroyed. The rate of this process determines the density of particles at the next stage of the expansion. This is an odd universe, a seething stew of high-energy photons and newly formed particles and antiparticles coming into being and then disappearing, creating a photon in the process.

As the universe expands, the energy available to make particles decreases and fewer massive particles (like protons and neutrons) can be formed. Instead, lighter particles, electrons, are formed. At the still-high temperature of the early universe, protons and electrons can interact to form neutrons. As the neutrons come into being, they can attach themselves to protons to form the nuclei of lighter-mass elements such as helium, lithium, and beryllium, as well as a special form of hydrogen, deuterium, which has an extra neutron. The current levels of each of these elements in the universe provide a tight constraint on this early stage of the universe, and measuring the amount of these elements is an important check for modern cosmological theories. The Big Bang model accurately predicts the amounts we see today.

As the expansion continues and the temperature drops, the universe is dominated by fast moving protons, neutrons and electrons. However, as the temperature decreases, the electrons slow down; at this point, with the new universe roughly 1 min old, they can be captured by the protons to form atoms. This era of recombination lasts only a few thousand years. The radiation, now freed from interacting with the stew of particles, can now travel freely across the universe: first light. This radiation is the cosmological background radiation that we see today, but it is greatly redshifted due to the expansion of the universe. Meanwhile, matter begins to clump together. Looking at the cosmic background radiation in detail reveals that current large clumps of matter—planets, stars, and galaxies—were originally small fluctuations on the otherwise smooth background radiation. Detailed observations revealed these lumps and bumps in the 1990s and early 2000s. (See Figure 15.2.)

After about 1 million years, the universe as we know it today was fully formed, dominated by condensed matter and free-roaming radiation, and expanding. The stars and galaxies still had to form through the rather slow process of gravitational collapse, but all the components we see around us today were formed. Tests of this basic model always confirm the details. The amount of helium and deuterium we see matches our understanding of the formation process predicted by the Big Bang model. The amount of clumpiness seen in the cosmic background radiation matches the amount of clumpiness predicted by the model. The Big Bang is well tested, the best available explanation for how the Universe came into being. Note, however, that the very initial stages of the process are, and will remain, unknown to us. There is no way to observe this early stage, because anything that happened before light could escape the new universe is, by definition, invisible. The general picture we have, though, is correct, because all the later stages can be tested through observation.

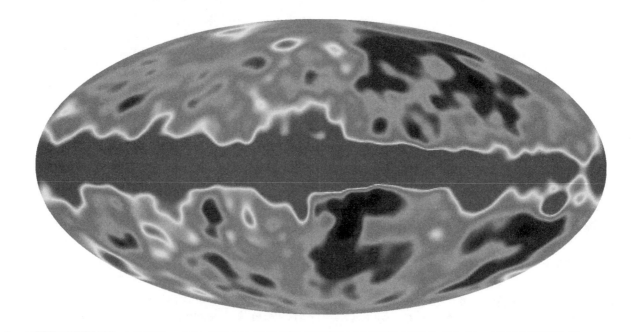

Photo courtesy of COBE/WMAP/NASA

Figure 15.2—Image of Cosmic Microwave Background Showing Fluctuations

Where We Are Going

The universe as we know it today was formed out of a seething stew of pure energy, via an expansion. So that's where we came from. But where are we going? Looking ahead, what is the ultimate fate of the Universe? Will it continue to expand forever? Will its expansion stop or somehow reverse itself? In the late 1990s all these outcomes were considered possible. We now know that only one of these outcomes is correct. But an understanding of the three scenarios allows us to better understand how cosmology works.

Gravity is the dominant force in the universe. It holds stars together, pulls stars into orbits in galaxies, and even holds together huge galaxy clusters. It also will largely determine the ultimate fate of the universe. If the amount of matter, and therefore gravity in the universe as a whole is too large, the force of gravity will be strong and will ultimately stop the expansion of the Universe by pulling the matter back together in a "big crunch." In contrast, if the overall density of matter is too low, then gravity will not be strong enough to stop the overall expansion; the universe will expand forever. If the density of matter is just right, then the force of gravity would just cancel the expansion, like a universal version of the thermodynamic equilibrium of stars. A universe that expands forever is known as an *open universe*. A universe that ultimately contracts is known as a *closed universe*. The seemingly special case of a balanced universe is known as a *flat universe*. Although some observations available before 1998 indicated that we lived in an open universe, other observations indicated we lived in a flat universe, and some theorists insisted we had to live in a closed universe. The Hubble expansion told us that the universe was getting larger at a constant rate. We had only to try to determine

the density of the universe to determine its ultimate fate. Much effort went into this search. The observations are difficult; as a result, the results tended to be uncertain. The best data pointed to a flat universe.

OUR CURRENT UNDERSTANDING

Einstein used his theory of relativity to model the universe. At the time he developed his theory, in the early twentieth century, the accepted cosmological theory allowed for a static universe, one that was not expanding. Because of this, he added a mathematical term to his equations—known as the cosmological constant—to counteract the gravity created by all the matter in the universe. This constant can be thought of as a force that pushes back against gravity, stopping the ultimate collapse of a static universe due to the force of gravity. When it was clearly determined through observations that the universe was expanding (remember Hubble's results in 1929), Einstein quipped that the cosmological constant was his "biggest blunder."

In fact, it wasn't a blunder after all. Two groups of astronomers, pursuing distant supernovae, announced in 1998 that the universe appeared to not be expanding at a constant rate: the expansion was accelerating. Because the supernovae they were studying were known to be of a constant brightness, if the universe were expanding uniformly, then these exploding stars should appear to be a certain brightness in proportion to their distance. However, they were all about 20% dimmer than expected. Immediately, it was thought that the fact that they were dimmer must be caused by some inherent property in supernovae of this type—or at least supernovae that exploded when the universe was younger. However, all studies showed that these supernovae were not inherently dimmer due to some physical property but were dimmer because they were farther away than expected given their measured Doppler shift. This could mean only that the Universe was not expanding over all time at a constant velocity, but, in fact, it was speeding up.

Cosmology was turned on its head. Hubble's law was no longer correct. The universe was not expanding uniformly; it was accelerating. The most obvious way for this to take place is for Einstein's cosmological constant to be nonzero. A nonzero cosmological constant would imply a universal force that accelerates the universe over time by pushing the expansion along faster and faster. This expansion force only has influence over very large scales, so it is not easily detected close by; by studying distant supernovae, its influence becomes detectable. It must be a property of space itself, a kind of "dark energy" that pushes space apart ever faster.

Because we cannot see it and because it is a pervasive energy field throughout the universe, it was dubbed dark energy. The dark matter that we know exists but cannot detect directly (we can detect only its gravitational influence on normal matter) and the dark energy that we have only just determined exists from the supernovae evidence together account for about 96% of the total mass-energy of the universe (remember Einstein's equation, $E = mc^2$, in which energy can be thought of as mass and vice versa). In other words, the normal matter we see—all the stars, dust, and even the planets—make up only about 4% of the total mass-energy of the universe. The remaining 96% is totally unknown to us. Astronomers and cosmologists have their work cut out for them. They must try to deter-

mine just what dark energy is and also what makes up dark matter. It will be a hard job. Neither can be detected directly; each is "seen" only through its influence on normal matter.

Another sticky problem was resolved by the discovery of the accelerating universe. Careful measurements of the ages of stars implied that the very oldest stars we could see were actually older than our best age estimate for the universe, given a uniform Hubble expansion. If the universe's expansion has been accelerating, then it is older than we think—it was expanding at slower rates in the past. Therefore, if the accelerating universe observations are correct, the ages of the stars now better fit with our estimates for the age of the universe (some fourteen billion years), which strengthens the probability that the Big Bang model is right.

Every subsequent check of the observations has confirmed the initial conclusions. We live in an accelerating universe. This also means that the universe we live in is open. It will continue to expand forever and will do so at an ever-increasing rate. This is somewhat disappointing from an aesthetic point of view. As the expansion carries on, the amount of hydrogen in the universe will decrease, and nuclear fusion reactions will finally end. Light from stars and galaxies will fade away. When the last small red stars stop fusing hydrogen into helium and slowly cool, bright stars will no longer twinkle in the skies over planets. Over time, objects will cool and darkness will prevail. Every once in a while, two cold stars could accidentally bump into each other and a flash of light would result, but it would not last long. Over time, galaxies would collapse into massive black holes as gravity wins over shorter scales. The final state of our universe appears to be a place where black holes slowly grow and the universe gets ever larger and colder. It is not a pretty ending, but it is amazing that we can determine our likely universal fate.

Although much work needs to be completed in astronomy before we understand the many fascinating phenomena we see, the general sense of how the universe got to its current state and where it is going now seems to be on pretty solid ground. Even though in science the only certain thing is uncertainty, we know quite a lot about the universe. Some would say that only one question remains. Are we alone in the universe? Right now we have no idea. The basic constituents of the universe are the same that make up our bodies, our air, our water, and our food. Surely, given billions of available stars, ours cannot be the only one that hosts a planet on which life took hold. The odds do not favor a universe where our planet is the sole harbor of life. The next chapter discusses this question—Is anyone out there?—the answer to which is likely to be the last amazing discovery in astronomy.

SUMMARY

Cosmology is the study of the origin, evolution, and ultimate fate of the whole universe. Some basic assumptions allow us to formulate theories on the origin of the universe that can be tested through simple observation. The assumptions are that the universe is isotropic, or the same in all directions, and homogeneous, or roughly uniform in content. We know from observations of galaxies that the further away a galaxy is, the faster it is moving. This Hubble law tells us we live in an expanding universe.

If the universe is expanding, then it must have been very small and hot at some time in the distant past, and we should be able to see emission from this period of time when the universe began its expansion. The cosmic background radiation we see today in the millimeter portion of the electromagnetic spectrum is the signature of the Big Bang, or initial cosmic expansion. This signal comes from a time when the universe became transparent to light. The lumps and bumps in this background radiation are the relatively dense regions of the universe that led to the clusters of galaxies we see today.

The universe, it appears today, will continue expanding forever and will do so more rapidly as time passes. The expansion of our universe is accelerating. This surprising result was actually predicted by Einstein's theory of general relativity, but he felt that it was a nonsensical result and added in a constant to prevent his equations from predicting an expansion. We know today he was correct.

The universe will expand faster and faster with the stars slowly using up their available hydrogen and helium. Ultimately, all light will be absorbed and no new light will be emitted. Mass will slowly coalesce together into giant black holes, making small flashes as they disappear. Our new observations of an accelerating universe lead us to the conclusion that there is a dark energy causing the acceleration, of which we know very little. Our observations of the motions of galaxies tell us that there is dark matter, of which we know very little but whose impact we can see through the force of gravity. In total, we know much about only the very small fraction of the universe that emits light of one wavelength or another. We have much yet to learn.

LIFE IN THE UNIVERSE

One of the most pressing questions facing humanity is whether or not we are alone in the universe. Can it be that of all the stars and planets in our galaxy and all the stars and planets in other galaxies, Earth is the only planet with life? Given the billions of stars in our galaxy and the billions of galaxies in the universe as a whole, it seems impossible that only Earth can host life. Even so, scientists have yet to find life on any other planet in our solar system, let alone life on other planets around other stars. Still, the possibility that life is out there, somewhere, drives researchers to continue to seek the answer to this open question.

By studying life on Earth, its properties, its origins and its evolution, biologists are beginning to understand what conditions are necessary to foster, support, and grow complex life. Astronomers are working to understand the origins of planets, how they change over time, and how these conditions can foster life. In the next hundred years, our observational capabilities may allow us to actually make images of planets around distant stars and study them in some detail. Will we find life, or will we find that we are alone in the universe? Either way, it promises to be interesting.

THE DEFINITION OF LIFE

Before we look for life, we should first define what it is. Even scientists have a hard time with this, but there is general agreement on the definition of life. First, life must reproduce. Trees make seeds, which sprout into new trees; animals have baby animals that grow to become adults; even algae and coral reproduce, making new copies of themselves.

Life must also change with time, or evolve. We know from fossils that dinosaurs once walked the earth, but none are here now. However, we do still have reptiles and birds, distant cousins of the dinosaurs that have slowly changed over generations to become what we see today.

Finally, life must interact with, or respond to, environmental conditions. Sunflowers track the Sun during the day, insects run and hide when they feel vibrations, and even single-celled organisms respond to such environmental surroundings as changes in light.

THE CHEMISTRY OF LIFE

Although life as we know it on Earth is amazingly diverse and complex, the building blocks of life are fairly simple. As we saw in Chapter 13, stars produce the interstellar medium that seeds the galaxies for new stars and planets. The solar system condensed out of such a cloud of matter, a mix of hydrogen, carbon, nitrogen, and oxygen, with smaller amounts of all the other elements.

Earth is about 4.5 billion years old. Geologists report that as early as 4 billion years ago, life had formed on Earth. When it first formed, the solar system was a much more violent place. Asteroids and comets smashed into Earth much more often. The comets brought water, forming Earth's oceans, and asteroids caused destruction, spewing heated gas, dust, and rocks down upon the newly formed Earth, along with the basic building blocks for complex organic (carbon containing) molecules: carbon, nitrogen, oxygen, and hydrogen. Comets, too, brought these basic ingredients.

THE ORIGIN OF LIFE

The early Earth was not a pleasant place. The Moon was much closer to Earth, causing tides of perhaps 1000 ft, instead of just the few feet we experience today. The Sun was significantly dimmer, providing much less light. Asteroids hit Earth much more frequently. Although not an ideal environment for us, it did allow life, however primitive, to take hold.

The exact origin of life is uncertain, because few clues remain from so long ago. But scientists have a good idea of the required ingredients. First, we need water. All life as we know it requires liquid water. Second, we need organic molecules. (*Organic molecules* are simply molecules that contain carbon.) Finally, we require some sort of energy to have life. Heat from undersea volcanic vents, light from the Sun, or energy from lightning strikes are all valid forms of potentially life-giving energy.

So, water, organic molecules, and energy are the necessary conditions for life. Anywhere we find these conditions on Earth, we find life. Perhaps if we find these same conditions on a distant planet around a distant star, we will also find life. Organic molecules make up the proteins that we find in all life forms on Earth today. There are huge numbers of organic molecules and many ways in which these molecules can interact chemically. It is this complexity of form and interaction that ultimately led to life as we know it. Scientists now think that the first life-related organic molecules, called *amino acids*, formed in the watery soup that was the early Earth's oceans or in a type of mineral deposit known as iron sulphide; the exact location and conditions are under active debate. Scientists now believe that 20 basic amino acids are the fundamental building blocks of all life. The interactions of just 20 molecules lead to all the complexity of life we see—trees, slugs, birds, algae, moss, and even ourselves. Thus we can define life as self-replicating, evolving, and interacting organized matter.

NEW THEORY

A report in the science journal *Nature* in 2004 presented a new theory regarding life's first foothold. This new theory has identified deposits of iron sulphide, a fairly common mineral, on the early Earth as the cradle of life. Iron sulphide deposits can form networks of honeycomb-like pockets. These pockets can then provide a place for complex molecules to interact and take up other molecules from the iron sulphide walls. Protected in a permeable shell of iron sulphide, the first cells could have formed from a soup of amino acids, water, and nutrient minerals. This interesting new theory could hold the key to our future understanding, but it must be rigorously tested before the idea is accepted.

We also find that all life passes on genetic information from generation to generation in the form of RNA and DNA. These complex molecules, known as *nucleic acids* (the "NA" of DNA and RNA), are composed of smaller molecules known as nucleotides. There are only four types of nucleotides; these are strung together in patterns along the RNA and DNA molecules. The patterns provide instructions at the cellular level for the formation of proteins needed by a particular organism. If it seems complicated, it is! The origin of life is an area of active research at the very cutting edge of science. Active scientific debate and research is ongoing, and we have to be ready to adjust our understanding as new results become accepted.

Although scientists are not sure how, at some point simple, single-celled life formed that contained genetic information in the form of DNA and was able to replicate itself. This led to simple bacteria, tiny single-celled life forms, and, eventually, the almost infinite diversity we see today. Importantly, due to a number of causes (such as radiation damage or just replication mistakes), the genetic information is not passed on perfectly from generation to generation. This means that there is always a chance of mutation, differences between each generation that can allow slow change, or evolution, to take place.

Even though these mutated changes are small, with enough time new organisms can be formed. Each family of organisms is generally called a species. Some have argued that the concept of species is outdated and represents our short lifespan, which can encompass only the briefest of periods here on Earth. Each life form alive today is connected to the first life on Earth and, therefore, to all other life forms, but few of the life forms alive today existed when life first began or even a billion years later. Each species is transitory, changing slowly over the millennia. Humans have arrived late on the scene to see a complex world of interrelated organisms that seem permanent and fixed from our perspective. Looking over the course of four billion years, we see that no species is permanent.

LIFE IN OTHER PLACES: RARE OR COMMON?

Given that the basic building blocks of life are fairly common and that the basic needs of life—water, organic molecules, and energy—are not too hard to get, shouldn't the universe be teeming with life? Perhaps it is. The recently established field of astrobiology seeks to answer this question while also learning more about the formation of life here on Earth.

When thinking about life in the universe, most people think only about intelligent life in the universe. Given that for most of Earth's history, bacteria ruled supreme, it is probably more likely we would find bacteria-like creatures than humans like ourselves. Just how likely is it that we will find intelligent life?

We can make a good guess by looking at the various occurrences that led to life on Earth and estimating how many other planets in our own galaxy (or the universe, though we would be hard-pressed to communicate with anybody outside of our own galaxy due to the great distance). Frank Drake (1930–), a pioneering radio astronomer, undertook just such an analysis and developed an equation, now known as the Drake equation, that guides our thinking about the possibility of finding life.

The *Drake Equation* is a chain of numbers that, when multiplied, gives us an estimate of the number of planets in our galaxy with intelligent life. It looks like this:

$$N_p = (R*) * (P_p) * (P_e) * (N_e) * (P_l) * (P_i) * (L_i)$$

Let's look at each piece of the equation. N_p is the number of planets in the Galaxy with intelligent life. $R*$ is the rate of star formation in the galaxy. This rate is usually averaged over the whole history of the Galaxy and is a number that astronomers are beginning to pin down. It is the most well-established figure in the equation. P_p is the probability of a given star forming planets. P_e is the probability that the star lasts long enough to allow life to form on the planet. N_e is the number of planets around this star that form at a distance from its host star where liquid water can exist. P_l is the probability of life forming on one of the planets in the habitable zone. P_i is the probability of intelligent life arising on the planet, and, finally, L_i is the lifetime of an intelligent civilization. Estimates of all of these values lead to guesses on the number of planets in our galaxy hosting life. The number ranges from just one (us!) to many millions, with a best-guess value of about 10,000 or so. We need not be too concerned, however; it is doubtful any are our next door neighbors. The Milky Way, our home galaxy, is more than 100,000 light years across and several thousand thick in the disk, and tens of thousands of light years thick in the central bulge. Spreading even 10,000 planets with possible intelligent life across that vast space means any two of them are very far apart. The number of planets with life in any form, not just intelligent life that we can communicate with, would be much larger.

Until the 1990s, we had no idea that planets even existed beyond our solar system. Now, thanks to the dedicated work of a few individuals, we know that planets exist around other stars. Already astronomers have detected more than 100 *extra-solar planets* (planets not located around our Sun), but none are like Earth. The techniques employed to find these planets favor the detection of large gas giants such as Jupiter or Saturn. However, future NASA missions will address the search for terrestrial planets like the Earth, which are much harder to see due to their smaller size.

COMMUNICATING WITH LIFE ELSEWHERE

If we do ever find life in the universe, especially intelligent life, we will certainly try to communicate with it. Some may question this effort, or even seek to prevent it, but it is a fundamental part of our character to want to share our knowledge and to hope to gain more. Can we ever hope to communicate with life elsewhere?

Just as distant objects in the universe can be seen here on Earth in both optical and radio light, we can also potentially send signals using these wavelengths. Each and every day we take advantage of radio light to send communication signals across great distances. The 21-year-old Italian Guglielmo Marconi (1874–1937) discovered radio communication in 1895. The self-taught scientist had experimented with electromagnetic equipment and convinced himself that signals could be transmitted a great distance by using a transmitter and a receiver. After initial experiments over very short distances, Marconi separated his transmitter and receiver by about 3 km, with a small hill in between. He had a servant stand at the receiver while he worked the transmitter. His servant had a rifle and was to fire the gun when he received the signal (a kind of clicking sound). Marconi fiddled with his transmission equipment and soon heard the rifle shot from behind the hill. Radio communication was born.

Radio communications quickly developed into a growth industry and many scientists and engineers worked to improve its capabilities. Ultimately, Marconi was able to send radio waves across the Atlantic Ocean, and today we now have radios in every car and home capable of receiving radio signals from distant transmitters, some thousands of miles away. But we can communicate further than that. Right now, the *Voyager 1* spacecraft is about 7 billion miles from the Sun, speeding away at about 325 million miles per year. Even at this distance, we can still communicate with the spacecraft. It carries a small radio transmitter and uses a high-performance antenna that is pointed back toward Earth. As long as it has power, we will still be able to communicate with it. This shows the power of radio communications.

Can we communicate with intelligent life elsewhere today? The Arecibo radio telescope in Puerto Rico is equipped with transmission equipment used originally as radar to investigate nearby planets and asteroids. It has tried sending signals toward other stars likely to host life like here on Earth (planets seemingly at the right location and perhaps with the right conditions—see the Drake equation). We are quite certain that any other Arecibo-like telescope in the galaxy would be able to communicate with our Arecibo if they happened to be pointing at each other at just the right time. The chances are extremely slim that this would occur, so most researchers working to communicate with intelligent life elsewhere in the galaxy spend their time listening.

A few years ago a computer phenomenon swept across the Internet, a desktop screen saver called SETI@HOME, which let amateur investigators help search for extraterrestrial communications by using spare computing cycles on their machines. With millions of people downloading the program, the organizers at the SETI (Search for Extraterrestrial Intelligence) Institute were hard-pressed to provide enough data for people to analyze. This shows just how exciting the possibility of detecting life is to the average person. You can still download the screensaver from the SETI Institute (www.seti.org) or get involved at a more technical level with the SETI League (www.setileague.org).

Some worry about what we will say to another intelligent species. We should be more concerned with understanding each other. Although significant effort has gone into designing first messages, there is no guaranteeing that either species will understand each other. Also, given the huge distances between us, it will be a challenge to learn from each other. Just knowing that some other beings are out there could be somehow comforting. One thing is certain: the detection of life, especially intelligent life, will be the most remarkable astronomical discovery of our civilization.

SUMMARY

As far as we know life exists only on Earth. Life can reproduce, changes over time and responds to environmental conditions. Life as we know it is based around the element carbon and relies on the presence of liquid water.

The origin of life on Earth is uncertain. However it got started, life needs water, energy and certain complex chemical molecules known as amino acids. These items were all present on the early Earth. Because the basic ingredients of life as we know it are fairly common in the universe, we expect that life is common, but we cannot verify this hypothesis. The Drake equation is a way of trying to estimate the number of planets with intelligent life in the universe. Each of the terms in the Drake equation is uncertain, so it can be used only to roughly estimate the number of planets with intelligent life.

Astronomers have discovered planets around other stars. Already, more than 100 extra-solar planets are known to exist. We still do not know if any of them harbor life or even if they can harbor life. It may eventually be possible to communicate with life on remote planets through radio wavelengths, but so far we have not found any signals from other life forms.

The telescope is one of the most fundamental tools of the astronomer. In its simplest form—two simple lenses—a telescope can enable astronomers to gather more light and with much better resolution than the human eye.

TYPES OF TELESCOPE

There are two fundamental kinds of telescope, the refractor and the reflector. Refractors use lenses to bend, or refract, light, whereas reflectors use mirrors to reflect light, sometimes employing lenses as well. Both have benefits and drawbacks.

Refracting Telescopes

Refractors are usually less expensive. This makes them the default telescope of choice for most amateurs, although a lower-end reflector can be priced competitively. Refractors of modest size can be used to view the planets, the moon, stars of many types, including binary stars, and, if large enough, fainter objects.

Figure A1.1 shows a cutaway view of a standard refracting telescope. A lens is mounted in the front of a long, hollow tube. The length of the tube is dictated by the focal length of the lens, which can also affect the quality of images the telescope provides. Light from a distant object enters the lens, which bends the light to a focus. Placing another lens at the opposite end of the tube will magnify the image produced at the focus of the main lens.

Refractors have one major drawback that seriously hinders their ability to perform research work and explains why reflecting telescopes are the telescope of choice for most professional research. The problem is known as

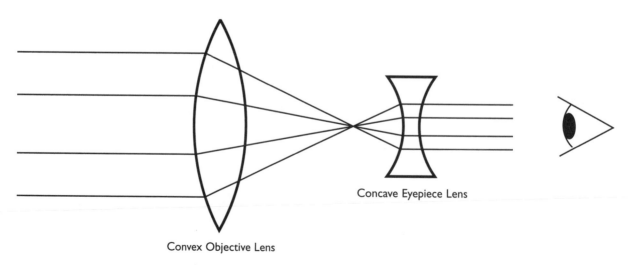

Concave Eyepiece Lens

Convex Objective Lens

Figure A1.1—A Simple Refracting Telescope

chromatic aberration, and it is a simple effect of the refractive properties of glass. Refraction through a given material differs slightly as a function of wavelength. Red light is focused slightly further away from the objective lens than blue light, leading to a slight blurring of images made with refracting telescopes. The problem is increased with greater-diameter lenses and also for objects further away from the center of the telescope's field of view.

Different solutions to this problem have been developed, such as the achromatic lens, which has an additional optical element, the achromat, inserted in the optical path to compensate for this slight focus difference. But every insertion of optical elements leads to scattered or lost light, and astronomers need every photon they can possibly gather. This is why most professionals prefer reflecting telescopes.

Finally, making very large lenses is exceedingly difficult. The glass must be free of air bubbles, something that is hard to achieve in large lenses even today. Air bubbles in the glass disrupt the traveling light and cause image errors and lost light. The lens must also be very strong. Because lenses in telescopes are supported by their outside edge, the glass must be strong enough to support the lens' own weight at the thinnest portion of the lens. These two factors taken together have limited the largest refracting telescope lenses to about 40 in. The most famous large refractor, which is still used for research, is the Yerkes 40-in. telescope, located near Williams Bay, Wisconsin. Its construction was completed in May 1897. (See Figure A1.2.)

Reflecting Telescopes

Attempting to solve the problem of chromatic aberration in telescopes, Sir Isaac Newton developed the reflecting telescope in 1668. Now called a Newtonian reflector in honor of this most famous physicist, it is still one of the simplest telescopes to design and build and also one of the least expensive telescopes to purchase.

By using a mirror instead of a lens, all light reflecting off the surface is brought to a focus at the same spot, unlike in refracting telescopes. Additionally, because mirrors are easier to make than lenses in most cases, larger mirrors can be purchased for the same cost as a smaller lens. More light means being able to study fainter objects, as most amateurs opt for a reflecting telescope.

Quality reflecting telescopes can be found for less than $250; at prices much less than this, telescope quality can make observing difficult. Many amateurs build their own reflecting telescopes, some even polishing their own mirrors as part of the process. Although this can take much time and effort, it can ultimately be cheaper than a purchased telescope and also be much more rewarding. Imagine observing the Andromeda galaxy, 2.2 million light years away, through a telescope you have built using a mirror that you slowly polished.

Photo courtesy of Alan B. Whiting

Figure A1.2—Yerkes Observatory, the Largest Refractor

A useful quantity for gauging different telescopes, both refracting and reflecting, is the so-called *f*-ratio. The *f*-ratio is the ratio of the lens size to its focal length (or for reflecting telescopes, the mirror diameter). The smaller the *f*-ratio, the closer to the lens the light is focused and the more compact the image is, concentrating the light in a smaller area and making a brighter image. Larger *f*-ratios produce larger, but fainter, images. Large f-ratio telescopes are typically used for observing planets, the Sun or comets, whereas small *f*-ratio telescopes are used to gather light from very faint objects.

Many amateurs debate endlessly the proper size and the proper *f*-ratio for a telescope. For general observations, a good compromise is often best, and I recommend a telescope with an *f*-ratio between 4 and 6 (often written *f*/4 to *f*/6). This range of values is a good compromise for both planets and faint objects. Many refractors, however, have much larger f-ratios. If you hope to see very faint objects, an *f*-ratio much larger than *f*/8 with a small-diameter lens (or mirror) will make it difficult.

TYPES OF TELESCOPE MOUNT

Once you have selected a telescope, the next choice is the kind of mount to use. Telescope mounts enable you to direct the telescope toward an object in the sky. They sometimes have motors that allow skywatchers to track objects as they slowly move across the sky.

The simplest mount is known as a Dobsonian mount, after its inventor, John Dobson (1915 -), an enthusiastic amateur astronomer and knowledgeable lecturer (Figure A1.3). Dobson still enjoys going to star parties and is one of the founders of an organization

known as the Sidewalk Astronomers, who work to bring the joy of observing the heavens to city-dwellers. A Dobsonian mount can be thought of as a lazy Susan and a cannon mount. The mount has many advantages, such as inexpensive construction, ease of use, stability, and reliability. There are some drawbacks, such as difficulty in using motors to drive the telescope automatically and reliable alignment, but for simply enjoying the views of the night sky, it is the best choice for a beginner.

The second major type of telescope mount is the alt-az mount (short for altitude-azimuth),

Photo courtesy of Teeter's Telescopes and Rob Teeter

Figure A1.3—A Dobsonian Telescope Mount

which is similar in style to the Dobsonian but mounted above the ground on a tripod. The mount can rotate in two directions: along the horizontal axis, called the azimuth, and the elevational axis, from the horizon up to the zenith, straight overhead. This mount has some disadvantages. First, the eyepiece can bang into the tripod legs when you look at objects close to straight overhead. Second, it is difficult to motorize these mounts so they can accurately track objects in the sky. Still, since most inexpensive telescopes come with this kind of mount, it is usually the first mount that amateurs will encounter. It is also the mount that most professional telescopes are now built with. (See Figure A1.4.)

The third major mount is the equatorial mount. The equatorial mount is similar to an alt-az mount, except that one of the axes is aligned parallel to the Earth's rotation axis, which enables accurate tracking of the sky by simply moving that axis with a small motor (Fig. A1.5). The other axis, although it does allow adjustment, is locked into position once the object of interest is centered in the eyepiece. These mounts have one drawback: they must be accurately aligned with Earth's rotation axis and adjusted for the latitude of the telescope location to function properly. Adjusting for latitude is fairly easy, but the polar alignment of the telescope can be time consuming and difficult. Modern "go-to"

Photo courtesy of NOAO/AURA/NSF

Figure A1.4—A Telescope on an Altitude Azimuth Mount

Photo courtesy of NOAO/CTIO/AURA/NSF

Figure A1.5—An Equatorial Telescope Mount

telescopes have greatly simplified this process by doing polar alignment automatically with a small computer and using motors on both axes to move the telescope. In the older design, the mount was custom made or adjusted for the latitude of the telescope. Equatorial mounts are greatly preferred by astrophotographers, because their motion can be more easily controlled than other mounts, making long exposures without blurring easier to obtain.

EYEPIECES

The eyepiece is where your eye and the telescope intersect. Eyepieces come in many designs and styles. Some have special coatings to minimize lost light or special optical elements to reduce chromatic aberration or to make the field-of-view distortion free. One key for the beginner astronomer is the ability to magnify objects seen with the telescope. Eyepieces do this, and the focal length of the eyepiece is the key factor. Eyepieces with smaller focal lengths will produce more magnified images for a given telescope. There is a formula to determine the magnification produced by a given telescope and eyepiece. The magnification is simply equal to the ratio of the focal length of the primary to the focal length of the eyepiece ($M = F/f$). For example, a telescope with a 100 in. focal length and an eyepiece with a 10 in. focal length would produce a magnification of 10, usually abbreviated 10×.

There are other eyepiece properties that play an important role in determining the quality of the image. First and foremost is the field of view. This is the amount of sky, in angular measure, that is seen in the eyepiece. The field of view for a given eyepiece is equal to the apparent field of view (quoted by eyepiece manufacturers) divided by the magnification.

Given the preceding example of the 10¥ telescope-eyepiece pair, let's assume that the eyepiece has a 30° apparent field of view. Use on the telescope described gives a real field of view of 30°/10, or 3°.

The eye relief of a lens is also important. Eye relief is the distance from your eye above the eyepiece where you can see the largest field of view. It is a bit difficult to calculate, but eyepiece manufacturers always provide this information for their eyepieces. If the eye relief is too small, you have to hold your eye very close to the lens, possibly knocking the telescope off source. If the eye relief is too large, it is hard to line your eye up with the light from the lens. Also, if you wear glasses, the eye relief has to be at least large enough to accommodate your glasses.

With all these variables, it is easy to understand why so many different kinds of eyepieces are available. There are also other accessories that can be used with small telescopes to improve the view. One of the most common is the Barlow lens, which simply introduces a single divergent lens before the actual eyepiece. This extra lens usually provides an increase in magnification by a factor of 2 or 3 by effectively increasing the distance necessary to bring the light that has passed through the objective to a focus.

Although the Barlow lens is a good addition to the toolkit of the serious amateur, beginners should sink more of their available funds into a larger objective or better mount. These have a far greater impact on the quality of viewing. A bigger objective means more light gathered and a brighter object. It also means better resolution. A better mount will make the telescope more stable, reducing wobble in the wind, and also make the telescope more functional.

COORDINATE SYSTEMS

Coordinate systems are the maps of the sky. Unlike land-based maps, which use longitude and latitude almost exclusively for positioning purposes, there are many coordinate systems used in astronomy. The two of interest to most beginners are the altitude-azimuth system and the equatorial system. Both have their uses, and it is good to be familiar with both.

The altitude-azimuth system is centered on the observer. As the observer looks around, the horizon is in the distance no matter where he or she looks. If the observer were at sea, the horizon would be more or less flat and appear to trace a large circle, with the observer at the center. Azimuth measures the angular distance around this circle, with 0° straight north, 90° straight east, 180° straight south, and 270° straight west. The other coordinate is altitude, which measures the angular distance from the horizon to the object in the sky. Straight overhead is 90°, and the horizon is 0°. To locate an object in this system, you simply draw an imaginary line straight down from the object to the horizon and measure the angular distance. If you hold your fist at arm's length, it takes up about 10° of sky. A finger is about 1°. Then measure the angular distance from one of the cardinal directions (N, S, E, W) to the point on the horizon below the object. This is the azimuth.

The altitude and azimuth of objects in the sky are constantly changing. Objects rise and set and move across the sky between these two events. This is one of the disadvantages of the coordinate system, but it is very useful for quickly directing other nearby observers to an object in the sky.

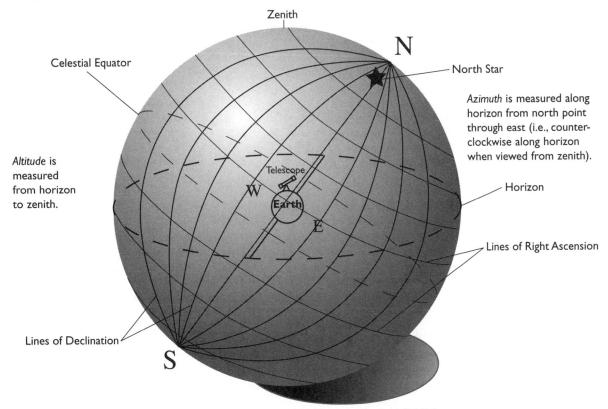

Figure A1.6—Azimuth and Altitude on the Celestial Sphere

USING STAR CHARTS

The sky changes during the night. To be specific, objects rise in the east and set in the west. By knowing the season and the time, you can use a star chart to find objects in the sky.

Star Hopping

Star hopping is a method used by amateurs to quickly find objects of interest in the sky. The basic method involves locating the object you want to see on a star chart and then identifying bright stars you can easily see with your naked eye that will lead you closer and closer to the object. As an example, let's use some bright stars to find a faint nebula known as the Ring Nebula. The Ring Nebula resides in the constellation Lyra. Luckily, Lyra contains an extremely bright star, the brightest in the Northern hemisphere, named Vega. Vega is up high in the sky in the fall and easy to find. Go outside pretty much any fall night and look toward the west. If you scan upward from the horizon, you will find a brilliant blue-white star, which is Vega. Once you have found Vega you will see a triangle of stars. The other two stars in the triangle are Beta and Gamma Lyra, and about halfway between the two is where the Ring Nebula can be found. Point your binoculars or telescope at Vega; then move it to either Beta or Gamma Lyra, and then slowly scan to the other of these two stars. By carefully paying attention to the field of view you will be able to find the Ring Nebula. It appears bright with binoculars, but you'll need a telescope to begin to see the ringlike shape. Star hopping can be used effectively to find a whole range of objects, and all you need is a good star map and some careful thought. The star charts provided in this book are good enough to find some objects this way, but you will need more extensive charts to find fainter objects easily.

THE CONSTELLATIONS

The constellations are one of the first things everyone learns about the sky. Most people know the constellation Orion or can identify the Big Dipper, part of the constellation Ursa Majoris. The constellations were originally used to tell stories.

One fact that would surprise the ancients who originally conjured the constellations is that they are not permanent. As the stars move over very long periods of time, the constellations will change too. Eventually Orion will not look like the striking hunter it is now, but perhaps it will resemble some other creature, person, or object.

Constellations are now defined not by the stars and the patterns that they make in the sky, but by internationally agreed-upon boundaries in the sky. Here is a list of the 88 official constellations.

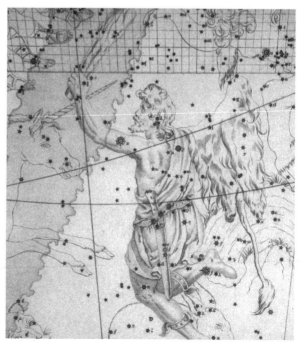

Photo courtesy of Michael Oates

Figure A1.7—Orion

Constellation Name	Genitive Form of Name	English Name	Hemisphere
Andromeda	Andromedae	Andromeda	NH
Antlia	Antliae	Air Pump	SH
Apus	Apodis	Bird of Paradise	SH
Aquarius	Aquarii	Water Carrier	SH
Aquila	Aquilae	Eagle	NH–SH
Ara	Arae	Altar	SH
Aries	Arietis	Ram	NH
Auriga	Aurigae	Charioteer	NH
Bootes	Bootis	Herdsman	NH
Caelum	Caeli	Chisel	SH
Camelopardalis	Camelopardalis	Giraffe	NH
Cancer	Cancri	Crab	NH
Canes Venatici	Canun Venaticorum	Hunting Dogs	NH
Canis Major	Canis Majoris	Big Dog	SH
Canis Minor	Canis Minoris	Little Dog	NH
Capricornus	Capricorni	Goat (Capricorn)	SH
Carina	Carinae	Keel	SH
Cassiopeia	Cassiopeiae	Cassiopeia	NH
Centaurus	Centauri	Centaur	SH
Cepheus	Cephei	Cepheus	SH
Cetus	Ceti	Whale	SH
Chamaeleon	Chamaeleontis	Chameleon	SH
Circinus	Circini	Compasses	SH
Columba	Columbae	Dove	SH
Coma Berenices	Comae Berenices	Berenice's Hair	NH
Corona Australis	Coronae Australis	Southern Crown	SH
Corona Borealis	Coronae Borealis	Northern Crown	NH
Corvus	Corvi	Crow	SH
Crater	Crateris	Cup	SH

Constellation Name	Genitive Form of Name	English Name	Hemisphere
Crux	Crucis	Southern Cross	SH
Cygnus	Cygni	Swan	NH
Delphinus	Delphini	Dolphin	NH
Dorado	Doradus	Goldfish	SH
Draco	Draconis	Dragon	NH
Equuleus	Equulei	Little Horse	NH
Eridanus	Eridani	River	SH
Fornax	Fornacis	Furnace	SH
Gemini	Geminorum	Twins	NH
Grus	Gruis	Crane	SH
Hercules	Herculis	Hercules	NH
Horologium	Horologii	Clock	SH
Hydra	Hydrae	Hydra (Sea Serpent)	SH
Hydrus	Hydri	Water Serpent (male)	SH
Indus	Indi	Indian	SH
Lacerta	Lacertae	Lizard	NH
Leo	Leonis	Lion	NH
Leo Minor	Leonis Minoris	Smaller Lion	NH
Lepus	Leporis	Hare	SH
Libra	Librae	Balance	SH
Lupus	Lupi	Wolf	SH
Lynx	Lyncis	Lynx	NH
Lyra	Lyrae	Lyre	NH
Mensa	Mensae	Table	SH
Microscopium	Microscopii	Microscope	SH
Monoceros	Monocerotis	Unicorn	SH
Musca	Muscae	Fly	SH
Norma	Normae	Square	SH
Octans	Octantis	Octant	SH

Constellation Name	Genitive Form of Name	English Name	Hemisphere
Ophiucus	Ophiuchi	Serpent Holder	NH–SH
Orion	Orionis	Orion	NH–SH
Pavo	Pavonis	Peacock	SH
Pegasus	Pegasi	Winged Horse	NH
Perseus	Persei	Perseus	NH
Phoenix	Phoenicis	Phoenix	SH
Pictor	Pictoris	Easel	SH
Pisces	Piscium	Fishes	NH
Pisces Austrinus	Pisces Austrini	Southern Fish	SH
Puppis	Puppis	Stern	SH
Pyxis	Pyxidis	Compass	SH
Reticulum	Reticuli	Reticule	SH
Sagitta	Sagittae	Arrow	NH
Sagittarius	Sagittarii	Archer	SH
Scorpius	Scorpii	Scorpion	SH
Sculptor	Sculptoris	Sculptor	SH
Scutum	Scuti	Shield	SH
Serpens	Serpentis	Serpent	NH–SH
Sextans	Sextantis	Sextant	SH
Taurus	Tauri	Bull	NH
Telescopium	Telescopii	Telescope	SH
Triangulum	Trianguli	Triangle	NH
Triangulum Australe	Trianguli Australis	Southern Triangle	SH
Tucana	Tucanae	Toucan	SH
Ursa Major	Ursae Majoris	Great Bear	NH
Ursa Minor	Ursae Minoris	Little Bear	NH
Vela	Velorum	Sails	SH
Virgo	Virginis	Virgin	NH–SH
Volans	Volantis	Flying Fish	SH
Vulpecula	Vulpeculae	Fox	NH

PROJECTS

Before the advent of photography, astronomers sketched what they saw in observing notebooks; amateurs today should still try this enjoyable pastime. Purchase a quality sketch book, trace circles on the paper representing the field of view of the telescope, and include room beside the circle for recording the date and time of the observations, along with supporting details (such as weather conditions or quality of the seeing).

A more advanced step is to try astrophotography. This is a fairly complicated activity and requires some relatively expensive equipment, but it can be highly rewarding. A high-quality 35 mm camera, with a special attachment for controlling the shutter, is essential. The camera must have a "B" exposure setting, or bulb setting, that allows the shutter to remain open until the shutter release is activated. Second, you need a camera mounting system to connect your camera to your telescope. This usually involves the purchase of a T-ring and a camera adapter. The T-ring allows the camera to be screwed into the camera adapter, which connects to the telescope where the eyepiece is normally mounted. Finally, for even the brightest celestial objects, the telescope must be properly balanced and tracking the sky using high precision motors. This will allow faint objects to be photographed without blurring. Many astrophotographers purchase special film, filters, or other devices to enhance their hobby, but what is needed most is a dark location and protection from wind.

Another way to enjoy astrophotography is to mount a camera, with or without a telephoto lens, to the tube of your telescope and use the telescope as a motorized mount to take long exposures of a portion of the sky. This method produces great images, particularly of large-scale objects such as our own galaxy, the Milky Way, its dust lanes, and its star fields.

Another way to record images is with a CCD camera. A few years ago these were prohibitively expensive and were used only by professionals, but with the advent of CCDs in digital cameras and video recorders, the prices dropped, and they are now regularly used in telescopic cameras. They also must be connected to the telescope using a special mounting system (usually supplied by the manufacturer) and be connected to a computer for control and storage of the captured images. The beauty of these devices is their ease of use, high sensitivity (many times more sensitive than even the best film), and reliability. For those who wish to pursue even more serious observations, they are ideal for scientific data gathering because they respond linearly to increased brightness, as opposed to film, which responds in a nonlinear fashion. This makes the images taken with a CCD scientifically useful. Many amateurs are pursuing research with CCDs, and many books are available with more information. They can be found on the Internet or by contacting your local librarian.

Last, but not least, are two specialized instruments that some amateurs enjoy using. The first is the so-called photomultiplier tube, or photometer (Figure A1.8). Used by

Photo courtesy of Michael Fletcher, OH2AUE

Figure A1.8—A Typical Photomultiplier Tube

professionals in the 1960s and even sometimes today, this device is a highly sensitive device that uses the photoelectric effect to greatly multiply light from a celestial object hitting a metal surface. They're limited in that they do not provide images; instead, they simply supply counts that are proportional to the amount of light gathered in a given period of time, but they are easy to use and can effectively measure star brightness with minimal effort. They are also relatively expensive and difficult to learn to operate properly, but the results they produce can be rewarding.

The second instrument is a spectrograph. Initially developed in the mid-1800s, these devices were rarely used by amateurs until recently, when larger telescopes became more affordable. Spectrographs take light gathered by a telescope and disperse, or spread, it so that the different colors can be seen separately. It is fairly simple to detect differences in light from different stars by comparing their spectrographs. One very active amateur spectroscopist is Maurice Gavin, who lives in England. His technique and his scientific results can be found online at http://www.astroman.fsnet.co.uk/spectro.htm.

DOING MORE IN ASTRONOMY

With the increased availability and ever-lower prices for telescopes, binoculars and other astronomy-related equipment, it is easier than ever to study the heavens. Amateurs make interesting discoveries each and every day, and some of these discoveries rival research results produced by professionals.

In 2001, for example, South African amateur astronomer Berto Monard discovered a new supernova in a galaxy known as NGC 1448. Here is an excerpt of an e-mail he sent to an Internet news group of fellow amateur astronomers who study variable stars (VSNET is the Variable Star Network, SN is supernova, IAU is International Astronomical Union, and UT is Universal Time):

From: Berto Monard
Sent: 19 September 2001 12:10

Subject: SN in NGC 1448

Dear VSNET and other observers,
I have pleasure in announcing my first visual supernova discovery, which has been con-firmed since. The SN will have to be named still by IAU, hopefully later today.

The following details apply:
Galaxy: NGC 1448 at position 03 44 32 -44 39
The position of this relatively bright supernova (suspect) in this relatively nearby galaxy (approx 15 Mpc) is about 15" North and 9" West of the galaxy nucleus. From this position it is not clear if it belongs to the disk or the bulge. Improved positions and descriptions will be announced in the circular.

There is a 14.8 V (approx) foreground star just to the North of the SN suspect.
My most recent observations of NGC 1448 in UT:

20010825.96 <14.6V
20010917.064 14.5V
20010917.108 14.5V
20010917.930 14.3V

Since then clouds have taken over here but I received reports that the SN has brightened further.
Enjoy your observations.
Kind regards,
Berto Monard
Pretoria

Notice that the first thing Berto did was announce that he made the discovery. He then provided details on where the supernova was located in the sky and details about how bright he measured the supernova to be. Finally, he notes that clouds have moved over his observatory and that astronomers else-where had let him know that it was getting brighter. Careful observation and the record-ing and distribution of information are the hallmarks of astronomy research.

Berto's experience is just a small example of the exciting world of amateur astronomy. There are thousands of people worldwide who regularly undertake astronomy projects and even publish their work in professional astronomical journals.

EASY PROJECTS

Sketching the Phases of the Moon

Many people take for granted that the moon goes through phases, making a full cycle in about a month. But just how long does it take? An interesting project is to determine through observations the amount of time it takes the moon to complete a cycle of phases.

To perform this experiment, start an observation notebook and record, each day or two for two to three months, the phase of the moon. Make a series of small circles in your book by tracing around a nickel to make a smooth line. Then shade in the circles to match the phase of the moon you observe. Remember that the moon is sometimes up in the daytime or early morning, not just at nighttime. Once you have 3 months of observation recorded, see if you can figure out how many days it takes the moon to complete a cycle of phases.

Tracking the Planets

The planets visible to the naked eye (Mercury, Venus, Mars, Jupiter, and Saturn) can be easily tracked over time relative to the stars. The word planet comes from an ancient Greek term meaning wanderer. A fun activity that does not require a telescope or binoculars is to follow the motion of the planets over time.

To begin, get a set of star charts that show you where the planets are. Two good sources are astronomy magazines and the Internet. Once you have found a planet (start by using Venus or Jupiter because they are usually easier to see), make a sketch of the planet showing its relationship to nearby bright stars. Instead of sketching the stars, you could make photocopies or printouts of star charts and plot the position of the planet in question on the chart itself.

As time progresses, you will build up an interesting chart that may begin to look something like Figure A2.1.

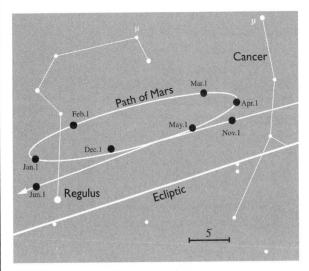

Figure A2.1—Retrograde Motion of Mars as Seen from Earth

This motion, in which a planet appears to move backward in the sky for a short period of time, was very difficult for early astronomers to explain. This is because they believed that Earth was at the center of the solar system. However, because Earth is actually in orbit around the Sun along with the rest of the planets, we occasionally catch up and pass a planet. This passage makes the planet appear to move backward for a short period of time (as we begin to move past the planet) and then begin to move again in the same direction it was originally seen to be moving. (See Figure A2.2.)

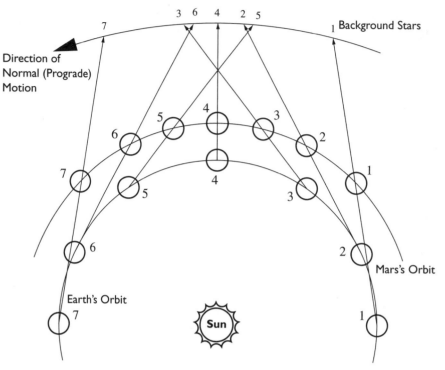

Figure A2.2—Retrograde Motion Looking Down on the Top of the Solar System

One note of caution: the retrograde motion takes place roughly once a year and is most dramatic for Mars, a planet further from the Sun than us, yet the closest to us. The effect is decreased for planets further away, such as Jupiter and Saturn. The planets closer to the Sun than Earth do not show retrograde motion.

Stellar Variability

A number of stars change brightness in easily observable ways. In fact, the first so-called variable star was discovered by David Fabricius, a German, in 1596. Its period was not accurately determined until 1638 by a fellow German, Johann Holwarda. The star is easily visible in binoculars and detailed charts to find it are available through the American Association of Variable Star Observers (AAVSO; details follow). However, some stars that vary in brightness are easily seen by eye. The best example is a star known

as Algol, an Arabic name that means "the demon's head." The star is also known as the winking demon because it dims dramatically every 68.75 h.

To undertake the project, go out every clear night and locate the constellation Perseus. The finder chart in Figure A2.3, from the American Association of Variable Star Observers (see bottom of image), shows the location of Perseus relative to the constellation Cassiopeia and points out the location of Algol, also known as Beta Persei.

Use the AAVSO chart to compare its brightness to the two nearby stars labeled [Alpha] and [Delta]. Alpha is slightly brighter than Algol at its maximum brightness, whereas Delta is just a bit brighter than Algol at its minimum brightness. (Note: the numbers next to some of the labeled stars indicate their magnitudes. [Alpha] is magnitude 1.8; [Delta]

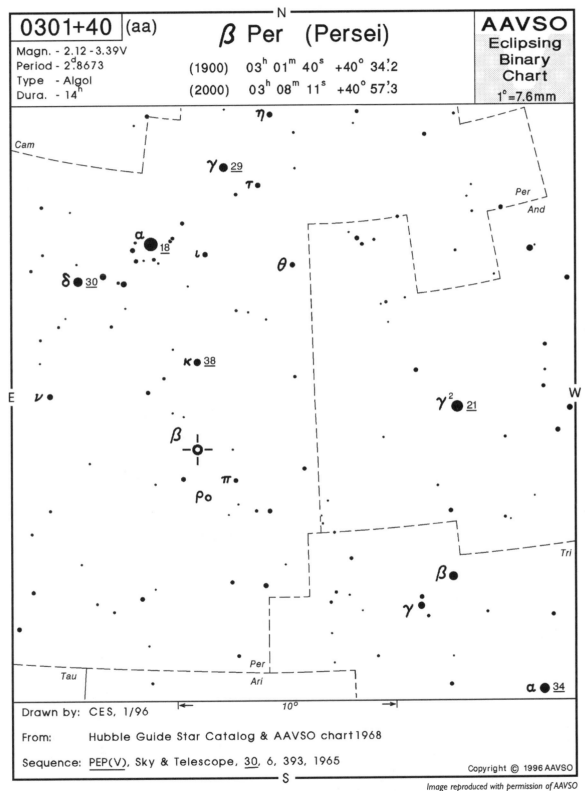

0301+40 (aa)	β Per (Persei)	AAVSO

Magn. - 2.12 - 3.39V
Period - 2ᵈ.8673
Type - Algol
Dura. - 14ʰ

(1900)   03ʰ 01ᵐ 40ˢ +40° 34′.2
(2000)   03ʰ 08ᵐ 11ˢ +40° 57′.3

AAVSO
Eclipsing
Binary
Chart
1°=7.6mm

Drawn by: CES, 1/96

From: Hubble Guide Star Catalog & AAVSO chart 1968

Sequence: PEP(V), Sky & Telescope, 30, 6, 393, 1965

Figure A2.3—AAVSO Star Chart for Beta Persei

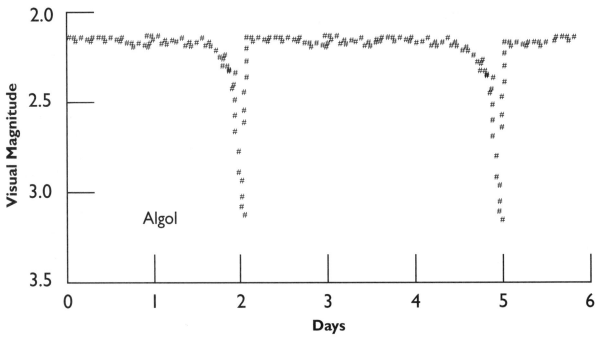

Figure A2.4—Partial Light Curve for Beta Persei

is magnitude 3.0. You can also use [Gamma] as a comparison.) Algol varies from a magnitude of 2.1 at its brightest to 3.4 at its faintest. It is an eclipsing binary system, where one of the stars partially covers up the other as the two stars orbit one another.

One way to make a record of your observations is to record the brightness as a function of time. A sample of this kind of plot, made with many observations, is shown in Figure A2.4. Your observations may look simpler, with only one or perhaps two observations taken per night (Fig. A2.4).

The goal of the project is to record by eye the brightness fluctuations of the star, not to accurately determine the period. As you make your observations, try to think about the two stars, both larger than the Sun, whipping around each other in an orbit that takes slightly less than 3 days. This system is just one of millions of equally awe-inspiring systems in our galaxy.

ADVANCED PROJECTS

Most advanced projects require the use of a telescope. This is because advanced work requires the study of fainter objects or observation at higher resolution.

Jupiter Observations

Using a telescope, trace the motions of Jupiter's moons by emulating the observations that Galileo made. For this project, prepare an observing notebook by tracing a series of circles down the center of the page (using a penny or a nickel). With your telescope, locate the so-called Galilean moons of Jupiter: Io, Ganymede, Europa, and Callisto. Trace their locations onto your notebook, labeling the day and time of your observation. Try to be as accurate as you can.

Continue to observe for a month or more. Try to determine the period of the moons' orbits. Can you note any colors in the moons themselves? Can you easily identify one moon from another between observing nights? *Sky and Telescope* regularly publishes a chart of the locations of the Galilean moons, which you can compare with your observations.

Solar Observations

THIS PROJECT REQUIRES A SOLAR FILTER OR THE USE OF A PROJECTION SCREEN TO PROTECT YOUR EYES. NEVER LOOK THROUGH A TELESCOPE OR BINOCULARS AT THE SUN. YOU CAN SEVERELY DAMAGE YOUR EYES.

Mount your solar filter to your telescope and go outside on a clear day. Set up your telescope and point it at the Sun. Be sure to block any finder scopes with an eyepiece cover, or you could accidentally injure yourself by looking into the finder. Pointing a telescope at the Sun requires a bit of practice, but you can use the shadow of the telescope on the ground as a guide. Try to minimize the size of the telescope's shadow on the ground, and you should have it pointed pretty close to straight at the Sun. Look into the eyepiece and make small adjustments to bring the Sun into the field of view.

Now study the surface of the Sun and see if you can detect any sunspots. During time of intense solar activity, there can be literally hundreds of small dark blotches or just a few large ones. During solar minimum, spots can be hard to find.

Record the locations of the spots in your observing notebook, noting the date and time of the observations. It is best to have drawn circles into your notebook by tracing around a drinking glass or mug first so that

sketching the Sun and its spots is fairly easy. Alternatively, the circle you draw in your notebook can simply represent the Sun's disk and not the field of view.

After making a sketch every few days for a month or so, you should begin to notice a pattern of motion for the spots. One complication you may encounter is that for standard amateur telescopes, the Sun is aligned differently in the field of view depending on the time of day you observe it. It is recommended that you observe the Sun as close to the same time each day as possible, perhaps observing it 4 to 5 min earlier each day to help compensate for Earth's orbit around the Sun. This will ensure that your view of the Sun through the telescope is aligned the same way each day. Alternatively, you can determine which way is north in your field of view if you have an equatorially mounted telescope by skewing the telescope in declination and making a small line on your sketch indicating North. Then you can align the sketches later. If you have an alt-az mount, it is best to observe the Sun at the same time each day.

To determine how fast the Sun rotates, try to estimate how long it takes a given spot to return to its original location. This period will be fairly close to that of the Sun's rotational period. Think about how your period is effected if spots drift slowly about on the surface of the Sun's disk.

This experiment was one of the first carried out with telescopes. In early April 1611, just months after the news of Galileo's telescopic observations was becoming known, Christoph Scheiner observed sunspots from a Jesuit college in Germany where he was a professor of mathematics and Hebrew. He published his work in a number of books, the most famous of which is *Rosa Ursina*, published in Rome in 1630.

Which Way Does the Moon Orbit Earth?

With all the motion going on in the sky, how do we know which way the Moon orbits Earth? This simple experiment will enable you to determine this for yourself. The first part of the experiment is to make measurements of the Moon each day you can and the second is to assemble them in a master drawing to plot the Moon's orbit.

Observations

Begin any clear night when you can see the Moon and it is less than about 45° above the horizon. If you observe the Moon when it is too high in the sky, its elevation will not correspond directly to its position in its orbit, as it does when it is lower on the horizon. Stand somewhere where you have a relatively clear view of the horizon and use your extended fist to approximate the elevation of the Moon. You could also make a small sextant using a plastic compass, but using your fist as 10° and your index finger as 1°, you can fairly accurately measure the angular altitude of the Moon.

Record in a table the date, time, whether the Moon was in the Eastern or Western portion of the sky, the altitude of the Moon, and also the phase of the Moon. You can make a small sketch of the phase if you like or use the name of the phase. Your table should look like this:

MAKING A SEXTANT FROM A PLASTIC COMPASS

A plasic compass can be used to measure the elevation of objects in the sky. Tape a straw along the flat edge of a plastic compass. This is what you will look through at the object you want to measure. In the small hole located in the center of the flat edge of the compass, tie a small string of about 8 in. in length. On the other end of the string, tie a few metal washers or a fishing weight. By sighting through the straw and pinching the string against the curved part of the compass with your fingers when the object in question is centered, you can measure the altitude above the horizon. Note that sometimes there are two numbers. You will have to determine which number represents the altitude by remembering that objects at the horizon have an elevation of 0, whereas objects straight overhead have elevations of 90∞.

Once you have assembled roughly 30 observations, best taken over 2 months with a few days between each observation, get a sheet of plain paper and make a 2 in.–diameter circle in the center of the paper. This will represent the Earth. Put a dot in the center of the circle. This is the North Pole of Earth, as if we were far above the North Pole. Now, off to the left of the paper, write the word Sun. The Sun's light is coming from this direction. Next shade the Earth so that the half of the circle closest to the Sun is bright and the half facing away is dark.

Date	Time	Elevation	E/W	Phase
2-11-05	8:30 P.M.	32°	E	Full
2-15-05	10:00 P.M.	20°	E	Waning gibbous
2-18-05	8:00 P.M.	40°	E	Quarter

Imagine yourself on the equator of Earth looking up at the Sun at noon: where would you be on this diagram? You would be on the part of the circle closest to the Sun, which would be at the 9:00 position if our circle were a clock face. Make a mark there and label it Noon. Make a similar mark on the opposite side of the circle and label it Midnight.

Now let's think about the horizon for a person at the noon position. The horizon can be represented as a line tangent (touching the circle at only one point) to the circle. Draw a straight line that is tangent to your noon position. This represents the horizon for that person. The Sun is straight overhead and the person can see half of the sky. The other half, the half of the sky to the right of the circle, is invisible to the person because Earth is blocking the view. But which way is east and which is west? Because in this diagram, Earth is rotating counterclockwise, the point on the horizon in the counterclockwise direction is east and the point in the clockwise direction is west. This is important, because you will have to locate the Moon above the eastern or western horizon for a person on Earth at the time you made each observation.

Let's keep going. Now we need to mark on the Earth the location of 6:00 P.M. and 6:00 A.M. 6 A.M. is at the 12 o'clock position and 6:00 P.M. is at the 6 o'clock position. Mark these with a small line and label them 6:00 P.M. and 6:00 A.M.

Plotting The Observations

Now comes the fun part: plotting your observations. Locate where around the Earth you were at the time you made the first observation. If you made it at 6:00 P.M., you would be at the 6:00 P.M. position at the bottom of the circle. The time 9:00 P.M. is halfway

between the 6:00 P.M. position and the midnight position, and so on. Lightly draw a tangent line at this location. This is your horizon. Mark the eastern and western horizons. Remember, the eastern horizon is in the counterclockwise direction. Then, taking a compass, measure up from the horizon the same angle you recorded for the elevation of the Moon. Make a small mark and then draw a line from the tangent point through your angular measure mark. Extend this line to the edge of the page. Now, measuring out 3 in. from the center of Earth, put a very small circle at the point where the two lines cross. This is your first Moon observation. Shade it in the same way you shaded the Earth and label it with the date of the observation.

Continue to plot all your observations. You may soon notice a pattern to its motion. Which way does the Moon orbit Earth? Is this surprising? Why should or shouldn't the Moon orbit Earth the same way as Earth's rotation?

RESOURCES FOR THE AMATEUR

There are many resources available to the amateur astronomer. With the growth of the Internet, much more is available now than ever before. It is impossible to provide a comprehensive list of the resources on the Internet or every single organization, but the following list will give interested readers enough to get going on their own.

Software

One of the best tools for any amateur is some kind of software that allows plotting or charting of the sky from your location. There are literally thousands of programs, some free, some inexpensive, and some rather costly. Here are three that are particularly useful.

Starry Night
(http://www.starrynight.com)

This program is a favorite. Starry Night is flexible, easy to learn, regularly updated, provides Internet connectivity to databases and information, and allows you to make Quicktime movies of astronomical events as observed by the software (not as it appears in the sky). It allows plotting of nightly sky charts of almost any scale. It even dims the screen if you are using it outside or next to your telescope.

The Sky
(http://www.bisque.com/Products/TheSky/TheSky.asp)

This software is one of the finest for integrating your computer with your GoTo/Electronically enabled telescope. Easy to learn and extremely flexible, this site currently provides a student edition at reduced price, as well. The Sky has a whole host of features from recording movies, to making specialized calendars (moon phase for example), to reports on objects visible tonight (or any time) and mirror-image reversal mode to match the view, as you will see it in a telescope. The company that produces this software provides more advanced software for amateurs to help them use their telescopes more efficiently as well.

Xephem
(http://www.clearskyinstitute.com/xephem)

This software is not for the beginner. This program can be downloaded for free and run on a Unix-based system. It provides three-dimensional stereo views of the solar system to help visualize trajectories (e.g., of comets), displays light curves from the AAVSO database, loads images in FITS format, accesses large databases with ease, and will actually perform photometry on images taken with a CCD camera or images input from FITS format.

Magazines

Sky and Telescope
(http://skyandtelescope.com/)

This magazine and Web site provide a number of resources of value. First and foremost are news reports of recent astronomical events or activities. Even professional astronomers follow the news in *Sky and Telescope*. The magazine provides information on making telescopes, historical articles, practical how-to articles on such topics as using CCD cameras or making great astrophotographs, and monthly sky charts for the northern and southern hemispheres. Finally, the Web site provides lists of resources useful to amateur astronomers, and the printed magazine has lots of advertising from companies that sell telescopes and telescope equipment—even astronomical-oriented travel opportunities.

Astronomy
(http://www.astronomy.com/)

An excellent resource for the beginner, the Web site and magazine are very much focused on introducing eager amateurs into the hobby of astronomy. The Web site provides introductory material, discovery materials, special beginner FAQs (lists of frequently asked questions), a glossary of astronomical terms, and also science news and recent results. The best part of this magazine is the excellently reproduced color pictures, which are published in large numbers.

Mercury
(http://www.astrosociety.org/pubs/mercury/)

The Astronomical Society of the Pacific publishes this magazine six times a year.

This active nonprofit scientific society is an organization for both professionals and amateurs. *Mercury* brings the two together by publishing articles of interest to both groups, without the pure science articles one would find in the *Astrophysical Journal*. The magazine also includes sky charts to help with skygazing and wonderful historical stories.

The Astrograph

(http://users.erols.com/astrograph)

The Astrograph is centered on the art of astrophotography and is published bi-monthly. They provide a low-resolution version of the current issue online, accessible to anyone, even nonsubscribers. Special articles focus on techniques and equipment.

Amateur Astronomy

(http://www.amateurastronomy.com/ index.html)

This iconoclastic magazine focuses on in-depth articles with a minimum of graphical overhead, thereby keeping their cost of publication down. Full archives are available online as well. It covers the largest and most well-known amateur star parties and gatherings.

BadAstronomy.com

(http://www.badastronomy.com/)

This website explains astronomy by finding poor explanations or just plain wrong explanations, pointing out how they are incorrect and then providing the correct explanation. There is even a companion book available that is a good resource for the interested amateur.

Clubs and Organizations

Getting together with people who are interested in astronomy is the best way to learn more about it and reinforce your own excitement. This is a list of organizations for amateur astronomers. They all have their own special focus, and you should take the time to investigate them before picking one (or more) to join. Many amateurs are members of all of these organizations

American Association of Variable Star Observers

(http://www.aavso.org)

This group observes variable stars, archives the observations, and makes the observations available to professional astronomers. It holds meetings, provides charts for observing variable stars as well as informative publications on how to observe them, and provides scientific results from observations of variable stars.

Association of Lunar and Planetary Observers

(http://www.lpl.arizona.edu/alpo)

This organization concentrates on helping amateurs observe and understand the Moon and planets as well as the minor bodies of the solar systems such as asteroids.

Astronomical Society of the Pacific

(http://www.astrosociety.org)

This group is a large, wide-ranging group of amateurs with interests ranging from observing the sky to education to professional research.

Astronomical League

(http://www.astroleague.org)

The League is a collection of small groups organized at the local level. It focuses on amateur astronomers and their issues and organizes meetings and star parties.

International Dark Sky Association
(http://www.darksky.org)

The goal of this organization is to protect the sky by encouraging the proper use of night-time lighting and the enactment and enforcement of sensible lighting codes. Everyone who loves the night sky should be a member of this organization.

International Meteor Organization
(http://www.imo.net)

The goal of this organization is to coordinate international observing campaigns of meteors. It hosts a yearly conference and provides large amounts of information on how to participate in their observing campaigns or develop your own.

Many comprehensive lists of astronomical organizations are available on the Internet. Use your favorite search engine, or try using Astroweb (www.cv.nrao.edu/fits/www/astronomy.html), a comprehensive list of astronomy and astrophysics resources available on the Internet.

RESOURCES FOR THE PROFESSIONAL

Many professional resources can be of interest or use to the amateur as well. Most major observatories and space missions provide informative Web sites with educational material, press releases, photos and background science information. Here are some of the most interesting sites on the Web. A comprehensive list is available online at the Astroweb (see above).

Telescopes

Space Telescope Science Institute
(http://www.stsci.edu)

This is the main page for the Hubble Space Telescope and the currently in-development James Webb Space Telescope. This site provides access to the data archives of the Hubble, educational resources, press releases and the current status of the James Webb Space Telescope. It even provides Hubble Space Telescope desktop wallpaper imagery.

National Optical Astronomy Observatory
(http://www.noao.edu)

The NOAO is a major facility of the National Science Foundation and provides telescopes both in the United States and in Chile for use by astronomers worldwide. The Web site provides access to press releases, educational material, and information for scientists planning to propose uses for the telescopes.

National Radio Astronomy Observatory
(http://www.nrao.edu)

The Very Large Array, Green Bank Telescope, Very Long Baseline Array, and Atacama Large Millimeter Array are all run and operated by the NRAO. Based in Charlottesville, Virginia, this organization runs the nation's radio telescopes. The Web page has an archive of images made with radio telescopes, press releases, educational materials and information for astronomers planning to propose uses for the telescopes.

Keck Observatory
(http://www2.keck.hawaii.edu)

The Keck Observatory is composed of the two (currently) largest telescopes in the world, the twin 10–m diameter mirrors installed on the summit of Mauna Kea in

Hawaii. The observatories are built from hexagonal mirror segments that are constantly adjusted to keep them in perfect parabolic alignment. The Web page includes pictures of the telescopes, press releases, news about the observatory, information for astronomers hoping to propose to use these behemoths, and career opportunities.

Chandra X-Ray Observatory
(http://chandra.harvard.edu)

This telescope is currently the world's premier X-ray telescope. The Chandra homepage includes the standard array of press releases, archival data, information for astronomers hoping to use the telescopes, educational material, and a well-made history of X-ray astronomy.

Societies

American Astronomical Society
(http://www.aas.org)

The AAS is the premier professional astronomy organization in the world. With more than 6000 members, the AAS hosts two meetings each year where members gather to share their research results. The AAS publishes the largest and most cited journals in the field of astronomy, *Astrophysical Journal, Astrophysical Journal Letters, Astrophysical Journal Supplement* and *Astronomical Journal*.

Astronomical Society of the Pacific
(http://www.astrosociety.org)

As mentioned in the amateur listings, this society has both professional and amateur memberships and publishes the professional journal *Publications of the Astronomical Society of the Pacific*, a monthly publication that highlights research results. The journal is one of the best sources for detailed articles on observatory equipment and telescopes and now features summaries of professional astronomy meetings.

International Astronomical Union
(http://www.iau.org)

The IAU is a worldwide organization composed of members from countries that have agreed to adhere to the membership rules of the IAU. The organization holds General Assemblies once every 3 years (Prague, 2006; Rio de Janeiro, 2009), organizes specialized conferences throughout the year, and is responsible for the definitions of nomenclature used in the field of astronomy and the naming of celestial objects.

Royal Astronomical Society
(http://www.ras.org.uk)

The professional society for English astronomers has long allowed foreign membership. The Society publishes *Monthly Notices of the Royal Astronomical Society*, a journal of professional research results. The Society holds meetings both in London and other locations in England and sponsors specialist meetings as needed. The society also publishes the interesting *Astronomy and Geophysics*, a full-color magazine published bi-monthly.

Other Sites of Professional Interest

NASA Astrophysics Data System
(http://adswww.harvard.edu)

The ADS is a digital library for physics, astrophysics, and instrumentation. The site provides access to abstracts of the professional literature with links to other resources of great utility to professional astronomers.

Astro-Ph

(http://xxx.lanl.gov/archive/astro-ph)

This Web site is a preprint server and often the source of the very latest results. Astro-Ph, unlike the journals mentioned below, has no peer-review process, so anyone can submit research results without the extensive editing and revision that the peer-review process usually involves. This can cause problems, because articles on discredited subjects, such as the "face on mars" or UFOs, sometimes appear.

Journals

Astrophysical Journal (including Letters and Supplement)

(http://www.journals.uchicago.edu/ApJ/front.html)

This Web site has current issues, archives, subscription information, and submission requirements.

Astronomical Journal

(http://www.astro.washington.edu/astroj)

This is a fine historical journal founded in 1849. It generally focuses on more observational results and less on theory, but it accepts publications in all areas of astronomical research. The Web site has archived issues, subscription information, and submission requirements.

Astronomy and Astrophysics (http://www.edp-sciences.org/journal/index.cfm?edpsname=aa)

This journal is the European journal of professional astronomy and astrophysics results. It accepts submissions from astronomers worldwide, but there are no page charges for papers with at least one European author. It is now published by a for-profit publisher; the site includes information on how to subscribe and submit works for publication but contains only limited access to archived articles.

Publications of the Astronomical Society of Japan

(http://pasj.asj.or.jp)

The professional journal of astronomy published by the Astronomical Society of Japan often contains interesting results, but it is not as widely read as other western journals. The Web site contains information on how to submit articles, subscribe, and access archival issues.

A more comprehensive listing of resources is available through AstroWeb, a regularly updated list of Internet resources on astronomy. That site can be found at http://www.cv.nrao.edu/fits/www/astronomy.html.

GLOSSARY

absolute magnitude
The apparent magnitude of a star that is 10 parsecs away from Earth.

absorption
The process of matter absorbing light.

acceleration
The rate of change of velocity, usually given in meters per second per second, or m/s2.

active Sun
When regions of activity appear on the Sun's surface, sometimes covering a large fraction of it. These active areas exhibit sunspots, flares, bright eruptions of energy, and prominences.

adaptive optics
Any of a number of devices used on ground-based telescopes to compensate for the effects of atmospheric errors.

albedo
The reflectivity of an object; objects with a large albedo are very reflective (like the Moon or Saturn's rings), whereas objects that absorb most light that hit them have a low albedo.

amino acids
The first life-related organic molecules, formed in the watery soup that was the early Earth's ocean or in a type of mineral deposit known as iron sulphide.

annular eclipse
An eclipse that occurs when the Moon is closer to Earth in its orbit, appearing slightly smaller and leaving an annulus, or ring, of the Sun still visible.

apparent magnitude
How bright a star appears from Earth, the combination of a star's inherent brightness and its distance from us.

arcsecond
An angle that is 1/3600 of a degree.

asteroid
A large chunk of rock, not large enough to be a planet but still large enough to block the light of a distant star. Most asteroids are located between the orbits of Mars and Jupiter.

astronomical seeing
The combined effect of air turbulence and temperature differences that causes blurred images for telescopes on Earth.

astronomical unit
A unit of distance equal to the average distance between Earth and Sun, about 93 million miles.

astrophysicists
Scientists who apply the laws of physics to objects in the universe.

astrophysics
The study of objects in the universe using the laws of physics.

atom
The smallest unit of matter that still retains the properties of a given element.

atmospheric pressure
The weight of the air in the atmosphere per unit area.

aurora
Impact zones, the spots where the solar wind is captured by Earth's magnetic field and guided along its field lines to just above the North and South Poles of Earth. In these regions, the high-speed particles interact with the atmosphere and cause air molecules to give off light.

autumnal equinox
The day in the fall when there is an equal length of daylight and nighttime. It usually takes place on September 23.

axis

A line about which an object rotates. Can be thought of as an imaginary rod stuck through the object, like a chopstick through a peach.

belts

The dark bands that appear above and below the large equatorial band that runs around Jupiter's middle.

Big Bang

The initial beginning of the universe.

Big Bang model

Theory that states that the whole universe grew from a small, hot, and dense state to the expanding universe we see today.

black hole

Infinitely dense objects, in which the gravitational field is so strong that light cannot escape from it.

blackbodies

Perfect emitters and absorbers of light used to calculate the distribution of light as a function of wavelength.

blackbody radiation

The light given off by blackbodies.

blind spot

The portion of the retina where the optic nerve attaches, preventing the reception of light.

Bonner Durchmusterung

A monumental catalog of stars created by Fredrich Wilhelm August Argelander (1799–1875) using a newly-constructed telescope in Bonn, Germany, to make observations of more than 500,000 stars.

celestial equator

The projection of Earth's equator outwards onto the celestial sphere.

celestial sphere

The imaginary sphere above Earth that appears to hold all the stars and planets.

chondrites

Rocky materials that contain small, spherical mineral formations named chondrules, which are formed through melting processes; these formations are held together with other minerals that did not melt.

chromosphere

The region where the bubbling surface of the Sun begins to interact with free space; it is relatively thin, about 1000 mi thick, but the gas in this region absorbs light from the photosphere and results in the formation of spectral absorption lines, which we can study from Earth using telescopes and spectrographs.

closed universe

A universe that ultimately contracts.

coma

The extended visible region of a comet.

comet

A bright object with a huge tail of gas and dust that rapidly moves across the sky, whose name comes from a Latin phrase meaning long-haired stars, a reference to their dramatic tails.

concave

Curved like the inner surface of a sphere.

constellation

A group of stars in the sky, usually identified with a mythological creature or character.

continuous spectrum

Colors seen in a rainbow.

convex

Curved like the exterior surface of a sphere.

core (solar)

Where all of the Sun's energy comes from. Due to the huge amount of material and the mutual gravitational attraction of the accumulated gas, the pressure at the Sun's core is several trillion times the atmospheric pressure on Earth's surface. Such a phenomenal pressure crushes atoms at the core close together. Due to the high temperatures, the atoms are also moving very fast. With a temperature of about 15 million degrees Fahrenheit and a density 10 times that of lead, the conditions are not something easily visualized or even imagined.

corona

The tremendously hot but not very dense region of the Sun's atmosphere located beyond the chromosphere. The gas in this region has temperatures in the millions of degrees Fahrenheit. It is quite large and extends far above the Sun, tapering off about a million miles above the photosphere.

cosmology
A formulation of theories about the origin, and change over time of the entire universe.

cuneiform
An early system of writing developed by Mesopotamian cultures.

currents
Flows of electrons.

dark matter
Material in the halo that we cannot see but that has influence on the overall gravitational field of the galaxy.

declination
A coordinate similar to latitude on Earth that is projected outward onto the celestial sphere and measures positions north and south of the celestial equator.

degree
A unit of angular measure equal to 1/360 of a circle.

density
A measure of the amount of mass contained in a given volume.

differential rotation
Rotation where objects further away from the center of rotation move at a slower angular velocity, like the planets orbiting the Sun or stars orbiting the outer regions of a spiral galaxy.

distortion
The blurring of an image by the turbulent atmosphere.

Doppler effect
The change in frequency of emitted sound or light caused by the motion of the emitting body.

Drake equation
A chain of numbers that, when multiplied, gives us an estimate of the number of planets in our galaxy with intelligent life.

dwarfs
The smallest stars at any given temperature (except for some special cases) located on the main sequence of an HR diagram.

eclipse
The blocking of one celestial object by another.

eclipsing binary stars
Stars that periodically appear to be dimmed but are aligned so that we would see one star pass in front of the other.

ecliptic
The plane of the Earth's orbit around the Sun.

electromagnetic field
Area surrounding an electrically charged particle.

electromagnetic induction
The fact that a moving electric field can cause a magnetic field and a moving magnetic field can induce electricity.

electromagnetic radiation
Commonly referred to as light, it is the fundamental carrier of information in the universe. It has a constant speed—the speed of light—and is characterized by its wavelength. Light is a traveling wave of electromagnetic energy usually formed by the repetitive motion of a charged particle.

electromagnetic spectrum
The entire range of wavelengths of light.

electrons
Negatively charged particles.

elements
Substances that cannot be broken down into other substances.

ellipse
The set of points whose combined distance from two selected points is a constant.

elliptical galaxies
Football-shaped distributions of stars, with little dust or star formation.

emission
The release of energy from atoms or molecules in the form of light.

emission nebulae
Nebulae that emit their own light (as opposed to simply reflecting the light of nearby stars).

epicycle
The observed reversal of a planet's direction of motion in the sky. Correctly explained by Copernicus' heliocentric model of the solar system.

equinox
A day when the Sun rises directly in the east and sets directly in the west. On this day, there is an equal amount of daylight and nighttime.

equivalency principle
Matter can be converted to energy, and vice versa.

erosion
The wearing away of rock through various processes.

extra-solar planets
Planets not located around our Sun.

Fermat's principle
A statement that light always travels a path between two points that minimizes its time of travel.

fertile crescent
The region in the Middle East that is now modern-day Iraq, where farming developed in the lush zone created by flooding.

flares
Dramatic and rapid releases of energy in the form of light of many wavelengths, including X-rays, which occur when magnetic fields break apart and reconnect.

flat universe
The seemingly special case of a balanced universe.

frequency
A measure of the rate at which a cyclic process takes place, usually measured in Hertz (Hz). If a record rotates twice per second, it is rotating at a frequency of 0.5 Hertz.

Fresnel diffraction
A special kind of interference pattern that can be observed (in one example) as the edge of the Moon blocks the starlight.

galaxy
Collection of billions of stars and their orbiting planets, gas, and dust.

Galilean moons
The four largest moons of Jupiter (Callisto, Europa, Ganymde, and Io); named in honor of Galileo, who first discovered them.

general theory of relativity
A physical theory developed by Einstein that states that all accelerations are equivalent, whether they are caused by gravity or through motion. The theory has implications in a number of physical conditions that exist in the universe, such as Black Holes or clusters of galaxies.

geocentric
Earth-centered; usually used in reference to a model of the solar system or cosmology.

giant molecular clouds
Dark dust clouds in the interstellar medium with a remarkable variety of molecules. These clouds are typically a few tens of light-years in diameter, are composed mainly of hydrogen and have very high densities, compared to the rest of interstellar space. (In absolute terms, the density of a giant molecular cloud is actually a better vacuum than we can create here on Earth in a laboratory.)

granulation
The pattern of hot gas rising and cool gas falling on the Sun, similar to water boiling. The Sun boils relatively slowly, with granules appearing on the surface over a period of 10 min or so and then falling back down over the same timescale.

gravitational collapse
If a cloud were cold enough, it was thought the force of gravity would be able to pull the material together into an ever-denser clump of matter, thus forming stars.

Great Red Spot
The most prominent characteristic of the surface appearance of Jupiter, a large, oval structure, which is actually a large atmospheric disturbance that moves through the belts over time.

greatest elongation
The greatest angular distance of a planet from the Sun.

heliocentric
Sun-centered; usually used in reference to a model of the solar system or cosmology.

heliopause
The outer edge of the Sun's heliosphere, where the Sun's magnetic field has dwindled to nothing.

heliosphere
The Sun's strong magnetic field, which extends far out into space, protecting all the planets from any magnetic fields in interstellar space and helping to deflect charged particles from entering the solar system.

homogeneous
The universe is smooth on the largest scales. We know that there is some clumping at the smallest scales, represented by planets and stars and galaxies, but on the very largest scales, the distribution of material is smooth.

Hubble's law
A rule that relates a galaxy's distance to its Doppler shift or, more properly, its velocity. A constant, now known as the Hubble constant, governs this relationship: velocity = H ¥ distance, where H is the Hubble constant.

hydrologic cycle
The path that water takes through the Earth's various systems and life forms.

index of refraction
The ratio of the speed of light in a vacuum to the speed of light in a given material.

inertia
The property that all objects at rest will stay at rest and objects moving will stay moving in a straight line unless acted upon by an outside force. The measure of an object's inertia is its mass.

initial mass function
A function that tells us just how many of each kind of star we might expect to see formed from a giant molecular cloud.

interference
A property of wave phenomena, such as water waves or electromagnetic radiation. It is caused by the fact that waves can add together or subtract from each other to make patterns that vary with time.

interferometer
A telescope composed of multiple smaller telescopes that generates the same resolution as a large telescope with a diameter equal to the maximum small telescope separation.

interferometry
A technique for combining the signals of many telescopes that generates the same resolution as a large telescope with a diameter equal to the maximum small-telescope separation.

interstellar clouds
Gas clouds found between the stars.

interstellar matter
The material we find between the stars.

interstellar medium
The interstellar space and the interstellar matter taken together.

interstellar space
The space between the stars.

ionized
When atoms and molecules lose one or more electrons and become electrically charged.

iris
A part of the eye that expands or contracts, limiting the amount of light that enters the eye.

irregulars
Generic classification of galaxies that do not look like elliptical or spiral galaxies.

isotropic
The belief that space is the same no matter where we look, that there is no favored direction and no place is special, and that there is no center to the universe.

Jovian planets
The four largest planets in the solar system (Jupiter, Saturn, Uranus, and Neptune); the group takes its name from the largest planet of all, Jupiter, which is named for the Roman king of the gods.

Kirchoff's laws
Basic rules that characterized the type of spectrum received from astronomical objects. Continuous spectra originated from hot, dense objects. Emission line spectra originate from hot, sparse gas. Absorption line spectra originate from a cool gas residing in front of a hot, dense object emitting a continuous spectra. Modern physics explains Kirchoff's laws quantitatively.

Kuiper Belt Objects
Objects of all different sizes found beyond the orbit of Neptune, in the region of the solar system where Pluto orbits.

latitude
Coordinates laid down in a grid on the spherical Earth that measure north-south positions. Latitude is measured in degrees, with the poles being 90° away from the equator, which has a latitude of 0°. Latitudes in the southern hemisphere are given as negative values.

life
Self-replicating, evolving, and interacting organized matter.

light-gathering power
The ability of a telescope to gather light. Only by increasing the size of a telescope can its light-gathering power be increased.

light-year
The distance light travels in 1 year, about 9,460,000,000,000 km.

local group
Our immediate cosmic neighborhood, dominated by the Milky Way and Andromeda galaxies, plus a few other isolated and small galaxies.

longitude
Coordinates laid down in a grid on the spherical Earth that measure east-west positions. Longitude is measured in degrees eastward or westward along the equator from a point directly south of Greenwich, England, which has a longitude of 0°.

luminosity
The measure of how much total energy a star is giving off, per unit of time, in all directions.

lunar eclipse
An event when Earth passes between the Sun and the Moon, casting a shadow across the surface of the Moon. Because of the Earth's atmosphere, the shadow is often reddish in color.

magnification
The increase in apparent size of an image seen through a telescope, microscope, or other lens, not equivalent to resolution.

magnitude
A unit of measuring the brightness of stars derived from an ancient system developed by early Greek astronomers, in which the brightest stars were named stars of the first magnitude and dimmer stars were stars of the second, third, or fourth magnitudes, and so on.

main sequence
The zone that cuts across the center of an HR diagram, in which most stars fall when the luminosity and spectral type, or temperature, of a star are plotted.

major axis
A line extended through the two foci that intersects with the ellipse.

mantle
Layer of Earth under the crust.

mare
Latin word for sea.

mass
A unit of measure of an object's inertia. The metric unit for mass is the gram.

metallic hydrogen
A region of very dense hydrogen deep in the interior of Jupiter that exists in a liquid state, but which also has characteristics of some metals because of the high pressure.

meteorites
Slightly larger pieces of rock that hit the surface of Earth, including any miscellaneous piece of space rock that hits Earth's surface, whether it originally came from a comet or not.

meteors
When Earth passes through the orbits of comets, which are littered with dust and small bits of rock, these "comet remains" enter our atmosphere, making dramatic streaks of light in the sky, informally called shooting stars.

minor axis
The line perpendicular to the major axis that goes through the center of the ellipse.

molecule
A group of two or more atoms held together by electric forces.

month
A period of time originally derived from the amount of time it takes for the Moon to cycle through its full set of phases, caused by its orbit around Earth.

nanometer
A unit of distance equal to 0.000000001 m, or about 0.00000004 in.

natural motion
A law stating that either something is at rest or it is moving in a straight line at constant velocity.

Near Earth Objects (NEOs)
Asteroids with orbits that take them near Earth, which potentially pose a direct threat to life on Earth; the risk is quite low but present nonetheless.

nebulae
Bright regions of gas and dust that appear cloudlike in space.

neutron star
A star that is formed basically through nuclear reactions that change protons into neutrons.

neutrons
Particles having neither a negative nor positive charge.

novae
Stellar explosions that result in the sudden brightening of stars by factors of tens of millions. They do not, however, blow apart their host star.

nuclear fusion
The process from which the Sun's energy comes. Due to the intense temperature and density at the core, hydrogen atoms can fuse together and become helium atoms, releasing energy. Four hydrogen atoms are needed to make one helium atom, but hydrogen atoms have only protons, whereas a helium atom has two protons and two neutrons. Two of the hydrogen protons convert to neutrons, which are less massive than protons. This small change in mass results in the release of energy, and this is where the Sun gets its energy.

nucleic acids
The complex molecules through which all life passes on genetic information from generation to generation (the "NA" of DNA and RNA).

nucleus
1. The central core of an atom. 2. The inner portion of a comet, sometimes called the core.

objective
The primary lens or mirror of a telescope.

occultation
The observable passage of one object in front of another.

oceanic spreading ridges
Volcanic spreading zones where new molten rock comes up from the hotter regions under the crust, known as the mantle, and forms new crust material.

Oort cloud
Clumps of material left over from the formation of our solar system; an area in the very furthest reaches of the solar system believed to be where comets originated.

open universe
A universe that expands forever.

organic molecules
Molecules that contain carbon.

outer planets
All the Jovian planets and the small, icy planet Pluto.

ozone
A gas made of molecules composed of three oxygen atoms that exists in the upper regions of our atmosphere and absorbs ultraviolet light.

parallax
The effect of apparent change in position that occurs when a distant object is viewed from different points of view. Parallax caused by the change in position of Earth can be used to determine the distance of remote celestial objects.

parsec
A unit of measure that is 3.26 light-years. A star 1 parsec away displays a parallax effect of exactly 1 arcsecond.

partial eclipse
Any eclipse when the surface of the Sun is only partially obscured by the Moon.

penumbra
The faint outer region of a sunspot (dark region on the photosphere of the Sun that normally forms in groups).

phases
The apparent changes in illumination of a celestial object over time.

photoelectric effect
A fundamental property of matter discovered by Einstein. Light, when hitting the material, can liberate electrons if the frequency of the light is above a certain threshold value. Increasing the amount of light hitting the surface increases the number of electrons liberated.

photons
Packets of energy that have characteristic wavelengths and energy.

photosphere
The part of the Sun that we see each day, where the gases that comprise the Sun finally become transparent and the light from the very hot gas can escape into space.

plane
An imaginary geometric construct that is perfectly flat, like a sheet of paper.

planetary nebula
A region of gas illuminated by and initially ejected by an old star (known as a white dwarf) that has a carbon core and a shell of helium fusion reactions.

plasma torus
Typically an object in the solar system, composed of plasma (a hot, ionized gas) in the shape of a torus (a doughnut-shaped ring of material). Jupiter's plasma torus is formed through a combination of Jupiter's strong magnetic fields and Io's active volcanoes.

polarization
A property of light that can be induced by electromagnetic fields or interaction of light with matter in which one plane of vibration is favored.

polarized light
Light that exhibits a favored plane of vibration for the electric and magnetic fields of the traveling electromagnetic wave.

prominences
Large plumes of material that originate near the photosphere of the Sun and expand away from it in spike-like projections.

propagation
The motion of something.

protons
Positively charged particles.

protoplanets
Small clumps of matter formed through the gravitational action of a planet.

protostar
An object that is in the process of stellar formation but has not yet begun nuclear reactions.

pulsars
Rapidly rotating neutron stars with strong magnetic fields.

quarks
Particles that make up protons and neutrons.

quasars
Galaxies with so much activity that they are visible clear across the universe.

quiet Sun
When the Sun shows little surface activity; during this period the surface shows granulation but no dramatic sunspots or large eruptions.

radiative region
The region of the Sun where energy is transported by the motion of photons, which ranges from the center of the Sun to within about 90,000 miles below the surface.

real images
Images formed on the opposite side of the lens.

red giants
Stars in which the core contracts, causing the hydrogen shell to increase in temperature and produce more energy, which puffs up the outer portion of the star, increasing its luminosity but decreasing the overall temperature.

reflecting telescope
A telescope that uses mirrors to gather and focus light.

reflection
The redirection of light by a given material.

reflection nebulae
Regions in the interstellar medium that are formed when light from stars scatters off the dust particles in interstellar space and directs some of the blue light toward us. A similar process makes our own sky appear blue.

refracting telescope
A telescope that uses lenses to gather and focus light.

refraction
The bending of light by a material.

resolution
The ability of a telescope to separate two closely spaced objects; not the same as magnification (also called resolving power).

resolving power
The ability of a telescope to separate two closely spaced objects; not the same as magnification (also called resolution).

retina
The back portion of the eye that is composed of cells that are sensitive to light and convert the incoming light waves to electrical signals that are sent to the brain along the optic nerve.

retrograde motion
When a given planet appears to make a slow reversal in its motion, completes a small loop in the sky, and then continues on in its original path.

right ascension
A coordinate system similar to longitude on Earth that is projected outward onto the celestial sphere, and measures positions east or west of the point on the celestial equator where the Sun appears to be on the vernal equinox.

scattering
The change in direction and character of light by the interaction of light with matter.

shepherd moons
The moons that have the most influence on the gaps between Saturn's rings; these gaps are caused by gravitational interactions with Saturn's many moons, which push and guide the ice chunks and rocks into particular orbits.

solar eclipse
An event that takes place when the Moon blocks the light of the Sun, casting a shadow onto Earth. There are partial, total, and annular solar eclipses.

solar mass
A particular unit defined by astronomers to use when speaking of the mass of stars or galaxies. One solar mass is simply the mass of our Sun.

solar radius
A special unit, scaled to the size of the Sun: one solar radius is equal to the radius of our Sun, or about 432,000 miles.

solar wind
A slow and steady loss of mass from the Sun in the form of a wind of charged particles, mainly protons and electrons, that originates in the hot region of the corona.

solid-body rotation
A special kind of rotation seen in the innermost regions of disks of spiral galaxies. The angular velocity remains constant with distance from the center of rotation.

solstice
A special day when the Sun rises or sets the furthest north or south during the year. The Winter Solstice usually takes place on December 21 and the Summer Solstice usually takes place on June 21.

spacetime
The joining of the three dimensions of space and the single dimension of time.

spectral lines
Particular colors of light seen from atoms when using a spectroscope.

spectroscope
A device that collects and then disperses light, so that its constituent colors can be identified.

spectroscopic binaries
Stars that are located so close together that even with the largest telescopes, we can see them as only one star. They can also be used to measure the mass of binary companions.

spectroscopy

The study of light by separating it by color and studying its particular interactions with matter.

spicules

Jets of gas that originate in the photosphere of the Sun and transport energy into the chromosphere.

spiral galaxies

Large disks of stars and dust with large central bulges.

steady-state model

An alternative theory of how the universe was created in which the universe is not expanding; it cannot predict all the observable facts we see without extreme complications.

stellar clusters

Groups of related stars.

stellar evolution

Process by which the temperature, luminosity, and other fundamental characteristics of stars are altered over time.

stellar nursery

A place where new stars are formed

stellar occultations

When Saturn (or any other body) passes in front of a much more distant star, and, from our vantage point on Earth, the star is covered up by either the rings or Saturn itself.

strong nuclear force

The force between protons and neutrons that holds the nucleus of atoms together.

subduction

The movement of the oceanic plates under the continental plates.

sublimating

Changing from a solid directly to a gas without becoming a liquid.

summer solstice

The day (June 21) when we have the greatest amount of daylight in the northern hemisphere, and the least amount of daylight in the southern hemisphere.

sunspots

The darker regions on the surface of the Sun that appear as dark blotches, the result of magnetic field loops at the surface.

supernovae

True stellar explosions that destroy the star.

tail

Broad, sweeping portion of a comet that lights up due to reflected sunlight as it orbits closer to the Sun, appearing bigger if the comet comes close to Earth; made of both gas and dust, they can give us some insight into the composition of the comets themselves.

tectonic plates

Shifting plates of solid material on Earth's surface that move over time and dramatically affect the appearance of the surface.

telescope

A device to gather and focus the light from distant objects.

total eclipse

An event that occurs when the face of the Sun is completely blocked by the Moon as seen from Earth.

transit

An event seen from the Earth when one object crosses across the face of the Sun. The best-known transits are those of Venus.

umbra

The dark central core of a sunspot (dark region on the photosphere of the Sun that normally forms in groups).

unpolarized light

Light that has no favored plane of vibration for the electric or magnetic fields that make up the traveling electromagnetic wave.

vernal equinox

The day in the spring when there is an equal amount of daylight and nighttime. It usually takes place on March 21.

very long baseline interferometry

The practice of using radio telescopes spread across the whole surface of Earth to provide the highest possible resolutions currently obtainable by any method.

virtual images

Images formed on the front side of the lens.

visual binary stars

Stars that appeared to be close to each other in the sky, some of which were shown to be orbiting one another.

wavelength

The distance between successive peaks or troughs of a wave.

winter solstice

The day (December 21) when we have the least amount of daylight in the northern hemisphere and the greatest amount of daylight in the southern hemisphere.

zodiac

An ancient star catalog from the Babylonian culture composed of 12 roughly equal constellations through which the Sun and planets were observed to move along the ecliptic.

zones

The light-colored bands that appear above and below the large equatorial band that runs around Jupiter's middle.

INDEX